HACKiNG HAPPINESS

HACKING HAPPINESS

HOW TO INTENTIONALLY ADAPT AND SHAPE THE FUTURE YOU WANT

PENNY LOCASO

WILEY

First published in 2020 by John Wiley & Sons Australia, Ltd
42 McDougall St, Milton Qld 4064

Office also in Melbourne

Typeset in LegacySerifStd-Book 12/15pt, Spi Global, Chennai, India

ISBN: 978-0-730-38499-1

NATIONAL LIBRARY OF AUSTRALIA

A catalogue record for this book is available from the National Library of Australia

Cover design by Wiley

10 9 8 7 6 5 4 3 2 1

Disclaimer
The material in this publication is of the nature of general comment only, and does not represent professional advice. It is not intended to provide specific guidance for particular circumstances and it should not be relied on as the basis for any decision to take action or not take action on any matter which it covers. Readers should obtain professional advice where appropriate, before making any such decision. To the maximum extent permitted by law, the author and publisher disclaim all responsibility and liability to any person, arising directly or indirectly from any person taking or not taking action based on the information in this publication.

CONTENTS

ABOUT THE AUTHOR

Penny Locaso is the world's first Happiness Hacker.

As an international keynote speaker, educational innovator and author, she is on a mission to teach 10 million humans, by 2025, how to intentionally adapt in order to future-proof their happiness and bring more joy into the everyday.

Grand missions like this are born from moments of courage. For Penny, the turning point was realising she had the success equation the wrong way around – instead of focusing on success to realise happiness, she started to focus on her happiness to realise success.

As a result, she left a 16-year career as an executive, ended an 18-year relationship, relocated her family interstate, and founded her company HackingHappy.co, which teaches the human skills required to thrive in complexity to community groups, educational institutions and large global corporations – including Google, Booking.com, Microsoft, Deloitte, SalesForce and Universal Music to name but a few.

Penny and her company HackingHappy.co's Intentional Adaptability Quotient® (IAQ) is the world's first educational program that measures how skilled you are in making intentional change in a complex environment that is evolving at speed. IAQ is a scientifically supported way to embrace slowing down and creating the space to bring intention to the forefront of decision making, amplifying innovation, wellbeing and happiness.

The IAQ concept resulted in Penny being accepted as a faculty member at the esteemed Singularity University. This position has her working alongside some of the best technology and Artificial Intelligence innovators in the world, enabling her to gain valuable insights into emerging technology in addition to decoding the human implications of rapid change.

Penny was voted one of the most influential female entrepreneurs in Australia, is an acclaimed TEDx speaker and is regularly featured in media publications such as The Huffington Post, BBC, Thrive Global, *SmartCompany*, *The San Francisco Chronicle*, StartupSmart, *The Age*, *The Sydney Morning Herald* and many more.

Above all else, she is an intentionally adaptable mother who is invested in her son's development and happiness and who uses her work and her imperfections to role model how to live a happy life.

She advocates fear(less)ness and practises what she preaches, even going so far as creating a global movement #Nakedforchange after a photo of her delivering a keynote in her bathing suit went viral on LinkedIn.

Penny proves time and time again that happy change is found when you surf the edge of your comfort zone – that's what this book will help you do.

HackingHappy.co

GRATITUDE

One of the simplest ways to elevate your happiness is through the practice of gratitude. It's scientifically proven that just taking a moment to be grateful for what you have, rather than focusing on what you don't, will make you happier.

So I'd like to indulge in a little gratitude as a way of acknowledging those who were instrumental in my hacking happiness journey and the realisation of a dream in sharing that journey in print with you now.

I am grateful for my son Saxon. Thanks for tolerating a mum who doesn't fit the mould and who makes you do crazy things like trek 120 kilometres through the Himalayas at age eight and for challenging me daily to be in the moment and look at the world through a different lens.

I am grateful for my dad, my mum, my sister and my brother. Thank you for calling me on my bullshit, keeping me grounded and supporting me in every crazy idea I have.

I am grateful for my uncle Don. Thank you for believing and investing in me and teaching me the hard lesson that happiness is not found in money.

I am grateful for my friend David. Thank you for helping me realise that the simple pleasures in life are where I am happiest. In nature, sharing a meal around my dining room table with friends and just playing soccer in the park with you, the dog and Saxon.

I am grateful to every individual who shared their story and vulnerability as a case study in this book in the service of helping others move closer to happiness.

I am grateful for my friend and collaboration partner Aden. Your vulnerability and willingness to experiment make my life and my work better. You continue to expose me to new practices and learning opportunities that make me surf the edge of my comfort zone. Thank you.

I am grateful for my friends Darren and Vanessa (a.k.a. the staff at Palmyra) who not only enabled me to escape and write this book at their beautiful property in Noosa but took care of me the whole time.

I am grateful for my friends Peter, Lucianne, Amanda, CJ and Julie: beautiful humans who have always got my back, challenge me to be a better person and are never afraid to show me what I'm missing.

Most of all, I am grateful to you, the reader. For being courageous enough to pick up this book, for being curious enough to open your mind to a different perspective and be willing to share your hacking happiness journey with me. I thank you.

INTRODUCTION

My Uncle Don was placed on a pedestal in our family. We were all in awe of his success and aspired to be just like him. He was a self-made entrepreneur long before it was ever considered an edgy career choice. He went from being a doctor to a commercial property developer, building and operating some of the first large medical centres in suburban Melbourne. He had a life we all aspired to: beautiful homes near the beach, fast cars, fine dining, expensive clothes and travel.

From a young age I would spend as much time as I could in his presence. On school holidays I would stay with him doing odd jobs in his medical centres for gold coins and immersing myself in his lifestyle, from the food he enjoyed to the music he listened to. I hold him responsible for my love of olives, anchovies, Kate Bush and Annie Lennox – things a country kid like me may have missed were it not for his influence.

The more interest I expressed in similar things to him and in educating myself the more he invested his time and money in my development. It was obvious he believed in me, and, as a teenager who was often off the rails, that belief made all the difference in the path I chose.

When I was 16 he came to me with an offer to attend a well-regarded private girls' school in order to complete my final years of high school and progress into university. It was a huge investment on his part and I knew it was an opportunity that could open doors for me and fundamentally shape a future of possibility.

My hard-working single mother was supporting three children on her working-class salary and could never have afforded such an education. My response was an easy 'yes', and shortly after he bought me my first computer (the original box-looking Apple Mac) to further accelerate my learning.

My family truly believed in my uncle's ability to succeed, achieve significant financial results and share the benefits, to the point that my mother and grandmother invested their life savings in his every business move. He was extremely generous in sharing his success and for quite some time it benefited the whole family. Until late one evening on 13 October 2011 when everything changed.

I'd just put my 14-month-old son to bed and the phone rang. It was my brother. I don't remember the words exactly – it was as if a huge fog moved in around me in that moment – the only thing I recall was the feeling that my Uncle Don was gone. For the first time in 36 years I felt myself collapse to the floor, curl up in a fetal position and sob uncontrollably.

The next day I found myself in a place where no-one ever wants to land ... at the morgue, identifying a body. I stood over my beloved 60-year-old uncle as the morgue attendant slowly pulled back a white sheet to reveal my uncle's grey ghostly face. As my eyes scanned down, I noticed in horror the chains locked around his neck. Empathetically the attendant explained that they had not been able to remove them in time for the viewing. A wave of extreme sadness came over me as I realised that my uncle had taken his own life in the most torturous way. His intent was to punish himself for the pain he believed he had caused with the collapse of his empire. The chains were weighted down with dumbbells. He had carried them in a backpack, walking a few kilometres in the dead of night, attached them around his neck and then quietly slipped himself into the murky waters off the edge of the Frankston Pier.

That moment changed everything and everyone in my family. My mother and grandmother lost everything. Not only their hard-earned life savings, but the only brother and son that they had ever known. They'd literally spent years toiling on our farms, saving their earnings, creating financial independence – and then overnight it was gone. For me, my definition of success imploded instantly. This was a man who seemingly had it all. A man who had never portrayed anything other than a calm, spiritual, grounded exemplar of good mental health.

If this was success, it sucked.

WAKING UP AND SHAKING UP

This story, understandably, haunted me. (And still does.)

Not surprisingly, like my role model Uncle Don, I had pursued the same path to success and was 16 years into my journey when he abruptly exited. I had accumulated everything I could have wanted in life: a nuclear family, a great career as an executive in a global corporation, a beautiful home with a white picket fence, European cars in the driveway and international travel whenever I wanted it. (Sound familiar?)

But there was a catch. I wasn't fulfilled, I constantly wanted more, and I was unsure of what 'more' was!

I wasn't *happy*. I was exhausted! And I certainly didn't want to end up like my uncle.

I spent the next two years questioning what success really meant. How had I arrived at the definition of success that I'd oriented my life around, what impact was it having on me and those I loved, and how could it have all gone so wrong for my uncle?

The more I reflected on the times in my life when I had been the most joyous, the more I realised there were consistent themes: I was happiest when I was:

- connecting with others
- solving human problems
- positively affecting the lives of others
- being in the moment.

Ironically, these were the things that were often sacrificed in my pursuit of success.

I soon came to the realisation that I was not alone in my discontent with success, nor in my pursuit of happiness.

There are so many people (you?) who seemingly 'have it all'. Professional career – check; nice home – check; a couple of kids – check; and maybe even a dog – check.

You've ticked all the boxes in life you were told would make you 'successful', yet you are unfulfilled and, sadly, unhappy – why?

I turned my seemingly perfect life completely upside down in pursuit of answering this question and helping others do the same. Within a seven-month period I left my highly successful 16-year career as an executive, relocated my family from Perth back to Melbourne (like moving from New York to LA), left an 18-year relationship and started my own purpose-driven company with the sole intent of positively impacting the lives of others. I gave myself the title of 'happiness hacker' (I'm claiming to be the world's first!) and set myself a bold mission to teach 10 million humans how to intentionally adapt in order to future-proof their happiness by 2025.

Through this journey, I came to understand that many of us are living our lives by a societal definition of success and it's making us miserable. We rarely create the space to press pause, take a breath and ask ourselves: what would success that made me feel good look like on *my* terms?

> Success does not make us happy; it is a by-product of being happy.

WHY I WROTE THIS BOOK

There are thousands of books out there selling silver bullets and seven steps to make millions, be happier and replicate the behaviour of high-performing entrepreneurs, executives and athletes. This is not one of those books. I don't prescribe quick fixes; I don't believe they exist. Anything worth having comes off the back of hard work, experimentation and persistence. Each path is our own and unique and I want to recognise that in the way I support you in bringing a little more joy into the everyday.

This book is an opportunity to look at the world, work and life through a different lens. To ask: what if the happiness you seek is not found in *wanting* what you don't have, but focusing on the things you are *avoiding*?

It is designed to challenge your desire for certainty and instead consider the magic that lies in the complexities and unknowns of today.

In the professional world, we've spent our lives curating perfect plans in order to manage change and mitigate risk – and now, in an age of exponential unprecedented change and distraction, *these rules do not apply*.

It's the courage to leap into the unknown, experiment, fail, learn and intentionally adapt that will enable you to unlock your happiness.

My intention is to provide you with a compass and set of tools to help you do just that.

Greater happiness comes through self-driven action, which is why this book is broken into two parts:

- **Part I** explores the 'happiness poverty' problem: why our definition of success is making us unhappy, and the opportunity that lies in not 'seeking' happiness but in looking at what we're *avoiding*. We unpack why we need to stop reacting and start intentionally adapting, and the skills we can amplify to do just that.
- **Part II** breaks down the concept of Intentional Adaptability into bite-sized pieces. You'll learn three critical skills to hack your happiness and experiment your way towards a thriving future.

Perhaps we are all secretly longing for a sign, even permission, to leap into the unknown and ride the edge of our comfort zones towards happiness—so take this book as that sign.

I want to mention that there are creators, educators and executives mentioned in this book as case studies who have had what looks like a blessed and privileged life. Some have had opportunities some of us can only imagine; some have accumulated wealth and high-priced possessions. So you may question, who are they to complain? How can they say they are unhappy? Why would they want to change?

As human beings, it's natural for us to judge and assume, but herein lies our own opportunity! An opportunity to be curious. I ask that as you read their stories you challenge any of these judgements as they come up. In my experience, having many material things doesn't make you a happy and thriving person. (Remember my Uncle Don?) These things don't protect you from anxiety or unhappiness; in fact, in many cases they can amplify anxiety due to the stress of trying to hold onto what you have even if it's not making you happy. Ironically, at the time of writing many people in this exact situation are now finding themselves at a forced moment of introspection due to the financial implications of the global coronavirus pandemic.

In my conversations with each interviewee, one of the consistent themes that comes up is the feelings of guilt for having so much and being perceived as ungrateful because they want *more*. Not more stuff, but more joy in the everyday, with less angst and less stress.

Everyone has the right to happiness, whether they have a little or they have a lot.

LASTLY, REMEMBER...

Hacking happiness is a journey – I'm still on mine! It's like a dimmer that gradually turns up over time based on the experiments you choose to undertake. Each turn of the dial is a moment that just doesn't seem to 'sit right'. Whether it's knowing you're not being the parent you want to be, or the leader you want to become, it's the compounding effect that propels you into action.

It's this action that brings clarity and exposes the path toward happiness that changes your life forever – for the better.

So what do you say?

Are you ready to hack your happiness?

HOW TO MAXIMISE YOUR JOURNEY

When I strike up a conversation with a random stranger and they ask me what I do, I always respond, 'I'm a happiness hacker'. This usually prompts a smile and a 'Tell me more!' Sounds pretty interesting, right?

Yes, it's an unusual job title, but it also says something about our society when there is a real need for a job that helps people find their happiness—because who doesn't want to be happy, and who doesn't feel that's a struggle today? In a world where so much of what we are fed comes from bad news and fear, is it any wonder that so many are seeking the holy grail of happiness?

> While hacking happiness sounds sexy and easily attainable, behind the scenes it is messy, challenging and uncomfortable—yet significantly rewarding for those who invest.

The best way I can describe it is like a yoga practice. This may conjure up images of crossed legs and esoteric chants, but anyone who practises yoga knows that it can be a true test of the mind and body.

The practice of hacking happiness is not dissimilar: you have to show up every day and experiment with different positions; you will have good days when you hold a pose forever, and other days where you fail and fall flat on your face. However, you will get better with consistent and persistent effort. It's not so much the outcome we focus on – that's a by-product – it's the trying that matters.

Ask yourself: when was the last time you committed to spending deep, focused time on you, on what makes you happy and bringing more of it into your everyday? Sadly, this seems a rarity, yet it's a necessity for thriving. So, if you continue on (and I hope you will) I have to warn you that, like all investments, hacking happiness carries a risk. The level of risk can be minimised through application, experimentation and ongoing practice, which is why I have included this little pre-read to help you understand how to get the most from your experience.

FIRST, WE HOLD UP THE MIRROR

Awareness is the first step to change. If we are unaware of what needs to change or of what we want to change, then how do we know to change it?

After over 20 years working with thousands in the space of change and adaptability I have learned that the best way to create awareness is to hold up the mirror. What do I mean? In the realm of hacking happiness, it's about looking at the behaviours we currently have and reflecting on how they might be affecting our ability to move in the direction we seek.

At my company HackingHappy.co, we value happiness over success and ignite a new wave of leaders with the skills to make intentional decisions about how they adapt in a complex environment. We pride ourselves on the curation of current data, ensuring that our work is always intentionally adapting.

Our extensive research in psychology, neuroscience and habit change has shown that we are a product of the things we repeat daily. That's why I want you to look in the mirror and see what you are doing at the moment to get you thinking and curious about what's possible if you make some tweaks.

With that in mind we start by assessing your level of Intentional Adaptability. The Hacking Happy Assessment takes around ten minutes to complete and it's free.

Jump online now at **IAQyou.com** and make a start.

I highly recommend that you do this before reading on, as it will provide a beautiful insight into you and where your opportunities lie for greater happiness. Ideally, it will provoke your curiosity to want to learn more.

Don't overthink your answers; just go with your first thought. Know that this is not a test. You're not seeking a 'perfect score', as in the realm of hacking happiness there is no such thing. Everyone starts from a different base and that base doesn't matter; what matters is evolution. You're seeking to understand more about yourself by looking inwards, thinking and reflecting.

Our goal is to create a basis for you to come back to at the end of this book, when you can reassess and observe where progress has been made and where new opportunities may lie.

THEN, WE ENABLE ACTION...

This book has been designed to enable you to take self-guided action through exploration and experimentation. As you will soon learn, I'm a no-BS kind of person. I find telling it how it is an effective way to communicate and enable informed choices, so that's how I'll roll.

If you choose to join me on this journey, I will provide you with a safe space to experiment, but not a comfortable one – because growth and meaningful change occur in discomfort. I'm here to support you in making intentional and sustainable adaptations in a complex environment that is evolving at speed.

My intent is to build your courage and confidence, enabling you to take back control of:

- your time
- where you channel your energy
- your happiness.

My passion lies in experimentation, as no two paths to happiness are the same, and I am not a doctor who can prescribe what is right for you.

What I can do is offer you happiness experiments that will enable you to make change in bite-sized pieces in order to test what works best for you.

At the end of each chapter, I have included a short section called **Experiment Now**. The intent of these sections is to encourage you to embrace the power of experimentation by applying what you have learned in the chapter. These experiments act as a kick-starter to your practice. For a deeper dive into the realm of application and experimentation.

At the end of each chapter you will also find a section titled **Reflect and Remember**. This brief section is designed to draw out the key takeaways from the chapter so that you can take a moment to reflect on what you have learned and reinforce its place in your memory if you so choose.

You will notice as you move through each chapter a sprinkling of **Happiness Hacks.** The intent of these hacks is to give you simple actions that you can experiment with straight away if you so choose.

LASTLY, WE SHARE THE HAPPY

I am by no means perfect, and nor do I profess to have *all* the answers. This is why I spend my days researching the latest in neuroscience, psychology and technology to find new ways to hack our brains, our behaviour and our environment to experience more joy in the everyday. I then use myself as a guinea pig and ask my students to do the same.

I've found exploring happiness in a community is way more powerful than going it alone. So now is the perfect time to share the happy. Consider bringing a friend with you on your happiness hacking journey; it's proven time and again that having someone else to keep you accountable as you change means that you are more likely to make sustainable change.

Perhaps consider joining the Hacking Happiness Collective that I've created on Facebook a safe space for unlike minds (like you) to explore, experiment and share practices that enable us to bring more joy into every day. Simply go to facebook.com/groups/hackinghappinesscollective/ to join us.

Who could be your happiness hacking buddy? Share with them what you are up to and invite them along for the ride. Consider experimenting together and sharing what you observed, what worked, what didn't and what you will do differently next time. You could even gift them a copy of this book. Look out for the Share the Happy symbol at the end of each chapter to explore how you can amplify your journey together.

I won't sugarcoat it: hacking happiness is hard work, but it's also fun. And once the door is open, you won't want to close it again!

So let's begin!

PART I

The Happiness Poverty Problem

Brace yourself, because in this section we will explore:

- why our definition of success is flawed and how it's affecting our ability to thrive
- how happiness is not found in what we want, but in what we are avoiding
- how our brains are being pushed into survival mode and why we need to stop reacting and start intentionally adapting.

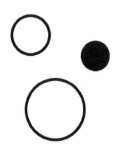

CHAPTER 1

Why success is a shit sandwich

Grab a pen and some paper, find a quiet spot with no distractions and sit for a moment. Get comfortable in your chair and close your eyes.

Now think about the word 'success'. What does it mean to you? What comes to mind? How does it make you feel? What images do you picture? Is it a beautiful home, an exotic beach house, a fast car, world travel... being a tech entrepreneur who's made billions, or a face on the cover of *Time* magazine? Whatever it is, draw it or write it down. Keep it unfiltered and keep it close by, as you will want to revisit this later in the chapter.

But first, I want you to have a look at what is there. How does it make you feel? Is it really your definition of success, or is it one you've been sold? How much of what you pictured lights you up inside, gives you meaning, energises you? Most importantly, how much of it *matters in the context of bringing you greater happiness*?

Let's consider an example. Sam is a senior executive in finance. Her image of success was centred around climbing the corporate ladder, leading large teams in even larger organisations, and having a big salary to buy the things she wanted: designer handbags, an expensive car, family holidays overseas...the list went on.

Yet when Sam looked back on this list – like I want you to do now – this is how she summed up what she saw:

> I have it all...yet I constantly feel like I want *more*. Nothing fulfils me. It's like I'm accumulating the want and shortly after my level of success just goes back to baseline. I feel like I'm back where I started...wanting *more*. I've fallen into the trap of status and prestige and I'm not sure those things even matter.

What Sam is referring to is backed up by a theory, developed by psychologists Philip Brickman and Donald T. Campbell, termed 'hedonic adaptation' (and later called the 'hedonic treadmill', figure 1.1), which basically describes how we as human beings get used to any positive external events in our lives. We assume that when we have that thing, win the lottery, buy the big house, get the job, we will be happier...but it's a trap that places us on a treadmill to nowhere. Studies have shown that our circumstances don't account for our happiness. When we achieve a desired thing, it spikes our happiness in the short term. But quite quickly we go back to our genetic happiness baseline. (In chapter 2 we explore in more detail the work of Sonja Lyubomirsky and our genetic happiness baseline.)

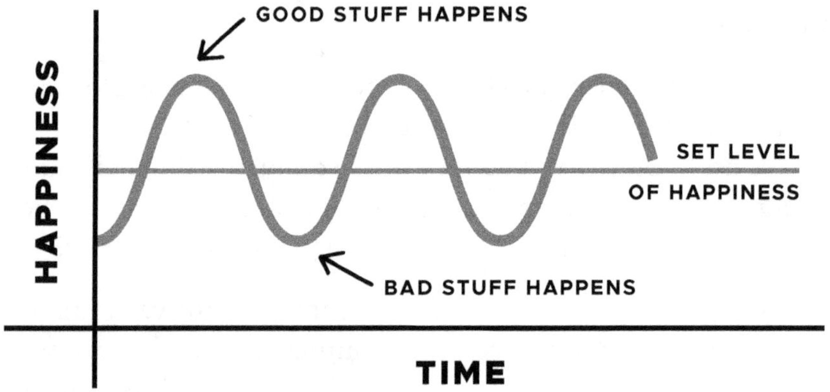

Figure 1.1: hedonic adaptation

Source: Positive Psychology https://positivepsychology.com/hedonic-treadmill/

According to the founder of positive psychology, Martin Seligman,

> Even if you could alter all of the external circumstances, it would not do much for you, since together they probably account for not more than between 8 and 15 percent of the variance in happiness. The very good news is that there are quite a number of internal circumstances that will likely work for you ... If you decide to change them (and be warned that none of these changes come without real effort), your level of happiness is likely to increase lastingly.

Does Sam's story ring true for you? How attached is your definition of success to the work that you do? Have you ever considered what success would look like if you focused on *who you are* as a human being rather than *what you do*?

> What if happiness and success are intertwined and only possible if we focus more on being and less on doing?

THE PATH TO POWER

The desire for success certainly provides aspiration and motivation in the game of life. Most of us start to form our definition of success at an early age, shaped by our environment, the people we look up to, the advertising we are exposed to and the influence of our friends.

We are raised to believe that if we do well in school and in university, we'll get a good job, which then leads to a career that delivers good money, potentially more societal influence and a higher standard of living, which is more likely to make us more socially attractive, which is more likely to increase our happiness. This is the linear view of success and its most basic linkage to our pursuit of happiness.

But does that actually make us happy?

Have we prioritised our ego over our happiness? Are we spending more time polishing our personal brand online and running on the busy hamster wheel than connecting to what truly brings us joy?

Take Steve, for example, a very successful senior executive in a global consulting firm. We sat down for a coffee after a workshop and he was on the brink of tears. He confessed:

> I've followed the path I was led to believe would make me successful. I work really hard...often at the expense of time with my family. I have all the trimmings in life, but I'm burnt out, miserable, and it's impacting my mental health. I drive past building sites and look at the bricklayers, the tradies, with envy. It's not usually a job we associate with success, but I think to myself that's the kind of work I want. Work where there is mateship, connection, hours that are set, where at the end of the day your work is literally finished and your time with family is sacred. I'm starting to wonder whether this is what success should look like.

Herein lies the problem.

> Our societal definition of success is firmly anchored in the accumulation of money and power.

Why? Capitalism, for one.

In a capitalist society we value money and power, which orients our behaviour towards *doing* in order to accumulate more of it. The more you do the more you have; and the more you have, the more influential you become, and the more likely you are to shape the future for the rest of us.

We have been led to believe that money and power equals success and this type of success leads to greater happiness. I'm calling *bullshit*!

The research shows that, once we can comfortably meet our basic human needs, the more money we earn, the more our happiness actually declines.

A GROWING CONCERN

Money doesn't make us happy. Full stop.

Look around you and consider the people you know, or observe in the media, who are earning good or even crazy money. Are they truly happy? Money may have afforded them a particular lifestyle, but has it delivered the holy grail of happiness?

Let's take the United States as a case in point. Their income per capita has increased markedly during the past half century, and yet their happiness is in *decline*. This drop is attributed to John Helliwell's five major variables that affect the happiness of a country (see figure 1.2, overleaf):

1. population health (measured by health-adjusted life expectancy, HALE)
2. the strength of social support networks
3. personal freedom (measured by the perceived freedom of individuals to make key life decisions)
4. social trust (measured by the public's perception of corruption in government and business)
5. generosity.

What's interesting is that none of Helliwell's measures relate directly to wealth, as Jeffrey Sachs points out in the report 'America's Health Crisis and the Easterlin Paradox'. Rather, it's meaningful connection, wellbeing and arguably what it truly means to be human that brings greater happiness.

Robert Waldinger is a Harvard professor who spends his days overseeing the longest study in history (75 years and counting) on human happiness. In his TED talk he reveals the greatest insight gleaned from all of the data collected is that those who invest heavily in social connection (not ego and financial gain) live happier, healthier and longer lives.

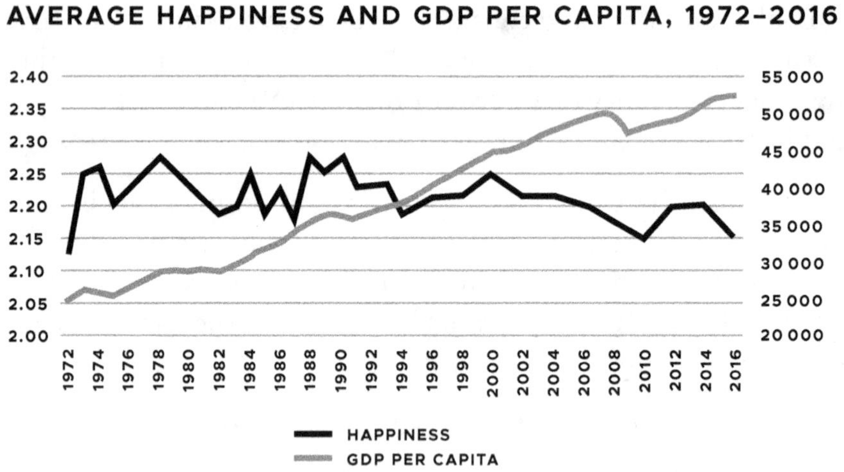

Figure 1.2: happiness versus income
Source: Helliwell, J., Layard, R., & Sachs, J. (2018). *World Happiness Report 2018*, New York: Sustainable Development Solutions Network.

We have been led to believe that the more money we earn, the happier we will be and that is correct up to the point of earning US$75 000 per year. (Which we could argue is the amount that allows us to meet our basic human needs.) A study undertaken by economist Angus Deaton and psychologist Daniel Kahneman showed that the 'lower a person's annual income falls below that benchmark, the unhappier he or she feels'. (No surprises there!)

Here's the kicker, though: the study showed that no matter how much above US$75 000 you earn, your degree of happiness does not increase.

In my own work with thousands of professionals, I have observed that often the more money we earn the more debt we take on in order to accumulate more things, better homes, better cars, better schooling. (Feel familiar?)

This debt often then locks us into what I call 'the golden handcuffs', where we become bound to a job we don't always like to service a lifestyle we thought would make us happy – and yet, all it does is create stress, financial burden and feelings of being stuck!

Let's connect back with Sam's story for a moment. After her constant desire for 'more' reached the point where it was like a slap in the face that could no longer be ignored, she started to challenge her definition of success. It took three years from the initial thought of disrupting herself for her to actually take action. (This seems to be a pattern with those seeking to make significant change in their lives; it takes time.) She was clearly stuck. When I asked her why, she stated that 'financial fear held me back'.

This was not a new story to me. I'd experienced the exact same fear myself. I don't think we realise how strongly we attach the money we earn (or the title we hold) to how successful we perceive ourselves to be. It's conditioned. Years into my hacking happiness journey, self-doubt kept presenting itself because my salary had not returned to the one I had left at the height of my corporate career. I kept questioning whether I should quit, whether I was failing in my reinvention even though my happiness had improved greatly and I loved what I was doing. Through some uncomfortable interrogation into my belief system I realised that I was subconsciously still measuring my success by the money I earned, and it was secretly stealing my happiness.

We've been sold a shit sandwich when it comes to success. Instead of enabling us to thrive, it's driving happiness poverty and a significant decline in the mental health of our society.

A MENTAL PROBLEM

The conflict between how we define success and how it affects the happiness of our society and our mental health is not new. William James, in a letter to H. G. Wells in 1906, wrote, 'The moral flabbiness born of the bitch-goddess SUCCESS. That—with the squalid interpretation put on the word success—is our national disease'.

A disease it is! There is growing concern globally that we are experiencing an anxiety epidemic in our digitally connected world, and that the hardest hit are the next generation. While global anxiety data to support this theory is elusive (due to the fact that many people suffer from more than one condition), as reported in *The Guardian*, researchers have found a way to measure how mental illness affects a population:

> One measure of mental illness that has become a gold standard over the past 30 years is the disability adjusted life year (DALY) – a sum of all the years of healthy, productive life lost to illness, be it through early death or through disability.

What's fascinating is how rich nations dominate this list, as shown in figure 1.3.

So we are arguably more successful, as we are wealthier, yet we are unhappier, more mentally unwell and, would you believe, lonelier than ever.

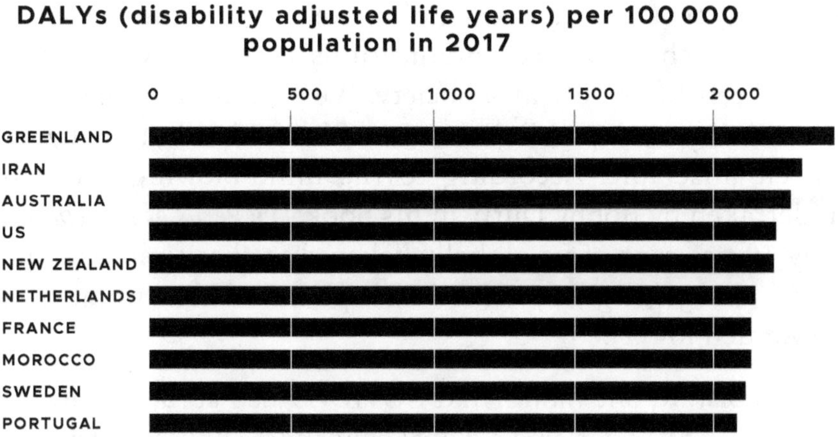

Figure 1.3: rich nations and mental illness
Source: Institute for Health Metrics Evaluation. Used with permission. All rights reserved.

According to a study by health insurer Cigna 50 per cent of Americans state they are lonely. In Australia it's one in four adults. What's most concerning is that Professor Holt-Lunstad's groundbreaking research has demonstrated that 'social isolation and loneliness significantly increases the risk of early death, and the magnitude of the risk exceeds that of many leading health indicators'. Is our success not only isolating us but sending many of us to an early grave?

> We've never been more technologically connected, yet humanly disconnected.

MORE = LESS

In January 2020, when I started writing this book, we found ourselves at the most abundant time in history. If we looked to nearly every social indicator – declining infant mortality, declining poverty, increased global literacy, and the declining costs of technology, communications and energy – we had never been better off as a society. We had an abundance of accessibility and possibility at our fingertips but many of us felt miserable. According to the mind-blowing research undertaken by Bobby Duffy in his book *The Perils of Perception*, only 10 per cent of us globally believed at that time that the world was getting better (and I suspect that that number is now much lower).

Fast forward one month and COVID-19 had abruptly entered our lives and was declared a global pandemic. Thousands around the world fell ill and died, livelihoods were lost and economies went into meltdown. Office workers were sent home to work remotely, lockdown became indefinite, physical distancing and self-isolation became the new normal and school was out. Partner this complexity with a society that was already feeling burnt out, anxious and humanly disconnected and you have the platform for a perfect storm. Abundance felt like it exited out the back door, and many were left fearful of the future.

We found ourselves at a forced moment of introspection. Mother Nature had sent us to our metaphorical rooms and given us time out. Time out to rethink the future of humanity and the role we have in shaping it. What we now have is a shift in where our abundance sits. We've been gifted an abundance of time away from the noise of the everyday to reset around what truly matters.

Pandemic or not, our time is our most valuable resource, and how we choose to spend it affects our mindset and our ability to weave happiness into the everyday. Billionaire investor Warren Buffett, in a conversation with Microsoft mogul Bill Gates and Charlie Rose, famously stated that he can buy anything in the world, but he can't buy time. Our constant pursuit of greater productivity has significantly affected our happiness.

Our focus on *doing* has compromised our state of *being*.

Busy-ness continues to hold us back as we unconsciously respond to distractions, while the things that truly matter and light us up are sidelined.

Society seems consumed with being more productive and more efficient so that we can squeeze more into every day. The pervasive use of technology to amplify our productivity has our brains overstimulated and our bodies stuck on the busy hamster wheel, unconscious of where our time is being sucked up.

Executives (like Sam and Steve) constantly tell me they no longer feel in control of their time or where their mind goes, thanks to the bombardment of attention-grabbing technology masked as productivity or knowledge-building tools. We have become more efficient and more productive so that we can do more *doing*...yet we've lost the space for *being*!

According to research conducted by Ashley Whillans and her team, time poverty is a real thing in the United States, with 80 per cent of people feeling they do not have the time to get what they want done in a day. The impacts on those who feel time poor are profound.

In her *Harvard Business Review* article 'Time for Happiness', Whillans shares:

> Those who feel time-poor experience lower levels of happiness and higher levels of anxiety, depression, and stress. They experience less joy. They laugh less. They exercise less and are less healthy...The research showed time stress had a stronger negative effect on happiness than being unemployed did.

In a nutshell, what you choose to invest your time in will determine whether you live in an abundant world or not.

OR LESS = MORE?

We are unintentionally walking backwards, away from our happiness, based on a flawed equation of success = happiness. It's time to give the bird to a legacy that is not acting in the service of humanity's ability to thrive. Let's flip the equation and see where it takes us...

happiness = success

How does that sound? According to Shawn Achor in his book *The Happiness Advantage*, research in both neuroscience and psychology supports a reverse happiness equation:

> We become more successful when we are happier. Doctors put in a positive mood before they make a diagnosis show almost three times more intelligence and creativity than doctors in a neutral state and they make accurate diagnoses 19 percent faster. Optimistic salespeople outsell their pessimistic counterparts 56 percent. Students primed to feel happy before taking a math test far outperform their neutral peers. It turns out our brains are hardwired to perform at their best not when they are negative or neutral, but when they are positive.

It took me 39 years to wake up to the disconnect between what I'd been led to believe would make me successful and what actually made me happy. Almost half a lifetime before I changed my conditioned perception of success and reshaped my life around a new paradigm. A paradigm based on weaving more happiness into my everyday using my controllables, my mindset and my behaviour.

For me, success and happiness are now intertwined and clearly centred around:

- being the best role model I can for my son
- making the time for joy and self-care daily
- doing work that positively affects the lives of others and is sustainable, with people I respect who challenge me to look at the world through a different lens and make me smile
- leaving the world a little better than when I arrived in it.

What list would you come up with to redefine success and shape your future?

REDEFINING SUCCESS

Remember our exercise at the start of this chapter? Well, I want you to do something similar now. Grab a pen and paper, find a nice quiet spot. But this time I want you to picture the word 'happiness'. What does happiness look like for you?

You can write down or draw the images that spring to mind that make you happy. Write words or phrases or doodles – it really doesn't matter, as long as it's meaningful to you. When I do this exercise in workshops and conferences around the world, I get people to pull out their mobile phones and find photos that make them happy, so if that helps get after it. Consider engaging a friend in this exercise and share your perspectives to further crystallise your ideas.

Done?

When I first started doing this exercise with large groups it was simply to build connections among participants in the room, but it soon became clear it provided a window to so much more. I started to notice that there were consistent themes around where people found happiness.

The seven happiness themes are (see figure 1.4):

1. human connection
2. animals
3. achievement
4. nature
5. presence
6. impact
7. experiences.

Now, looking at your list or the images you've pulled up from your phone, which themes do they align with?

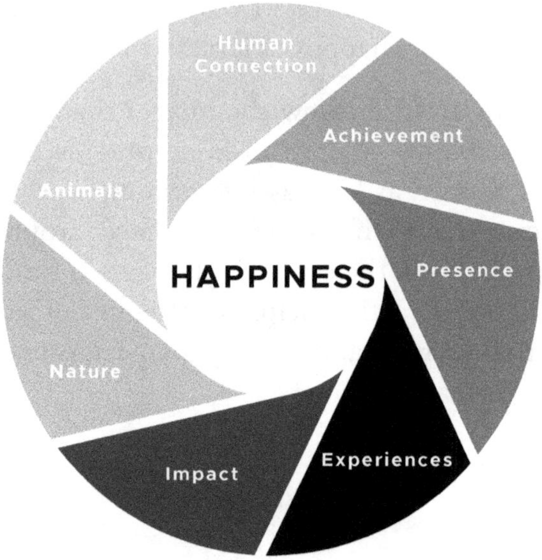

Figure 1.4: where is happiness found?

More interestingly, how much of what you've identified is related to work? (My guess is not much.) When we explore these themes in a workshop setting I ask people what they observe. The most common response is that *none* of these things relate to work. This is a perfect example of how outdated our definition of success is. Without a doubt, each and every one of these themes can be connected to work in some way if we get creative enough. Many workplaces now allow pets in the office; human connection is a choice; walking meetings outdoors are often more productive than meeting around a table; and the list goes on.

If these themes are where happiness is found, ask yourself how much of this is going on in your everyday life. Imagine if we leveraged this simple insight into how we shaped success in not only our work but in our lives?

Success is a by-product of doing the things that make you happy more often, which are the things that align to the themes above!

It's time to screw 'success' and redefine it on your own terms.

Time to challenge the flawed societal definition of success and reduce the overwhelm and angst it creates for so many. What if we start with what makes us happy and find a new way of defining success? What if we could weave more happiness into the everyday?

You simply cannot be successful if you are not happy. So let's leverage this simple insight to shape our work and our lives now – because our future depends on it!

IN ACTION

Just one more thing before we move on, because this is important. Remember Sam from the start of the chapter? Well, she no longer works in a corporate finance role. At the time of writing, she is in a state of transition where she says she feels 'liberated and uncomfortable'. When I asked what the catalyst for her finally taking action was after three years of longing, she said it was the realisation that she had a choice. A choice to change.

It wasn't until she had undertaken a workshop with me that the realisation hit her. I had mentioned to her in that session that it is not my place to judge how others define their own success; my only ask is that it is conscious and intentional.

When I asked Sam what success now looks like for her, having gone through the process of redefining it, she said it's centred around

> making intentional change, brave choices to do what I want to do, not choosing the safe path, avoiding the golden handcuffs, choosing who, when and what work I do, pushing the boundaries of what I think I can do and making enough money to cover the basics.

The path to money and power is a choice, and that choice comes with compromise. That compromise may very well be your happiness.

So what will you choose? The misery of the safe, known path, even if it's not serving you? Or will you activate courage, step into the uncertainty and surf the edge of your comfort zone, knowing that happiness is somewhere on the other side?

Stay or go?

EXPERIMENT NOW

1. Grab a blank piece of paper and a pen (preferably coloured pens). Creativity is a beautiful way to amplify your thinking.
2. Create space, turn off all distractions and give yourself 15 minutes of uninterrupted thinking time.
3. Ask yourself: 'What makes me happy?' Think of the times in your everyday life where you experience joy, contentment, pleasure, fulfilment. What were you doing, who were you with, what was the feeling? Freestyle (in the table), capturing words and pictures on the paper to articulate what makes you happy.
4. Consider how you redefine success on your own terms. Let go of the societal definition of success and think of what success would look like on your terms if you wove more of the things that make you happy into your everyday.

Happiness looks like (draw and scribble)	
New definition of success (define success on your terms)	

5. Now consider one small action you can take every day to help you turn your ideas into action and bring a little more happiness into your life. It can be as simple as introducing more walking meetings to cultivate greater human

connection with nature, a daily random act of kindness or carving an hour out of your day for a new experience or just to be with family. Write down your simple action below.

REFLECT AND REMEMBER

* The attainment of success is driving happiness poverty and a significant decline in the mental health of our society.
* Today we are arguably more 'successful', yet we are unhappier, more mentally unwell and lonelier than ever.
* You cannot be successful if you are not happy.
* We base everything on a flawed equation of *success = happiness,* whereas it should be *happiness = success*.
* Success is a by-product of doing the things that make you happy more often.
* The path to money and power is a choice, and that choice comes with compromise; that compromise may very well be your happiness.
* It's up to you to redefine success by looking at what makes you happy in the everyday.

SHARE THE HAPPY

Consider undertaking the redefining success experiment with your partner, if you have one, or a close friend, and compare what you come up with. Learn from each other and commit to action together.

CHAPTER 2

Screw the plan; embrace the uncertainty

When I decided to leave the comfort of my corporate job, I was amazed by the number of my respected peers who openly shared that they thought I'd lost the plot by exiting without a clear plan of what was next. I was an anomaly back then – no-one left the safety of the golden handcuffs unless it was to jump into a newer, more diamond-encrusted set, higher up in the chain in a different company. Yet the more they told me what I was doing was crazy, the more right it felt to jump into the unknown and work out how to build the parachute on the way down.

I now realise that what I was doing made many feel extremely uncomfortable (which is perhaps exactly how you feel about the change you want to make). It was shining a spotlight on a change they themselves longed for but just weren't ready to make. My actions compelled my peers to project their fears onto me and unknowingly mask them as concern.

Often when we do something that others long to do (but are afraid to do) they will tell us all the reasons why we shouldn't and couldn't. Fear projection is a real thing and we allow it to stop us from hacking happiness because it comes from those who are close to us – those we trust, whose opinions we respect.

In my self-disruption journey to realign to what made me happy, I did all the things I'd been told never to do in the professional world. I screwed the plan up and embraced the uncertainty. The result?

Fast forward five years, and it's now these same peers who reach out regularly, longing to make the same change and asking me how I've done it. How I reinvented myself completely in what appears to be a tight time frame, and how they can too.

> Change is hard, and it's scary, but we need to accept and embrace that growth occurs in discomfort, while avoidance leaves potential and possibility on the table.

HAPPINESS HACK

Next time someone tries to project their fear onto you, just listen, observe and say thank you. Will you choose to let their fears become yours and stop you from doing something you've longed for? Or will you choose to let it go and step forward into what brings you joy?

THE PAIN OF A PLAN

Large traditional corporations have historically built their success on managing and mitigating risk. When I worked in the corporate world managing large-scale change projects, for example, there was nothing I did without a 500-plus line item project plan, a risk-mitigation strategy and a budget that was pre-approved. I had been conditioned to believe that without a plan, I would fail – and failure was not acceptable and certainly not something to be celebrated. In fact, it would *limit* your career and your career choices. It would be a red flag with the words 'She can't do it' in bold-type font.

So many of the beliefs we have about planning and managing risk go against the grain of exploring what makes us thrive. Often what you have been led to believe will make you successful actually works *against* you in your path to happiness.

For years I'd been paid in my career to have the answers. I was a professional, and it was my job to be all-knowing. I now realise this was exactly what was holding me back. Why? Because when we assume the position of the 'expert' it affects our mindset; it limits our ability to be open to challenging our belief system (which is often formed off a sample size of one), to unlearning. We assume that what we've done before will work when applied to new problems, but how can you know what the best approach is to a challenge you've never tackled before?

> We learn by doing, by messing up, dusting ourselves off, reflecting and intentionally adapting.

It's fascinating to me that people assumed that I had a clear plan in place before I left the corporate world, about what I was going to do and how I was going to do it. This was the Penny they knew, and it was the social conditioning playing out again. The truth is I had absolutely no idea what I was going to do next. That's right: none. But I had spent so much of my life planning for the future that it stopped me from enjoying the now and, damn, we know tomorrow never comes.

However, there were a few things I knew to be true. I wanted to:

- have a positive impact on the lives of others
- spend more time connecting and being in the moment than worrying about 'what if?'

- leverage my passion for creating meaningful change and helping others realise potential they didn't know they had
- leave the world just a little better than what it was when I arrived in it.

That was all I had. As I look back, it was exactly what I needed to make a start on hacking happiness. What I knew to be true provided a compass to step forward (even in small steps) and an acceptance that there was not and never would be a perfect plan towards happiness. Waiting for it to appear would only hold me back. I came to the realisation that certainty is an *impediment* to growth – embracing the unknown is where the magic lies, yet so many of us avoid it.

The path forward appears when we allow our actions to breed the clarity.

AN UNKNOWN EDUCATION

With no set plan or idea about what was next I decided to find people who could help me discover the answers I was looking for. Human beings who were doing work they loved, who had gone before me and made an intentional choice to not take the safe path but instead take the path towards what truly mattered to them, not knowing where it would lead.

I jumped online and started searching for entrepreneurs led by passion. It didn't take me long to unearth a growing collective of conscious capitalists and social entrepreneurs. I was fascinated, coming from a traditional corporate background, that this space of doing commercially sound business while actually making the world a better place and positively affecting lives existed. It was news to me. I started sending emails to random strangers in this community, telling them I was in a state of transition with no idea what was next, with a passion to make the world better and an offer to buy them a coffee if they were willing to share their wisdom on how they had created a career pursuing what brought them joy.

All of these human beings were open to creating the space to help a stranger find a path to greater happiness. (I only had one 'no'.) Each coffee connected me to someone new and to their networks, and many of these people are now friends and supporters. This is where my real education in hacking happiness began. I was learning there was no silver bullet, no easy path, as no two journeys were the same. The common thread was that these individuals were willing to try, to experiment, to fail, to adapt, to unlearn, to risk it all in order to live the life and do the work that brought them joy.

UNLEARNING

Now might be a good time to introduce the concept of 'unlearning'. It was a term that I had never considered in my corporate days, but it's acutely critical to understand if you wish to explore your happiness. Why? Because creating space for a different approach, a new way of being, requires us to let go of old beliefs. It's these old ways that act as a barrier to growth and possibility.

What does unlearning mean? In an academic context Bo Hedberg, Paul Nystrom and William Starbuck define unlearning as 'the intentional elimination of knowledge, which is obsolete and may detract from new knowledge acquisition'.

In my terms it's about letting go of your ego, embracing uncertainty and challenging your belief system to continually ask the question 'If I was wrong about that, how would I go about proving it?' and then acting upon it.

Now, you can't simply unlearn by erasing something you know from your brain—once it's there it's there. However, according to researchers in their paper 'Unlearning before creating new knowledge: A cognitive process', you can consciously 'reduce the influence of old knowledge for the sake of creating new knowledge and/or patterns of thinking'. Building this skill is pertinent to your ability to let go of what got you to where you are and being open to what could be.

If by chance you believe that you are one of the rare beings where most of what you know is actually fact, I would challenge you to take a look at Bobby Duffy's book *The Perils of Perception*. His research across 40 countries shows how deluded we are as a species about the world around us and why we are often wrong about nearly everything. I implore you to challenge yourself to consider that your beliefs are shaped by your environment and experiences; you are a sample size of one in a world of billions, and just because you believe something does not make it a fact. Don't let your beliefs stand between you and unlocking your happiness.

HACKING HAPPINESS EXPLAINED

So what do I actually mean when I say 'hacking happiness'?

Hacking happiness is not about finding a way to skip down the streets laughing and painting rainbows every day. That's bullshit. It's just not possible, because life has many uncontrollable elements and the reality is that bad things will happen; it's inevitable ... I mean, who could have predicted the coronavirus and the impact it would have on our way of life?

While we can't control everything, we can control how we choose to respond – and that is what will ultimately affect our ability to experience a higher level of happiness.

> Hacking happiness is about giving yourself permission to ride the wave of every emotion that life throws at you and know that you have the skills, support and resources to come out the other side a little better than you were before.

There is a misconception that happy people are happy 24/7 – but the reality is that those who live the most joyful lives are those who allow themselves to fully experience all feelings, rather than suppress negative feelings because they are seen as bad.

Psychologist Jordi Quoidbach explores this idea further through a concept called 'emodiversity'. Emodiversity is how emotionally diverse we are; it's our capacity for allowing ourselves to experience many different positive and negative feelings. UC Berkely's *Greater Good Magazine* detailed the first study of 35 000 people, finding that:

> ...emodiversity is linked to less depression....for all types of emodiversity: positive (experiencing many different positive emotions), negative (many different negative emotions), and general (a mix of both). In fact, people high in emodiversity were less likely to be depressed than people high in positive emotion alone.

So herein lies my first warning (which may come as a surprise): hacking happiness can create an unexpected emotional response, and it's likely to make you cry and doubt yourself. Know that this is completely normal!

A way of being, not doing

Apart from the fact that being happier:

- feels good
- gives us more energy
- enhances our social connections
- makes others feel good

science also shows that happy people are more flexible, innovative and productive in their work. They lead and negotiate more effectively. They bounce back quicker, are healthier and live longer. Now, damn, who doesn't want that?!

According to research undertaken by Professor Sonja Lyubomirsky, 50 per cent of your happiness is genetically determined (this is the genetic happiness baseline mentioned in chapter 1), which means it's fixed, you are born with it; 10 per cent relates to your circumstances, and the remaining 40 per cent? Well that's up to you!

The thoughts, actions and behaviours you undertake in the everyday will determine how that remaining 40 per cent plays out. I'm a firm believer in focusing on what you can control and not what you can't, which is why when I talk about hacking happiness my focus is on supporting you in experimenting with the 40 per cent you have available to you.

How can you challenge yourself, your mindset and behaviours to be happier every day?

How do you want to show up in life? What repeatable things can you do, day in and day out, that will enable you to be the happiest version of you?

One of my biggest supporters was my dear friend Jenni. She was my champion in the corporate world and my cheerleader when I stepped into the entrepreneurial world. While we were always half a world apart due to our respective careers she had a knack for jumping into my inbox exactly when I needed a little boost. She passed away from cancer five years into my happiness journey, one month shy of her forty-fourth birthday. As I spent time with my beautiful friend in the last weeks of her life, as she faced the reality of her situation, she truly showed she was a master of hacking happiness.

Happiness is not a goal, nor is it an end state: it's a way of being.

Jen had a choice: a choice to either wallow (and rightly so) in a situation that seemed so cruel and wrong, or to be grateful for the wonderful life she had lived and be in every moment she could in the time she had left with those she loved.

She chose the latter. In facing death, she realised that the things that she had been avoiding pointed directly to where her happiness may be found. In a letter written by Jen to her beloved husband, which I had the honour of delivering as part of her eulogy, she eloquently stated:

> My lesson when I was diagnosed with this cancer was that I tried to be a warrior, to be solo and always be in front… I thought I wasn't worthy enough and needed the recognition of others (in my case, through my work) to be successful and be loved. The reality was that I am worthy of love, I am surrounded by it, and never needed to doubt it. Live a life that is magical, don't hold back if I am not here, miss me but celebrate my life and live it with genuine love, without fear as things will work out.

We need to stop 'seeking' happiness and start looking at what we're avoiding. We all have the same 40 per cent of our own happiness that's up to us, that we can influence. How we choose to show up in the everyday will determine what that 40 per cent will look like. We have an opportunity to step into the things that we know bring us joy, and stop avoiding them because they can be uncomfortable, provide uncertainty and bring up feelings that we would prefer to suppress or ignore. Happiness is messy yet magical. It is found in leaning into the hard stuff, and exploring the feelings we would rather ignore when they show up. The opportunities for more joy in the everyday sit in unpacking uncomfortable feelings, so that we can move through them in a way that allows us to come out the other side just a little better than we were before.

So where do we begin?

EXPERIMENT NOW

How do we embrace uncertainty, let go of the perfect plan and create a compass that enables our actions to breed the clarity? We unplan happiness by exploring what we know to be true in the context of the change we seek.

1. Start with the end in mind. Where you think you want to be in 12 months is not where you will end up, but putting a stake in the ground is helpful in moving forward. Visualisation has long been proven powerful in realising change, so close your eyes and visualise what happiness looks like for you in just 12 months' time. Where would you be, who would you be with, what work would you be doing, how would it feel, what impact would you be having on yourself and others? When you're ready, open your eyes and list anything that came up for you in the 'Happiness looks like' column on the far right-hand side of the table.
2. Now under the 'Reality looks like' column in the table, I want you to write down your current situation relative to the aspiration you wrote down in the 'Happiness looks like' column. For example, Happiness looks like: '3 evenings a week where I am engaged with my partner or family without distraction from 6.30 pm till 8.30 pm, enjoying quality connection'. The reality might be, 'I come home distracted every night constantly checking my phone, being short with those I care about and never really in the moment'.
3. Use these insights to unpack what has held you back from moving from your current state to what happiness looks like. Your opportunity lies in the gap between your aspiration and reality. Note down what you've been avoiding. Be completely honest with yourself, as filters will dilute your ability to hack happiness. What barriers within your control have you allowed to stop you from moving closer to a happier state of being? For example, FOMO — fear of missing out. If you're not constantly connected to your phone you might miss something and it might affect your ability to succeed... but at the same time it could be taking you away from the things that make you happy, like being present and in the moment.

Reality looks like

What I've been avoiding

Happiness looks like

Three small actions to breed clarity

Actions, observations and insights

4. Surf the edge of your comfort zone and write down three small, simple actions you can experiment with to start addressing what you've been avoiding in order to move you closer to happier in the everyday. Change in bite-sized pieces is the best way to build the courage and confidence to step into bigger, riskier yet more rewarding change over time. It might be as simple as, 'Put my phone on aeroplane mode in another room between the hours of 6.30 pm and 8.30 pm 3 nights a week'.
5. Go forth and experiment using the actions you noted.
6. Observe over the coming weeks how your actions make you feel and how they affect your mindset and behaviour. Take the time to reflect on this and make notes in the space provided.

REFLECT AND REMEMBER

* Change is hard, it's scary, but we need to accept and embrace that growth occurs in discomfort, while avoidance leaves potential and possibility on the table.
* We learn by doing, by messing up, dusting ourselves off, reflecting and intentionally adapting.
* The path forward appears when we allow our actions to breed the clarity.
* Hacking happiness can create an unexpected emotional response and it's likely to make you cry and doubt yourself. This is completely normal!
* Happiness is not a goal, nor is it an end state; it's a way of being.
* We need to stop 'seeking' happiness and start looking at what we're avoiding.

SHARE THE HAPPY

Undertake your Happiness Unplanning with a friend or your partner and share your perspectives and the actions you identified. Set a date in a few months' time to reconnect and share what happened when you took your actions and how it has affected you. This is a great way to hold yourself to account.

CHAPTER 3

From reacting to adapting

Let's address the elephant in the room. The change you seek is freaking scary; 'terrifying' might even be a word to describe how you feel when you think about it. Damn, this is your life we're talking about, and it matters. I get it! I've stood in those shoes, I've sat in the pain of uncertainty (many times), questioning 'have I made the right decision?', 'will it work out?' (I'm actually in that space right now as the 2020 COVID-19 pandemic is in full swing.) These feelings, these questions, they are completely rational to consider.

Here's the thing though: fear (of things that are not life threatening) is a signal of how *important* something is to you. You're afraid because you feel so invested in the outcome, you want it so bad, but the fear that it may not work out stops you from leaning into the possibility.

> The irony when it comes to change is it's often not the act of change we are afraid of; it's the fear of what we have to lose or give up as part of the process.

It doesn't matter that what we're giving up is making us unhappy. It's still familiar, it's known, it's comfortable, and this creates a barrier to stepping into what we could *gain*. You feel frozen, stuck – let's be honest, you're probably finding any excuse you can to put roadblocks in the way of taking action! So know this: if these feelings resonate, it's a sign you are absolutely in the right place.

We do not find ourselves here because we seek to be normal. What is 'normal' anyway? Normal doesn't exist, normal is about conforming to how you think others want you to be. Normal is not aspirational, it's comfortable. In fact, I'm challenging you to consider that normal might end up being the very thing holding you back from being happy.

So do you want to be normal or do you want to be happy?

A PATTERN FOR CHANGE

A few years into navigating my hacking happiness journey, I started to notice a clear pattern. Every time I spoke in front of an audience or ran a workshop there was one question that kept being asked:

> 'How do I realise the life I want and still navigate the pace and scale of change that's occurring?'

At work, or as a leader, you may find yourself tasked with helping others navigate the pace and scale of change, but honestly you're struggling with how you do this for yourself, let alone anyone else! Everyone tells stories of their jam-packed days where we are reacting to the noise of life. Seriously, how do you get the time to think, to create, to *be* when every day is full to the brim?

The pace of change in our society is getting faster and even more disorientating and, as we've observed, this directly correlates with a decline in our mental wellbeing and ultimately our happiness. So what to do?

My curiosity about this problem led me to a 2011 article in the *Harvard Business Review* that explained a concept called an Adaptability Quotient (AQ), which measures the ability to adapt in a complex, fast-changing environment. Your AQ proves more important than your EQ (Emotional Quotient) and IQ (Intelligence Quotient) in the context of the unprecedented future we face. It is considered the new competitive advantage in a world that is evolving at speed.

When I first read this article, things started to make a lot of sense. After all, being adaptable was a skill that continued to play a huge role in my ability to hack happiness. Finding what makes you happy requires experimentation, learning and adjusting to new conditions. We need to be able to adapt to our changing environment, as what makes us happy unfolds as a process – it's not an end goal you suddenly get to – and it is different for everyone as we all start at a different point. Equally, this kind of adaptability is key to what I had observed in managing large-scale change in the corporate world for 20-plus years. But there was a catch.

Adaptability alone didn't go far enough in addressing the question that I kept getting asked: 'How do I realise the life I want and at the same time navigate the complexity of the pace and scale of change that's occurring?'

Look around you: we as human beings are constantly adapting as our environment changes. (For example, remember how quickly we had to adapt to global lockdowns and social distancing in the face of COVID-19.) It is this ability to adapt that has kept us alive and has enabled us to evolve as a species. In today's world where we're dealing with rapid-fire exponential change, the extrinsic motivation to adapt is in abundance; we adapt because we feel we have no choice. The environment (external factors) dictates that we change to avoid or minimise unpleasant consequences.

Adaptation has become about surviving, not thriving.

In the world of addictive technological advancement (and, at the time of writing, a global pandemic), companies and governments actually use human habit formation to drive our behavioural change. So much of our adaptation is now unconscious and driven by others – others who may not have our best interests at heart. Technology is often developed to be maximally addictive so that the companies providing it can gain insane wealth and power, rather than using tech as a tool to amplify human potential and happiness. (Sounds a lot like that messed up societal definition of success discussed in chapter 1!)

The smart phone is a perfect case in point. It's become an extension of our bodies, to the point where many of us become anxious when it is not in our line of sight. It's created extreme FOMO (fear of missing out); if we don't constantly check our phones we may miss something important at work, in life. We have unconsciously adapted: what was originally a device to make calls now feels like it's necessary for our survival.

You may be surprised to learn that one of the most popular jobs in Silicon Valley these days is that of 'attention engineer'. This position, not surprisingly, originated in the casinos of Las Vegas. The role of the attention engineer is to understand how habit formation works in the brain and then use this insight to develop technology that forms new habits that keep you coming back again and again. It's externally engineered adaptation. (Yes, wow!)

We are great at adapting (without even realising it) when we are forced to do so to avoid pain, but our ability to intentionally adapt in order to *thrive* is often a challenge.

Many of us are so full in our days and in our heads that we are not connected to how we actually feel, to what internally makes us happy and how we can intentionally adapt to enhance that.

How do we leverage our *intrinsic* motivation, the motivation that comes from within, to drive our adaptation?

We have to stop reacting, and start intentionally adapting.

THE INTENTIONAL ADAPTABILITY QUOTIENT

I thought long and hard about the recurring question ('How do I realise the life I want and still navigate the pace and scale of change that's occurring?') and started to explore how I could use my personal insight and skill in hacking happiness to develop a compass for other people to use. Something that enabled change in bite-sized pieces and turned the dial up on happiness in the everyday. That's when the Intentional Adaptability Quotient was born.

Your Intentional Adaptability Quotient (IAQ) is the measure of how skilled you are in making *intentional* change in a complex environment that is evolving at speed.

Measuring the change in your IAQ® over time helps you to develop the skills to effectively navigate the pace and scale of exponential change in order to thrive, not just survive.

It's not about speeding up and squeezing more into an already full day or brain; it's actually about slowing down, creating the space to think and bring intention and meaning to the forefront of how you make decisions.

When I couldn't find anyone teaching a concept like this, I went out and created it. I leaned into the fear of not having the perfect answer or a plan and decided to surf the edge of my comfort zone. The courage to experiment was central to my ability to create a highly impactful and sustainable way for individuals to be happier. I approached my idea like a scientist and created a hypothesis:

> You can teach someone how to amplify their IAQ in order to thrive.

I then considered how I might go about proving this hypothesis. I decided I would start by developing a behavioural profile of someone who had a high IAQ. What would someone with a high IAQ do in the everyday? What would an intentionally adaptable mindset look like?

I'm a hacker and my approach to everything is to always start small and simple. I sat down and noted in a spreadsheet the mindset and behaviours I had used and supported others in developing to hack happiness. I then reflected and considered what skills we would need to be able to turn up the dial on these behaviours in order to become more intentionally adaptable.

Out of these exercises came an IAQ model (which we'll look at shortly) and a set of experiential educational programs developed to test my hypothesis. I created an online Hacking Happy Assessment to start collecting data to gain greater insight into how I could help others hold up the mirror to where their IAQ was at and enable them to measure their shift over time.

> I then did something some might consider crazy, but I honestly believe crazy is only crazy until it is proven possible... and damn, we need more crazy in the world!

I went out to a number of my corporate clients and told them what I was trying to do and how I thought skilling people in IAQ could make them happier, more innovative, more engaged at work and more mentally well, and, as a by-product, more productive. I asked them to join me in my IAQ experiment to help me build a high-impact educational program and assessment tool that would enable their people to thrive.

To my surprise Microsoft, Deloitte, KPMG, National Australia Bank, Mercer and a Melbourne-based grammar school (a school that wanted teachers and students learning IAQ in the same classroom) all said yes! (How amazing is that?)

Building the skill

Now, before I share with you the IAQ Model (see figure 3.1) and the results of our experiment to date, I want to be completely honest. This process is ongoing and evolutionary and if you choose to progress you too are now part of the experiment.

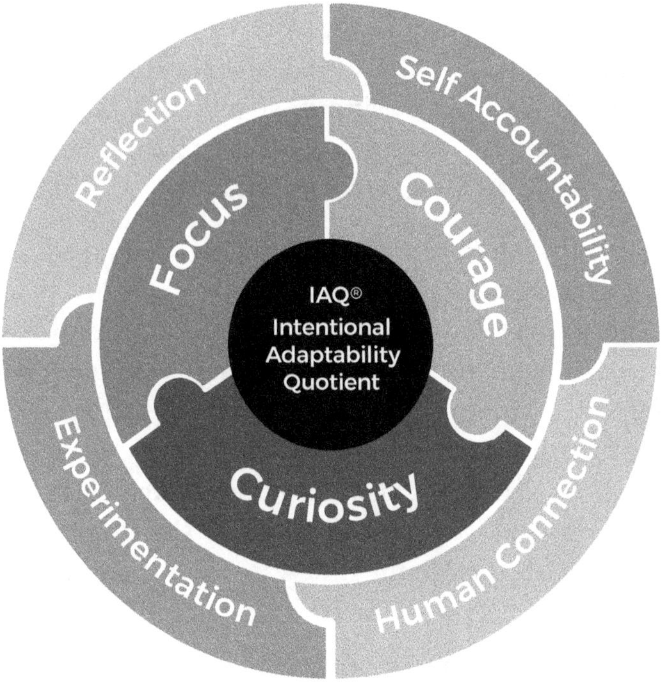

Figure 3.1: the Intentional Adaptability Quotient Model

I, like you, am learning as I go and intentionally adapting how I evolve and teach IAQ as a means to hack happiness. I'm sharing this because this is the reality of any Hacking Happiness journey; it takes experimentation, and an investment of time partnered with the development of the IAQ skills.

When I teach IAQ, I focus on the amplification of three key skills (the inner circle of the model) to enable greater clarity around what makes one happy and provide a framework for bringing more of it into the everyday. So what are the skills that enable you to turn the dial up on your IAQ? They are:

1. focus
2. courage
3. curiosity.

As I've mentioned, it's early days in the IAQ experiment, but one insight has been profound in the work we've done to date. In our highly connected world we are suffering from a 'busy' epidemic, and our prioritisation of being busy and constantly operating in a state of doing is creating a significant barrier to innovation, learning, mental wellbeing and happiness.

When I first started teaching IAQ I thought curiosity seemed like a logical place to begin. To my surprise, time and again senior leaders in the IAQ classroom kept stating, 'I'm too busy to be curious'. Busy people were telling me they were at capacity and, while they knew they needed to be curious to disrupt themselves and their organisations, they just didn't have the time and the mental capacity. This insight was a game changer. It became clear that any investment being made in future skill-building without addressing the busy epidemic first was wasted. This is why, when we teach IAQ, we start with focus.

IAQ skill 1: Focus

Building your skill in focus is centred around enabling you to intentionally focus in a world that is now designed to distract you.

It's about learning how to step away from the noise of busy, of constantly doing, and create the space to be, to think clearly: to determine what truly matters to you in your life (including your work), what brings you joy, and experiment with behaviours that enable you to do more of it every day.

IAQ skill 2: Courage

When we've removed the barrier that busy creates we can lean into the second biggest barrier I have identified to intentionally adapting – FEAR. Courage is centred around teaching you how to shift your mindset around fear and failure. Rather than seeing fear and failure as barriers to change, we focus on using them to shape the change you seek. We don't want to avoid fear: we want to feel it, understand where it shows up in our bodies and what triggers it, share it with others and use it as an opportunity for growth.

IAQ skill 3: Curiosity

I always think of curiosity as the reward in the IAQ Model. It's the reward for removing busy and fear as barriers to the change you seek. When you've created the space, the clarity and the skill to be more focused and have realised the benefits of harnessing your fear, curiosity provides the basis to unlearn and explore possibility.

Curiosity is an innately human skill; we are born with it. However, the traditional schooling, university and corporations that we push people through have significantly affected our ability to activate our curious being. When I teach curiosity, I teach it as a state of being, not something you do in your spare time (of which people tell me they have none! Agree?). I teach people how to be curious in the everyday, how to have more curious conversations, and ask more curious questions than state opinions, because we know no-one learns anything by talking all the time.

Future shapers

I like to think of the Intentionally Adaptable as the future shapers. These are the people who make a conscious choice to not inherit a future designed by somebody else but to intentionally mould it themselves.

Those who have a high IAQ:

- take control of their time because they know that it is their most precious and valuable resource
- are not afraid to say 'no', and they say it often; they understand that the more they say 'yes' to others the less able they are to say 'yes' to themselves
- create the space to be less busy and more positively engaged (more on this later)
- are comfortable in the stillness because they know it's where the brain does its most powerful work
- thrive in uncertainty and complexity and trust the discomfort of not accepting the first solution that presents itself to a problem
- use fear as a green light to ride the edge of their comfort zone because they know that growth occurs when we are uncomfortable
- make the time to cultivate deep human connections because they know opportunity and possibility lies at the other end
- surround themselves with 'unlike minds': those who challenge them to look at the world through a different lens
- have a level of curiosity that finds them surprising themselves often.

From inside to outside

Think about how you learn. What have you ever done for the first time that you have done exceptionally well? My guess is, not much! That's because we learn by doing. Skill is developed with:

- practice
- mistakes
- intentional adaptation

which is why when I teach IAQ, I use an experiential learning process. A process that enables you to determine what works best for you.

IAQ is designed to develop self-sufficient perpetual learners who can reinvent themselves time and again off a foundation of meaning and knowledge of what makes them happy. You do this through the amplification of skills in the outer circle of our IAQ model:

- **Self Accountability** is about learning how to focus on what you can control, not what you can't. It's about taking control of your mindset and behaviour in order to shape that 40 per cent of your happiness that is within your sphere of influence.
- **Human Connection** is about exploring how opportunity, mental wellbeing and happiness are amplified when we are more humanly connected.
- **Experimentation** is about learning to get comfortable with trying new things that feel uncomfortable and even impossible. We learn and grow through experimentation, even if the experiments don't work out as intended.
- **Reflection** is about how, if we don't take the time to reflect and ask ourselves what worked, what didn't and what we're going to do differently next time, do we adapt for the better?

As you progress on your hacking happiness journey throughout the rest of this book, you will notice that the start of every experiment that follows will require you to progress by either being Self Accountable, Humanly Connected, Experimenting or Reflecting (or perhaps a combination of these).

A CASE FOR CHANGE

Before we get onto the Hacking Happy Assessment, I want you to meet John and hear how an awareness of IAQ affected his ability to take action around what matters. Read on and see whether you can connect with John's story.

John was a senior executive who had climbed the ranks of a global organisation. His next big move was likely into a CFO or CEO position. He and a group of his peers had formed a working group that met monthly to explore pretty much the exact same question I kept getting asked… 'How do we navigate the pace and scale of change in order to thrive?'

Each month John and his peers would connect and discuss the tools they had come across that could potentially help them answer this pressing question. John had discovered the IAQ concept and model and found it interesting. He and his peers decided to take the free Hacking Happy Assessment at hackinghappy.co (more on that in a moment) and have a conversation around their scores and what actions they could take to amplify their IAQ. John was so surprised and intrigued by the process that he reached out to me personally to share the insights of this experiment over a virtual coffee.

I asked John what he and his peers were hoping to gain from undertaking the Hacking Happy Assessment and he said,

> We were looking for feedback. We wanted to know that we were not alone and it was okay to not have all the answers as to how we should disrupt ourselves for greater happiness. We wanted to know where we should start. Where were the obvious development opportunities? We assumed that we would all come out with high IAQ scores as we were used to change—we'd lived and breathed it—but we were wrong.

John told me that the Hacking Happy Assessment was like holding up a mirror to the fact that we are creatures of habit. What he and his peers realised goes back to my earlier point around why I developed Intentional Adaptability: a lot of their adaptation was not intentional. They were good at change when they were told they had to change by the business:

> We realised we are very good at running away from things but not great at knowing what we should run towards. Actually, we have no idea what to run towards. The Hacking Happy Assessment made us question how we stop things being done to us and enable things to be driven by us.

I share John's story because I feel it provides a compelling case for why one would want to explore the concept of Intentional Adaptability to deliver greater happiness. Students who have undertaken skill-building programs in IAQ have shared many benefits, including that it:

- provides a compass to effectively navigate the complexity and uncertainty of exponential change
- helps unlock potential students didn't realise they had
- enhances creativity and innovation
- enables deeper human connection and amplifies relationships

- provides a feeling of empowerment and control over one's life
- enables greater fulfilment in the everyday
- improves mental wellbeing and reduces feelings of anxiety
- activates a mindset that challenges one to look at the world through a different lens.
- changes lives for the better. (This is my favourite one.) It's not always immediate but, over time, it's as though once the subconscious becomes aware of IAQ it can no longer ignore the opportunity it presents.

I myself could add to the list of benefits, but this journey is not about me. It's about you! The benefits you experience could be totally different and yet equally compelling, which is why I so love the concept. It's not a one size fits all; it's about helping you experiment with what fits best for you. Cultivating focus is the best place to start that first step in your IAQ practice, and that's exactly where we are heading next.

First, be aware...

The first step in any change we seek starts with awareness. You can't make change for the better if you aren't aware of what needs to change. This is part of the reason why I developed the Hacking Happy Assessment. I wanted to enable you to hold up the mirror to your IAQ, and challenge you to create a little space to think about your mindset, your behaviour and what matters to you.

This is where we begin and it provides a powerful basis for us to work together through experimentation to understand where your opportunities lie and what you can play with to amplify your happiness.

Then, be warned…

Amplifying your IAQ is a lot like yoga. It's a life practice, not an end state. There is no 100 per cent; it's about evolution. It's about showing up and practising daily – 'getting on the mat', as we would say in yoga. You will have good days and bad days in your practice, and that is exactly as it should be. Positive change occurs with consistent and persistent practice, and this is the space we play in with IAQ.

While IAQ as a concept is evolving daily, I want to make one thing very clear: it may not be for everyone *right now*. What do I mean?

My belief is that it is very hard to apply IAQ as a compass if your basic human needs are not being met. If you do not have access to food, shelter, safety or water then your brain is operating in survival mode, and all of your mental resources are consumed with trying to solve those critical challenges first – understandably.

Working out how to thrive is sidelined when you're struggling to physically survive. IAQ is designed to enable self-actualisation, which we can only work on when our basic human needs are met.

EXPERIMENT NOW

* Go to IAQyou.com (if you have not done so already) and follow the simple steps to complete your Hacking Happy Assessment.
* Have a look at your IAQ score, which is emailed to you once you complete the assessment. Take the time to reflect on any insights into where your opportunities for amplification lie.
* Take 15 minutes of undistracted quiet time and answer the following questions:

What surprised you?	
What one thing did you learn about yourself?	
What one thing would you like to change or amplify as a result of taking your Hacking Happy Assessment?	

REFLECT AND REMEMBER

* We are great at adapting when we are forced to do so to avoid pain, but we often find it challenging to drive our own adaptation proactively to thrive.
* Your Intentional Adaptability Quotient (IAQ) is the measure of how skilled you are in making *intentional* change in a complex environment that is evolving at speed.
* IAQ focuses on amplifying three key skills—focus, courage and curiosity—and the sequence in which you develop them is equally important.
* IAQ is designed to develop self-sufficient perpetual learners who can reinvent themselves time and again based on what makes them happy. The amplification of the skills of self-accountability, human connection, experimentation and reflection enable that.
* Building your IAQ enables you to identify and consciously stop running *away* from things and clarify what you should run *towards*.

SHARE THE HAPPY

Take your Hacking Happy Assessment with a friend or partner and share what you learned about yourself in the process and what action you intend to take to turn the dial up on your IAQ as a result. This is also a great team exercise if you are a team leader.

PART II

Hack Your Happiness

This is where we get our hands dirty and unpack each Intentional Adaptability Quotient skill to enable you to build a basis for being more happy more often.

We start with *focus* by challenging you to consider why busy = bullshit and how to amplify your ability to *be* rather than constantly *do*. Being positively connected to ourselves, each other and the environment provides a platform for more joy.

We then move into *courage* and consider why fear is one of the greatest levers you have available to you to shape the life you've always wanted. We also explore how small acts of bravery practised consistently over time will enable you to build the courage and confidence to step into bigger change, life change, which opens your head and heart to more fulfilment.

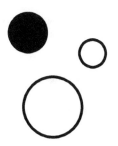

Finally, we deep dive into *curiosity* and explore how it is the foundation of innovation and evolution, yet we are practising it less than ever, and how we can flip this paradigm by cultivating our curious being as a daily practice.

Ready?

IAQ Skill 1—Focus

How to focus in a world that's designed to distract you, and create the space for more of what matters.

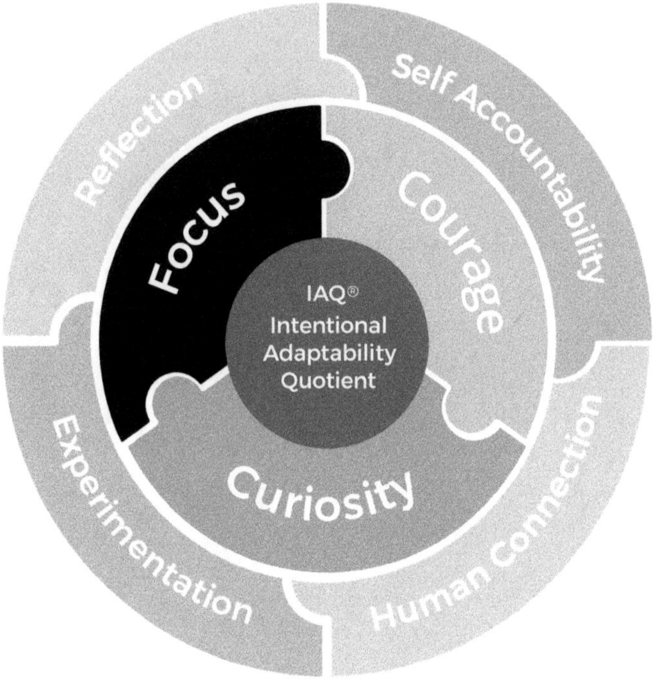

CHAPTER 4

Focus: Busy = Bullshit

In my past life, I would find myself run down with a bad flu around once every three months. It was frustrating! Instead of resting and trying to recover (so the virus didn't keep returning), I would prop myself up in bed, tissue box beside me, coughing and spluttering. I continued to tap away on my computer and push my health to the edge of its limits to maintain my level of busy. I mean, who has the time to be sick, right?

I was committed to my busy; I believed in it to the point where not even burnout could stop me from my need to be constantly in a state of *doing*. It wasn't until I started to question this unsustainable cycle, step back and observe what was going on around me that I realised busy was my gateway drug to burnout, and I was not alone.

According to the World Economic Forum, burnout in the workplace is increasing at an alarming rate. It's estimated that the annual impact on the global economy is £255 billion (AU$472 billion). Ouch! What's even more disturbing is that in 2019, the World Health Organization classified burnout as a syndrome, which solidifies its existence as a medical condition. It is predicted that within a decade burnout will be a pandemic. (Not sure many of us will want another one after going through COVID-19!)

We have created a 'burnout generation' with *Harvard Business Review* research uncovering that '50% of millennials and 75% of Gen Zers have exited roles in the past for mental health reasons'.

We live in a world where most of us are operating in a constant state of overwhelm and exhaustion. Why is it that so many of us have what we need, yet we push ourselves to the brink of burnout in pursuit of more? Our wanting more is making us sick!

> There are no winners in a race conducted on a hamster wheel.

THE DOING DELUSION

How often do you get through your daily to-do list? How often do you get through it, without adding more and more to it for the next day? If you are one of the busy *doing* majority, then that answer is likely 'very rarely'.

Do you believe that if you squeeze everything plus a little extra into 'now', then in the future more time will magically reveal itself? If you get all those competing things off your to-do list now, then later you can jump into the other list of things that light you up, the fun stuff, the activities that you long to do but never seem to get around to doing... right? Happiness researcher Ashley Whillans refers to this human affliction as 'future time slack': we convince ourselves that in the future we will have extra time that we don't have currently.

> We decide to make some sacrifices now with the promise of enjoying more time later. But of course, when the future comes, we don't have more time. We just repeat the same mistake.

Doing more now in the hope that more time will magically appear in the future is a fast track to busy burnout.

Dr Annie McKee calls this 'Sacrifice Syndrome' and, not surprisingly, it's significantly diminishing our ability to thrive. She explains that we:

> give and give until there's nothing left. The human organism doesn't do well under such conditions. Our brains literally begin to shut down. We filter information, keeping only that which we feel we must have in order to survive. We become hyper-focused on potential threats. We don't see reality clearly.

Tunnel vision is a real phenomenon: the more we jam in, the less our brain allows us to notice what's going on around us. Basically, we derail normal brain functioning and diminish our capacity to connect with our environment and enable our creativity.

> We have deluded ourselves to believe that a constant state of doing will deliver success, when instead it's become our disease.

BUSY DIS-EASE

Not busy is not cool! When I ask a large audience who in the room feels 'not busy' and one person proudly raises their hand, the room all turn their heads in awe of this enigma. What is it about not being busy that makes so many of us uncomfortable? Ask yourself: when you take away the busy in your day, what is left? How does the thought of it make you feel?

In 1946, highly acclaimed neurologist and psychiatrist Dr Viktor Frankl called the white noise between busy and not busy 'Sunday neurosis'. He described it as:

> that kind of depression which afflicts people who become aware of the lack of content in their lives when the rush of the busy week is over and the void within themselves becomes manifest.

What's perhaps most disturbing is that if we fast forward to the present day, Sunday neurosis is rare. Why? Because we've found an unexpected solution: we now fill our weekends to the brink of busy so that we don't have to sit in stillness. Boredom is almost nonexistent because the idea of being alone with our own thoughts for many is excruciating. A perfect case in point was the COVID-19 lockdown. Overnight we stripped away the everyday noise for millions and just moved it into the home, heaping the complexity of isolation, home schooling and feelings of crisis on top. Rather than take pause and use this moment of disruption for inflection, many operated in overwhelm, reacting by just reshaping their busy in a new environment until it became unsustainable. It's what we are avoiding (i.e. *being*) that provides the greatest opportunity to reset practices that have not been in our service for far too long.

> We are hard-wiring ourselves for doing and it comes at the compromise of what is humanly innate to thriving — being.

THE PRODUCTIVITY ILLUSION

In 2019, I was running a program with a group of corporate professionals called 'The Busy Equals Bullshit Challenge'. Out of curiosity, I asked why they had come. One by one their responses were the same: 'I came because I feel crazy busy, it's making me feel anxious and I want you to teach me how to become more productive'. There it was, that word: 'productive'. A word that for many conjures the illusion that success is perhaps just on the other side of its elusive secret. I was curious to understand what they meant by the word 'productive', so I asked, 'Correct me if I'm wrong, but you came here feeling insanely busy, it's making you feel overwhelmed and anxious often – and you'd like me to teach you how you can squeeze *more* into an already full day?' To which their response was a resounding 'YES'.

> We are led to believe that if we are more productive, more efficient in every aspect of our lives, we will be more successful and create more space in our universally limited resource of a 24-hour day.

That's why every waking moment of the day is filled, podcasts are listened to at 1.5 to 2 times the speed, 'busy bragging' is a real thing (how many 'busy-offs' have you encountered, perhaps in a lift with peers?), sleep is often restless and creativity and innovation are stifled.

I want you to consider for just a moment how much time your drive for relentless efficiency has freed up. Reflect back on the time since you obtained your very first smart phone (the iPhone, for example, was introduced in 2007). How many productivity devices, applications or efficiency-creating technologies have you utilised in your work and your life since that time? *I'm guessing quite a few.*

Now consider how much time these technologies have given you back in your day. Do you now find you fall into the category of the un-busy few, with loads of spare time available as a result of employing these new 'productivity' resources? What are you doing with that newly found free time? Where is it going? And if that's the case, I'm going to challenge you on that because... why did you pick up this book?

Okay, I may be stirring a little, but you get the point: we rarely meet people who have an abundance of free time thanks to all the technology they have introduced in their life. Ironically, it's often the complete opposite. The more time-saving, productivity-hacking technology we introduce, the more we just seem to fill the space with more doing.

Perhaps now is the time to ask ourselves what if productivity was an illusion and Busy = Bullshit?

The fact is that there is a multibillion-dollar marketing machine driving the productivity race. Just look at Apple, for example.

On 5 June 2018, Apple announced that they would introduce a new iPhone feature called Screen Time, which would allow users to take back control of their devices and see how much time they were spending in connected voids. (A connected void is where you find yourself aimlessly thumbing your device, and perhaps an hour later you either can't recall why you even picked up the device in the first place, or are down a path totally unrelated to where you started. It adds no value to your life other than sucking your time away.) Screen Time was arguably implemented as damage control, a result of the mounting evidence of technology being used to manipulate behaviour for addiction, and of how ill-equipped we are to deal with the onslaught of technologically enabled distractions (often masked as productivity enhancers or connection enablers).

I actually wonder what would happen if Apple provided the ability to flip the Screen Time view, and showed people how little time in each day they are actually spending disconnected from technology and more connected to themselves and other human beings? Where did this belief come from that we need to maximise the potential of every waking moment by making it efficient? What is the cost of productivity at the compromise of being, connecting with other human beings, exploring and experimenting?

There is a magic and now human point of difference that lies in active pursuits of inefficiency. Think about the inefficient indulgence of sitting in the pain of deep thinking to solve a hard problem that you've never worked on before; the inefficiency of being spontaneous, or creating the space to get lost, or sitting in a conversation with no intent other than allowing it to unfold.

Inefficiency is often the friend of creativity and innovation—and we have squeezed the life out of it. It's time to explore how we indulge in intentional inefficiency in order to unlock our potential.

BUSY EATS HOBBIES FOR BREAKFAST

It appears that many of us have now tarred the trusty hobby with the inefficiency brush and sidelined it for more productive pursuits. If I asked you to tell me about one of your hobbies, what would you say? And if you are one of the few who still has one, do you find yourself squeezing (or sidelining) your hobby around all the other noise in your day? What is most likely to get your attention: the hobby or the stuff you busy yourself doing so you can get to the hobby at some stage?

And what do you even consider a hobby to be these days? Strangely, most people seem surprised when I make it clear that a hobby is not going out for coffee or drinks with your friends, that it is a creative outlet that brings us pleasure and joy: swimming, reading, climbing mountains, drawing...

Unfortunately, busy is eating our hobbies for breakfast! Hobbies are slowly disappearing, as is the concept of leisure time.

> We don't have time for hobbies anymore, yet switching off the busy and creating the space for hobbies can actually recharge our batteries and improve our performance.

Gaetano DiNardi in his article 'Why you should work less and spend more time on hobbies' states researchers have found that

> creative activity like hobbies are positively associated with work-related recovery experiences (i.e. mastery, control, and relaxation) and performance-related outcomes (i.e. job creativity and extra-role behaviours). Creative activity while away from work may be a leisure activity that provides employees with essential resources to perform at a high level.

So from this point on, I want you to reconsider how you see hobbies. It might even be worth sharing this research with your boss!

> A hobby is not something you squeeze in around all your other stuff or, worse, still sideline altogether, but something that needs prioritising in order to enable recovery and, most importantly, your happiness.

HAPPINESS HACK

What are your hobbies? Make a list now so that you can prioritise. If you don't have a hobby, create a list of those that interest you. There are no excuses for not doing this activity! Google or chat to some friends to help get some fresh ideas. What one action will you take to try one hobby on your list? I recently paid $20 on Udemy.com to learn how to draw and have carved out just 15 minutes a day for this practice. It's been a creative game changer.

Remember, any action, no matter how small, is a start. We are here for progress not perfection!

BE POSITIVELY ENGAGED

Before we go any further, I want you to do this quick exercise. Consider how many times you think you have said or typed the word 'busy' in the last 48 hours?

I have asked this question of thousands of participants and audience members over the past years, and on average 90 per cent share that they use the word busy between one to five times a day. (How did you compare?) Have you ever stopped to consider (if you use the word 'busy' as a consistent daily practice) how it's affecting you? How it's affecting your work, your life, your relationships and, most importantly, your ability to truly thrive?

These simple questions are designed to hold up the mirror to how your use of the word 'busy' might be what stands between you and the space for more of what matters.

In 2018, I was talking with a new friend, Julie Trell, and I started to share with her how busy I was. She immediately interjected and told me she 'didn't do busy'. She explained that she made an intentional choice to stop using the word 'busy', that instead she says she's 'positively occupied'. I laughed out loud at first, then I checked myself and thought, 'Hang on, that's so interesting'.

I started to wonder what would happen if I tried to drop the 'busy' from my vocabulary, too. From that day forth, when someone asked me how I was I would respond 'I'm positively engaged' (my own little tweak to Julie's idea). I was astounded at how this simple change in language affected the depth of my conversations.

Instead of the conversation being shut down before it began (I mean let's face it, busy is not really a conversation opener), people would actually stop dead in their tracks and say to me 'What?' To which I would respond, 'My life is full doing things that I love'. They would then probe further in surprise and ask

'What are you *really* doing?' I would say, 'I choose not to be busy; instead I choose to create the space for the things that light me up. Sometimes that's engaging in more human connection, other times it's blocking out time in my diary to think and work deeply without distraction'. I would then challenge them to try removing 'busy' from their vocabulary and see what happens...which, interestingly, many did.

So this is my challenge, or my gift, for you. Busy has become an on-trend state of mind, a vocabulary staple, in the digitally connected world. So what would happen if you removed it from your vocabulary?

> One of the greatest lessons I have learned on my journey to hacking happiness is that the language you use will determine your ability to make change.

The more often you use positive language in your internal and external dialogue the more likely you are to feel good, which, according to the research of Barbara Fredrickson, gives you an edge in your daily happiness and your ability to learn more effectively:

> The psychological broadening sparked by one positive emotion can increase an individual's receptiveness to subsequent pleasant or meaningful events, increasing the odds that the individual will find positive meaning in these subsequent events and experience additional positive emotions.

Our brains are more open when we allow ourselves to experience positive emotions, and we are able to process information quicker, solve hard problems more effectively and experiment with new approaches. Isn't that what we all want?

HAPPINESS HACK

Ditch the word 'busy' from your vocabulary for one week. I dare you! You may like to experiment swapping it for 'positively engaged', or select your own, positive word or phrase to fill the void of the word 'busy'. Note what happens over the week. How does this change make you feel? How do other people respond?

CRACKING YOUR BUSY CODE

Now we have eliminated the word 'busy' from your vocabulary, I want you to consider what it's been hiding. When I ask people to share with me what they'd really like to say instead of 'busy', statements such as 'I'm exhausted', 'I'm struggling to get what I need done', 'I wish I could just say no' or 'I'm not happy, I just feel it all never ends' come up.

> We use the word 'busy' as a smokescreen to hide from ourselves and others what we are really thinking, feeling and wanting to say.

So it's time to hold up the mirror to your own behaviour and assess what you have been really saying when you use that term, 'busy'. This is a perfect example of how we find the opportunities for greater happiness when we unpack what we are avoiding. The aim is to create awareness of what is really going on inside your head and how that affects you, both internally and externally. It's only when we truly understand what sits behind our busy that we can reduce the white noise, and focus more on thriving.

In my experience working with thousands in the space of busy, there are six 'busy codes' that we all seem to hide behind. As you read through them, see which ones you identify with.

Busy code 1: anxiety

An amazing psychologist using virtual reality to cure people of phobias said to me once during an interview that 'busy perpetuates busy. It is only a matter of time before a busy mind will go to anxiety'. It seems (not surprisingly) she was right.

When I am standing in a room filled with people talking about the topic of being busy, and I ask them to raise their hand if they have **never** experienced anxiety or had a friend or family member experience it, how many people do you think raise their hand? Not one, that's how many.

It feels like anxiety is everywhere, yet interestingly, in a world where there is data on everything, the evidence to substantiate that there is an anxiety epidemic is actually hard to come by – and believe me, I have looked.

According to Harvey Whiteford, professor of population mental health at the University of Queensland, survey data on anxiety in high-income countries indicates that the levels haven't changed, they've flatlined. Furthermore, Whiteford explains the two big changes driving what feels like an anxiety epidemic are the increased awareness and de-stigmatisation of mental health challenges. Global marketing resources invested in normalising mental health issues have driven a significant increase in the number of people seeking help. That's a good thing, right?

But the thing that we are not accounting for is the number of people suffering who are not captured in the data; those who still do not admit their anxiety or actively self-report suffering. According to the World Health Organization nearly two-thirds of people with a known mental disorder never seek help from a health professional. I come across many of these people in the professional world, people who still worry that their disclosure of constant anxious feelings will be career limiting. Equally disturbing is how the incidence of anxiety will grow as we deal with the aftermath of the COVID-19 pandemic, with its societal and economic implications.

Epidemic or not, we know that anxiety is a huge challenge for the connected busy world and it isn't getting better.

Without a doubt anxiety is definitely on the rise in the next generation. Interestingly, 'busy' is becoming a common term alongside of it. The principal of an elite girls school in Melbourne mentioned to me in conversation recently that she had a concerning busy problem in the school, with children as young as eight sharing that they were too busy to complete the workload requested of them. Clearly busy parents are producing busy children and perhaps are not even aware of it or the long-term implications.

The New Zealand government has become so concerned with the rise of mental health issues among its people that in 2019 it introduced a mandate whereby if you as a government official want to introduce a new policy, you have to demonstrate how that change will positively influence the wellbeing of society. What a novel idea that one could argue could be easily replicated by other governments globally to tackle a growing problem.

Interestingly, anxiety is a completely natural feeling – it's how our body responds to stress. It's that uncomfortable 'what if?' feeling that can drive fear or uncertainty around what's coming next. We all experience it from time to time, like before public speaking or when moving house, and this little bit of anxiety can be a good thing. It can help motivate us to take action as we seek to minimise its presence. The challenge is when it doesn't go away, it's constant and it starts to affect our ability to function in the everyday.

Busy code 2: distraction

Consider for a moment how often you work on a single task, without any distractions. For example, writing a report, analysing data or sitting in a meeting, completely and utterly immersed in that single thing for an hour without checking your phone or your email or anything else. If you're thinking 'I don't remember the last time' or 'maybe it was a month ago' then you, my friend, are not alone! In fact, 66 per cent of those who have taken the Hacking Happy Assessment discover that their busy is code for distraction.

Our level of distraction could very well be the biggest productivity challenge organisations face in the future. According to the Udemy's 2018 Workplace Distraction Report, almost 70 per cent of workers concede that distraction is a real challenge for them whilst they are at work. Not surprisingly, Millennials and Gen Z are most likely to feel distracted with more than a third of them (36 per cent) spending two or more hours eye balling their device whilst at work.

Our attention has become a highly valuable commodity.

So valuable in fact that Netflix CEO Reed Hastings stated at an industry summit that his company's real competitor is... sleep! You heard right: sleep. It's the only place left to grab a little more of your attention in a busy world. Hastings stated, 'You get a show or a movie you're really dying to watch, and you end up staying up late at night, so we actually compete with sleep. And we're winning!'

Nir Eyal wrote a best-selling book in 2014 titled *Hooked*, which disclosed the secrets of how Silicon Valley tech companies (such as Netflix) created an extremely lucrative industry out of building habit-forming technologies. *Hooked* was written as a roadmap for startup founders to replicate a proven technology product design model that covertly programs our brains to form addictive behaviours – for both good and bad. Yes, you should be concerned, but also optimistic because you own your attention and where you choose to direct it is up to you. Eyal's subsequent book, *Indistractable*, flipped the paradigm to enable us to stand up and take control of our distraction and redirect our time more effectively.

In order to tackle distraction, we need to first be aware that not all technologies are created equal, and not all technology is bad. To the contrary, there are some amazing products that act in the service of amplifying human potential and wellbeing, like the one I'm using now to help write these words. Focusmate has been a game changer for me. You simply book in a 50-minute accountability session and block in time to complete a task without distraction, on a video call alongside a stranger. Being accountable to someone else when you are trying to make change has proven highly effective. It's as simple as turning up at the scheduled time, sharing with your new friend what you will focus on and then getting down to business for 50 minutes. I set these sessions for 5 am most mornings and it's what gets me out of bed. I absolutely love it!

My issue is with technology that is designed for addiction, and my concern is that this type of technology is growing at a rapid pace because our attention is worth money, and lots of it. Partner this insight with the fact that our brains generate dopamine when we unconsciously engage with technological distractions, and our behaviour is driven towards instant gratification. We want and actively seek out the quick fix. It's like a drug, and it propels a busy mind as we look to find answers to anything that pops up in any moment of the day quickly... filling almost every available space.

Busy code 3: quick fix

Let's do something a little different to get you thinking. I want you to pause and go and find the answer to the following question. What happens to the brain when you focus? Take all the time you need and when you feel like you have an answer you are satisfied with write it in the space below...

Done? Great. Now I want you to think about how you answered that question: how long did it take? Where did you find the answer, the internet (most likely via our friend Google)? Herein lies the magic, but equally the problem ... the answer to almost any question is now just a click away.

What would you have done pre-internet? (Yes, gasp, there was such a thing!) And back to the earlier point on the benefits of inefficiency, how would that search for a solution in hard-to-find places have affected our brain's processing power and our willingness and ability to solve difficult problems long term? The type of problem solving that requires deep thinking, experimentation, discomfort and failure, out of which disruption and innovation are born?

Let's use the discovery of Viagra as an example of how deep focus on a specific problem can deliver unexpected and hard results (pardon the pun). The researchers that discovered Viagra were not looking for a solution to erectile dysfunction. They were focused on testing a drug called sildenafil as a cure for hypertension and heart disease. After a series of tests the researchers concluded that the drug would not deliver. However, they redirected their focus when participants in the research group shared that, while their heart issues may not have resolved, issues in other regions of the body seemed to have improved significantly. By 1998 Viagra was an approved drug and it now generates revenue in excess of US$1 billion per annum.

Now, I'm not suggesting that we ditch the world wide web completely. I'm proposing that our drive for an instant answer to almost every question is wiring us and our brains towards the quick fix.

According to Nicholas Carr in his Pulitzer Prize finalist book *The Shallows: What the internet is doing to our brains* there is a downside to our instant answer mindset. When we undertake an internet search, hyperlinks are presented and your brain asks the question: 'To click or not to click?' This constant decision-making interruption prevents us from immersing ourselves and getting lost in the words, which means what we are reading rarely stores in our deep knowledge. As Carr puts it:

> The redirection of our mental resources, from reading words to making judgments, may be imperceptible—our brains are quick—but it's been shown to impede comprehension and retention, particularly when repeated frequently.

Busy code 4: loneliness

You probably don't consider yourself a loner because you have a network of friends, yet you quite often might confess to feeling alone. Am I right? (Well, ironically, you are not alone there.) Is your busy code for loneliness? Are you filling every void – the free space when you wait for the train, in the coffee shop and home alone on the couch – with your tech because you don't want to look alone, let alone feel it? Filling every moment in the day might make you feel connected, like you belong, yet deep down it's actually disconnecting you from human interaction.

Terms like the 'Isolation Generation' or 'the Loneliest Generation' have been coined to describe the rise in loneliness in Millennials. According to a YouGov survey of 1254 American adults, '30% of Millennials said they always or often felt lonely, compared with 20% of Generation X and 15% of boomers'.

Loneliness researcher (yes, there is such a thing) John Cacioppo in his conversations with *Lost Connections* author Johann Hari shares, 'People must belong to a tribe'. Hari goes on to say that, 'just like a bee goes haywire if it loses its hive, a human will go haywire if it loses its connection to the group'. Cacioppo's research on loneliness had uncovered:

> That we—without ever quite intending to have become the first humans to ever dismantle our tribes. As a result, we have been left alone on a savanna we do not understand, puzzled by our own sadness.

We have never been more technologically connected yet humanly disconnected, and with social distancing and self isolation the norm thanks to COVID-19 at the time of writing, this challenge is amplified! We are more invested in appearing to have great relationships online than we are in cultivating them offline.

Just think of the last time you posed for a selfie, to try and make it look like you were having fun! My favourite case in point was when I went with my friend to a hot spring retreat for the day. Surprisingly, phones were not banned in the tranquil sanctuary. This meant that while sitting in the hot pools we were surrounded by couples and friends who were not engaged in enjoying the experience together, but instead were taking nonstop photos to get the perfect one to share on social media.

We don't feel connected because we are not really connecting the way we were designed as human beings. What's even more disturbing is that human connection is a key skill for the future and we are doing it less than ever. The less we humanly connect, the less skilled we are at reading each other's body language and being able to empathise and understand one another. The less skilled we are at that, the less likely we are to have difficult conversations, to problem solve and build resilience. Not surprisingly all of these points link back to our ability to create a foundation for mental wellness.

Busy code 5: self-validation

Here's an interesting one. Would you actually admit that you enjoy the feeling of being busy?

Does saying 'I'm busy' make you feel important, needed, like your work is meaningful and there's loads of it? Does the idea of not being busy make you feel uncomfortable because it may mean you are perceived as unproductive or perhaps not important because your plate is not full? Do you love the saying 'if you want something done ask a busy person', because that's you?

If this all resonates then perhaps your busy is code for self-validation. What do I mean?

Busy makes you feel needed; it makes you feel good about yourself because you love to please others with your doing. However, your busy may in fact have no end point. Your days and you are completely maxed out, and long term how sustainable is that? Not to mention, without any stillness or down time, how do your brain and your body recharge?

Just ponder that for a minute...

Busy code 6: FOMO

Do you find yourself saying yes to every opportunity out of fear that you might miss out on something amazing or because the delivery of a 'no' might be perceived as a career-limiting move? If the answer is 'yes to the yes', then your busy is likely to be code for FOMO.

Dictionary.com describes the fear of missing out (FOMO) as 'an anxious feeling you get when you feel other people might be having a good time without you'. The term has only existed since 2004 and was first coined by Patrick J. McGinnis in the *Harvard Business School* magazine. FOMO was born out of the age of social media, mobile technology and the rise of the internet. In the distraction age, FOMO drives us to constantly check our social media pages to see what our friends are up to.

What you're missing has never been more visible or overwhelming. Author Greg McKeown explains that smart phones, social media and consumerism are causing us to be

> more aware than at any time in history of what everyone else is doing and, therefore, what we 'should' be doing. In the process, we have been sold a bill of goods: that success means being supermen and superwomen who can get it all done.

But we must consider the cost of never saying 'no'. What value does your 'yes' have when you give it to everyone? Arguably ... not much.

FOMO has become so pervasive that in 2010, software entrepreneur Anil Dash wrote a blog proposing we flip our FOMO mindset to one of JOMO – a.k.a., the joy of missing out. JOMO is about accepting that in the digitally connected world you are always going to miss something – and often, many things.

> The reality is that it doesn't matter what you miss. What matters is where you choose to show up (your physical presence) and what mindset you bring to it (your mental presence).

It's really about choosing not to feel guilt when you make an intentional decision to experience more joy in your life by missing out.

Dash believes there is a clear shift in our society away from the soul-sucking fangs of FOMO and toward an abundance of JOMO:

> Being the one in control of what moves me, what I feel obligated by, and what attachments I have to fleeting experiences is not an authority that I'm willing to concede to the arbitrary whims of an app on my mobile phone ... That's a joyful thing.

HAPPINESS HACK

Time to hold up the mirror. Reflect on what it is that you are really saying when you use the word 'busy' and why you're afraid to be honest about it to yourself and others. You may want to use the Busy Code Checklist below to tick off which ones resonate most for you to help you unpack what's really going on inside when you use the word 'busy'.

The Busy Code Checklist

- ☐ anxiety
- ☐ distraction
- ☐ quick fix
- ☐ loneliness
- ☐ self-validation
- ☐ fear of missing out (FOMO)

Insert your own busy code ______________________________

THE UNCOMFORTABLE TRUTH

Now we land at a moment where we expose the uncomfortable truth. Where our act of pulling back the curtain on our busy highlights the pain we are trying to avoid, the sadness that our behaviour is sidelining.

> Our ability to unlock our happiness sits in exposing and addressing the things that make us uncomfortable.

Avoiding is no longer a pathway to thriving. It's time we drew a line in the sand, stepped into the discomfort and created the space to focus on the stuff that brings us more joy.

Ready?

EXPERIMENT NOW

Let's start by creating the motivation to get your JOMO on by exploring what you would be doing with your time if you weren't so busy. What's standing between you and making that happen? Where would you focus your time if you had more of it freed up?

I want you to complete the following sentence. Don't filter your answers; just list what comes up for you. We are simply seeking to light a spark through awareness.

If I wasn't so busy I would...

Now I want you to consider what (within your control to influence) stands between your current state and you doing more of the things you would love to do (if you weren't so busy). Reflect on what you felt your busy is code for, as now is a good time to look more deeply into what came up. It's likely that your busy code is a key part of what's holding you back from creating space for more of what matters.

What's stopping you from creating the space for more of the above?

What one small action can you take to create just a little more space for more of what matters?

REFLECT AND REMEMBER

* Doing has become our dis-ease and it's providing a fast track to burnout. Is this what we really want?
* Productivity is the enemy of creativity and innovation. The indulgence of inefficiency in some aspects of our lives can unlock potential we didn't realise we had.
* The language you use will determine your ability to make change. Drop the word 'busy' for just a week and observe what happens.
* Be aware of what your busy is code for. Which of the six busy codes do you identify with?
* What are you really saying when you use the word 'busy', and what's stopping you from being honest with yourself and others about it?
* Embrace JOMO—the joy of missing out. The reality is that it doesn't matter what you miss; what matters is where you choose to show up (your physical presence) and what mindset you bring to it (your mental presence).

SHARE THE HAPPY

Take on the one week Busy = Bullshit Challenge with a friend or with your team members. It's as simple as agreeing not to use the word 'busy' for one week and then reconnecting (ideally in person) to reflect and discuss what came up for you.

CHAPTER 5

Focus: From doing to being

The theory of human evolution by natural selection was first shared with the world by Charles Darwin in 1859. Survival back then was about being the best fit for the environment; those who could not adapt to the changing environmental conditions would not only be left behind, but wiped out. My, how things have changed!

Thanks to advancements in technology and cultural norms that embrace diversity and seek to include the disadvantaged, the ability to survive extends well beyond the biologically strong. While survival has historically been a worthy pursuit to ensure human beings continue to walk the earth, for many of us, now that our basic human needs are met (air, food, water, safety, shelter) we seek more than just existing. We're seeking the ability to thrive.

We find ourselves at an interesting point in time. This moment was best described by Ruby Wax when she said: 'Evolution doesn't mean the species gets better, it just means we become better adapted to our environment, sometimes at a great cost'.

Our unconscious adaptation to enable the quickest (easiest) path to productivity and ultimately success has backed us into the survival corner. A corner where our focus, courage and curiosity (the skills of IAQ) are significantly diminished to ease the pain of just keeping up. We're seeking comfort and speed at the expense of thriving.

The reality is that there is no quick or easy route to Intentional Adaptability.

> You have to take the hard route, the indulgently inefficient route, the route with no guarantee of a set outcome other than unlearning, growth and greater being.

As champion weightlifter Jerzy Gregorek put it: 'Hard choices, easy life. Easy choices, hard life'.

So I'm asking you to trust that slowing down and focusing more on the journey, the right now, than the end result will enable a shift from surviving to thriving. It won't be easy, but it will be rewarding.

FROM EXPERT TO EXPERIMENTER

Let's start by confronting a limiting belief that holds many of us back from trying new things: the idea that you need to be an expert in order to be good at something. The truth is that every expert was once a beginner who was willing to experiment. In the age of adaptation, we need to swing the pendulum from looking to the expert for answers, to valuing the experimenter who is willing to find a new answer that was not considered before. In this case, that experimenter is you!

Curating an experimental mindset is grounded in the practice of focus. Building your focus muscle starts with an openness to going against the grain: it's about choosing to be intentionally different. Remember, you're not seeking to be busy; you're seeking to just be.

To be deliberate, considered and giving of your attention to just one thing at a time. Sounds pretty simple, right?

Well, if it was easy then everyone would be doing it – and let's face it, most of us are not! It's highly likely you will find focusing a challenge. I want you to notice when it becomes hard and remember one simple thing: *Amplifying your skill in focus is about practice, not perfection.*

THINKOLOGY IS YOUR ADVANTAGE

Now is a good time to introduce a concept I call Thinkology. There are varying definitions of this term, but the way I like to put it is:

> Thinkology is the practice of creating the *focused space* to take something complicated apart *with the intent* of putting it back together in a way that *has greater meaning or impact* to you or the world around you.

Focused thinking (without distraction) partnered with intention forms the foundation of taking back control of where your attention goes and who receives the value of it. I guarantee if you don't consciously choose where your attention goes, someone else will – and it's likely it won't be in your service.

Thinkology as an intentional practice builds our focus muscle, which enhances our ability to be fully present and in the moment more often. In today's world that's not only a huge point of difference – it's an immense advantage, as the quality of your thinking, your ability to problem solve and innovate is significantly amplified.

Like most things in this book, the best way of getting to grips with how to do something is to, well, just do it. So let's have a play with Thinkology. We're going to activate your focus, bring your attention to you, and find out how you can move from doing to being.

First, think back to the history of evolution and the fact we are the last surviving species of human beings. *Homo sapiens* was the term used by Carl Linnaeus in 1758 to categorise our species. The term '*Homo sapiens*' originates from Latin, where 'homo' means human being while 'sapiens' means 'discerning, wise, sensible'. (Kind of ironic, really, when one could argue that these three things seem to be lacking in humanity at the moment!)

In short, *Homo sapiens* can be interpreted as *wise being* (literally 'wise man' but that isn't very inclusive so I changed it!). Now why does this matter? Because if we want to focus on *being* we need to get clear on what it means to be a *human being*.

> In the world of doing, sadly it appears that many of us have lost connection with what it means to be human.

HAPPINESS HACK

Remove all distractions and allocate 30 minutes of your time to answer the question 'What does it mean to be human?' If you get stuck or run out of ideas, I want you to stay right where you are until the time is up. Stay bored because that is where our brain does its best work. (It's seriously why you get your best ideas in the shower—the toilet also used to be a great spot for that, but now most of us are on our mobile phones in there.) Observe how you feel in the stillness when nothing comes to mind. You may want to ask yourself, 'How am I feeling, why am I feeling this way, how does this relate to my human being?' In the spirit of Thinkology I would encourage you to come back to this question a couple of times over the coming week. Sit with it undistracted, add to it, change it around. Allow your response to evolve.

DEFINE YOUR BEING

I've been curious about the question 'What does it mean to be human?' for a while, and I've come to realise this is a powerful question to explore with others as well. Over time, using the practice of Thinkology combined with this question has created an interesting behavioural adaptation. I have become so focused on understanding what it means to be human in today's world that I have now woven it into the first question I ask people when I meet them (an example of how focus + courage + curiosity can work together).

Instead of asking someone the stock-standard question of 'What do you do?' (which I believe is just another way for us to put people into a box by applying our unconscious bias, which limits the depth of understanding of another), I now ask them 'Who are you as a human being?'

I mentioned earlier that being is about choosing to be different, choosing to bring the real you to the fore. This is one way in which I do that!

HAPPINESS HACK

Take your exploration of what it means to be human one step further and apply the Thinkology practice to ask yourself 'Who am I as a human being?' You may be surprised at how you choose to define yourself and how that highlights the roles you play in life and the things that challenge you and equally bring you joy. What's also interesting is how your answer to this question evolves over time. Enjoy!

LEVERAGE THE UNEXPECTED

So what happens when we ask this question? Well, that's where things get interesting.

Most people are taken aback. (Are you?) This is because we don't expect it. It's pretty random, right? Now imagine if you weren't reading this book, but I had asked you that in person, in a meeting for the very first time. You likely have that scripted answer to the question 'What do you do?' ready to roll out instead, so 'Who are you as a human being?' catches you by surprise.

What I'm looking for when I ask 'who are you as a human being?' is a window into human connection and an opportunity to practise focus because the answer interests me. Most people respond with 'wow, that's a great question' and it makes them pause, think and truly consider their answer, which I love because the answer requires *their* focus and engages them more deeply in the conversation.

The result is fascinating as it immediately shifts the dynamic of that conversation. This question develops a deeper level of trust, as the responder feels you are truly interested in them. They talk about things that aren't work related – and they talk about them quickly. They share things that truly matter to them: their family, their interests, their passions.

I'm not suggesting this approach to first introductions is for everyone. One woman once told me that she felt the question was inappropriate – and that's fine, I'm always open to feedback. However, I haven't stopped using the question, as by far the majority love it and it has truly strengthened my relationships.

GET INTENTIONAL

My friend Dom Price works as Atlassian's workplace futurist, and by his very nature he loves experimenting. So I asked him how he brings intentionality to his time. He shared:

> The only constraint that we all share is time. So I pose the question how do we challenge ourselves to use our time wisely because we know the focus on efficiency is not working. I choose to have a portfolio approach to how I invest my time and I'm unapologetic for it. I don't say sorry 'cause I'm not.
>
> I have a meeting at the start of each quarter with my boss where I share with him the split of how I will spend my time around the core themes of me, my team and the organisation. This is about setting the expectations so that we are aligned on where I'm focused. Sometimes we negotiate and that's fine but I still only have the same amount of time available.
>
> I'm also very clear on what I am investing in that will not deliver short term returns; it's more about planting seeds for the long term. This allows me the head space to explore new things I'm curious about that may be beneficial but there are no guarantees of a payoff, but if we don't experiment we won't know.
>
> This approach works for me and whilst I appreciate I am in a fortunate position this fortune has been earned through hard work, a willingness to ignore what's normal and take risks.

The practice of intentionality is at the heart of our ability to thrive. Just saying the word 'intention' brings our brain to a place of focus.

When I talk about intention I'm talking about building your skill in being deliberate and purposeful in the actions you choose in the everyday. It sounds like common sense, right?

Unfortunately, as my beautiful sister Donna says to me often, 'common sense isn't as common as it used to be'. It will come as no surprise that it's challenging to act with intentionality, with so much distraction vying for our attention and the speed at which many of us are operating.

The faster we move, the more we rely on our subconscious and our past experiences to influence our actions, rather than taking pause, slowing down and considering whether there could be a better way, or even asking ourselves, 'Is this what I really want?' Running from one meeting to the next with no space in between is a perfect example. My question to you is 'How much of your daily doing feels intentional?' Do you actually know what percentage of your day is split between unconscious doing and intentional being?

> Awareness is the first step to change, so understanding the split of doing versus being enables us to explore where the opportunities lie to increase our effort in being intentionally focused.

BE AWARE

In a nutshell, focus is about choosing and practising what you give your attention to, right here, right now. To amplify your skill in focus (so that you do not get distracted by the white noise of busy) we start by better understanding what it is that we currently spend our time repeatedly doing (often unconsciously).

As a concept of Greek philosopher Aristotle has famously been summed up: 'We are what we repeatedly do. Excellence, then, is not an act, but a habit'.

Becoming aware of our habits (or the activities we repeatedly undertake), particularly the ones that are not serving us, and focusing on how we can positively shift them in bite-sized pieces, provides a solid basis for a little more happiness in the every day.

James Clear, in his bestselling book *Atomic Habits,* shares that

> changes that seem small and unimportant at first will compound into remarkable results if you're willing to stick with them for years...the quality of our lives often depends on the quality of our habits.

Our aim, therefore, is to expose the habits we have that are not acting in our service, commit to change, experiment with new habits, and consistently practise to find what works best.

Create habits that work for you

Our behaviours are our greatest points of leverage to enable sustainable change, to reset our mindset and make happiness habits subconscious. So how do we disrupt our bad habits and replace them with new ones that enable the life we want?

Firstly, we know relying on willpower alone to stop a bad habit just won't cut it. Your willpower is actually a finite resource. It will run out and often may have already done so by the time the bad habit is occurring. We need to look at how we can remove the power from the bad habit and replace it with a better habit.

There are three simple hacks we can use to do this. I recommend reading through them all first and noting which ones jump out at you. Some will work better for you than others, and that's fine. Remember, it's all about experimenting and discovering what does and does not work, because one size fits all is not a solution in the realm of hacking happiness!

Remove the habit trigger

Observe what is kicking off the unconscious behaviour that is not serving you. This is about bringing awareness to what is activating the behaviour. Is it a place, a time, a person, a thing? An example might be my son going to bed at night and me turning on the TV and unconsciously getting up and grabbing something to eat even if I'm not hungry. I realised my trigger was the TV combined with alone time on the couch. So I stopped sitting on the couch alone to watch TV at that time and instead placed my book on the reading chair for when my son went to bed and picked that up instead. I didn't even think about getting food because I had eliminated the trigger.

Set up your environment

This is about making the bad habit harder or impossible to do. For example, I wanted to stop drinking coffee for a week to see what happened, so I put the coffee maker out of sight and got rid of all the coffee in my house, making it impossible for me to make coffee at home.

Replace the activity

This is the thing that happens in the middle, between what we call your trigger and your payoff. At home alone at the end of the day, I would find myself reaching for a wine at 6 pm, so to stop the habit I started taking the dog for a walk instead. The trigger was the shutting of my computer, which remained the same; I just walked to the front door and grabbed the dog lead instead of going to the kitchen and grabbing a wine glass. The payoff was that I felt I was still clocked off and disconnected from my work, and I was more relaxed without the extra calories.

> Whatever you choose to experiment with in order to hack your habits, make sure you apply the following repeat and reinforce rules to ensure you set yourself up for good habit sustainability.

Repeat your new habit

Program your subconscious to automatically act based on the frequency by which you undertake a habit. The frequency of that repetition will determine how quickly you can embed your new habit. For example, if you've set up a habit that you will undertake weekly, it will take quite a while to embed, whereas if it's something you do daily (or even multiple times a day) then it will become automatic faster.

Reinforce your new habit

For a habit to stick, it has to be a positive experience. There needs to be an anticipation of a good feeling in the run-up to doing it. One of the ways to achieve that is to track your progress. There are many free habit tracker apps available such as Habit Bull to help you track your progress and motivate you along the way.

HAPPINESS HACK

Download a habit tracker app, input one or two habits you would like to embed and try tracking them daily for 2 months. If your phone is too much of a distraction, go old school and create your own habit tracker on a piece of paper. It's as simple as drawing up a table with the habit you want to embed, the days of the week and a space to tick off your progress. Observe what happens.

SHINE A SPOTLIGHT

In the last chapter I asked you to consider what you would be doing with your time if you weren't so busy. I wanted to create an awareness of what you long for, but are doing little of. The intent was to provide the motivation for change by shining a spotlight on things that light you up. I followed that up by asking you to reconnect with what it means to you to be human and who you are as a human being, so that you could gain clarity on what you value, and what gives you meaning. These moments are about putting guideposts in the ground so that we can now ask ourselves: 'What are we actually spending our time doing?'

Where is your attention currently directed? What is stopping you from doing the things that bring you joy, and how can you intentionally adapt your behaviour to create more space for those things?

Using our Thinkology practice alongside the Time Value Assessment in figure 5.1 we can create the space to better understand where our time is being spent in the average day.

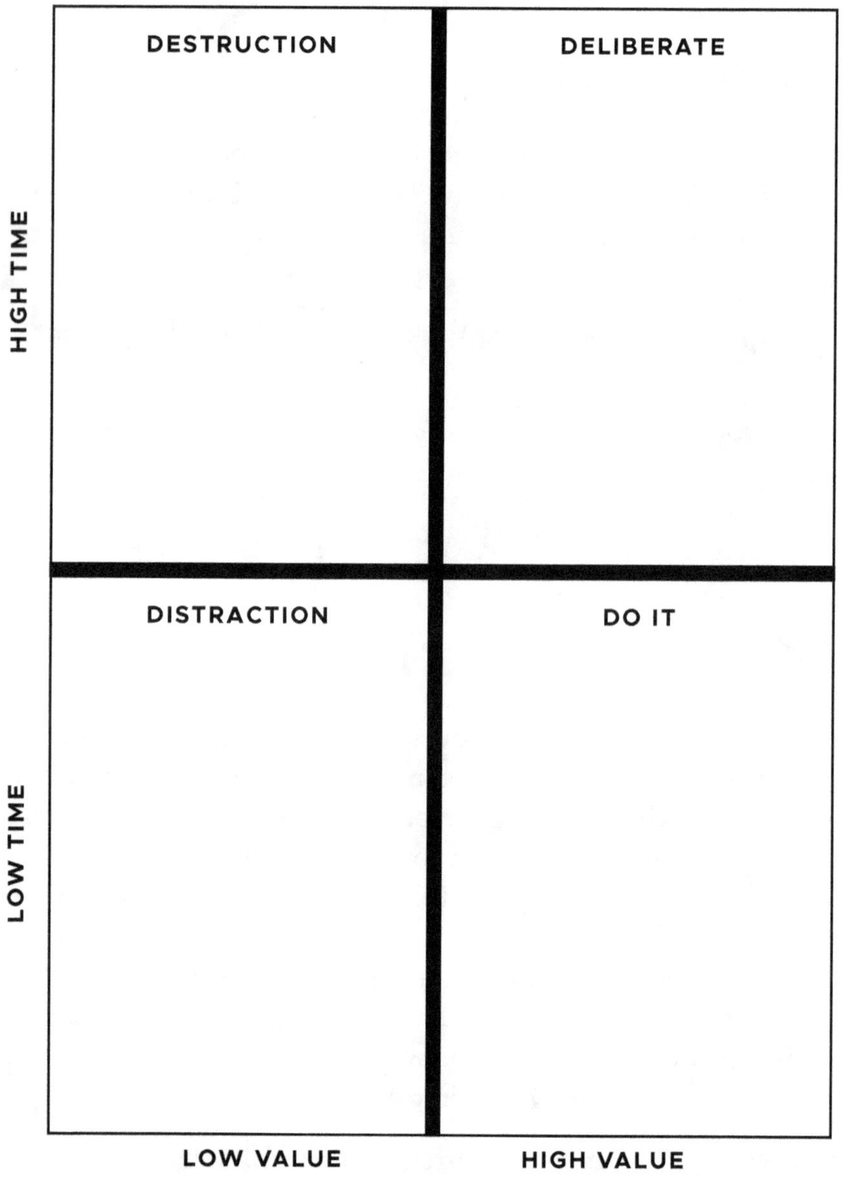

Figure 5.1: the Time Value Assessment

This involves placing each activity that you undertake regularly in one of the four boxes in figure 5.1. Where you place an activity is based on your assessment of how much time it takes, versus the value it delivers to you (in the context of what really matters or gives you meaning). So let's explore what goes where and why.

Distraction (low value, low time)

These are activities that take what feels like little blocks of time, but in aggregate can cost you significantly – think about jumping in and out of social media or email for minutes at a time. I used to do this a lot until someone said to me that 'email is someone else's to-do list getting passed around'. This made me realise that email for me is a low-time task with low value. Consider this just 90 minutes a day consistently in and out of your inbox is almost 49 eight-hour working days in a year. Think of what you could do with that time even if you reduced it by half?

While small in nature, distraction activities are repeated frequently, which turns them into habits. Distraction habits more often than not suck time (and drop you into that connected void we spoke about earlier) that you could be using to focus more on the things that bring you joy.

You may be thinking this doesn't apply to you because you're a great multitasker, able to do many things at once effectively. I'm here to tell you the science says otherwise. It's well understood that the brain cannot focus on multiple things at once. Switching from task to task (getting distracted) impedes performance as well as affects your learning ability, memory and more. Now, I'm not saying every distraction is bad. A little distraction is fine if it's intentional, however a lot of consistent distraction can be a barrier to your potential and your happiness.

Destruction (high time, low value)

'Destruction' as a term seems pretty serious and I've used it with intention to grab your attention. The activities you place in this quadrant are things that consume a lot of your time but add little value to you. Often these are activities we don't want to do that we end up doing as a result of our inability to say 'no'. We fear the repercussions of delivering a 'no', of letting the other party down even though we know saying 'yes' to them will take us away from the things that we truly want to do.

A great example of this in the workplace is meetings with no clear agenda or set outcome, or monthly reports that take hours to create and then no-one reads them. It's not that these activities don't serve you at all – they must in some way, or you wouldn't do them. Maybe doing them helps you avoid the pain of a hard conversation?

Our ability to execute our 'no' with confidence and courtesy is one of the greatest opportunities we have to create more space.

Do It (low time, high value)

These activities are a no brainer because they are actively in service of the things that matter to you and take little blocks of time to action.

For me, a great example of this would be walking the dog. It takes 30 minutes out of my day, helps me get moving, energises me, clears my head for better thinking when I return to my desk and connects me with other human beings as I go to the park.

Also in here is expressing gratitude at the end of each day with my son. Quality time with my son is one of the things I value most and gratitude is scientifically proven to make us happier. So, at the end of each day, my son and I take just five minutes to share three things we are grateful for. It's habitual, it's fun and it's aligned to what matters to me.

Deliberate (high time, high value)

Writing this book is a great example of this. The process requires intention partnered with significant focus, without distraction, in large blocks of time. Deliberate work is equally challenging and rewarding and the results are profound. Cal Newport uses the term 'Deep Work' (in his book of the same name) and defines it as

> professional activities performed in a state of distraction-free concentration that push your cognitive capabilities to their limit. These efforts create new value, improve your skill and are hard to replicate.

I would also argue that Deliberate work as a practice does not have to just sit in the domain of 'professional activity', but can be equally valuable in personal pursuits such as hobbies.

HAPPINESS HACK

Now it's time to unpack how you spend your days to help you create more space for more of what matters. Track what you do in an average day. Plot each activity on the Time Value Assessment (if there's not enough space for you, draw your own) to gain awareness of where your opportunities lie to shift your behaviour.

FIND TIME FOR MORE OF WHAT MATTERS

The Time Value Assessment is often an eye opener. Most of us realise how little if any activities sit in the Deliberate space and perhaps only a few in the Do It. Why? Because so much time is unconsciously spent on Distraction or Destruction due to habits that don't serve us!

As video game developer John Carmack said, 'Focus is a matter of deciding what things you're not going to do'. Adding more to a full day is not a solution to overwhelm; we must look at what to take away and only then consider what we intentionally add in its place to amplify our happy.

> To enable more focus, we need to ditch the Distraction and Destruction, and create more space for Do It and Deliberate activities.

Schedule limited times throughout the day when you will allow yourself distractions. For example, I only check email twice a day for 30 minutes each time. I've set up the following out of office message to manage others' expectations of me when it comes to how I respond to email. What's interesting is how many people have taken this auto response and copied it for themselves. If it helps, go right ahead!

> We Practice What We Teach therefore I dedicate the majority of my working days to deliberate work and client connection. This means I only check emails twice a day. If you'd like to book a keynote or workshop for your team or community please contact the HackingHappy.co Magic Wand at ... If your enquiry is urgent, let's go old school and give me a call on ... I love human connection!

HAPPINESS HACK

Building barriers between you and distractions is a great place to start to create a little more space. Here are some hacks that have worked for me that you could play with.

* Buy an alarm clock and make a hard no phones in bedrooms rule. (This one's a game changer!)
* Set your phone to lock you out for certain periods of the day. Mine goes to sleep at 7.30 pm and wakes at 7.30 am.
* Plan phone-free activities such as walking the dog, time with friends, family and meetings.
* Remove applications like email and social media from your phone so that you can't jump in and out of them unconsciously all day.

FROM DESTRUCTION TO DELIBERATE

When was the last time you said 'yes' to something you didn't want to do? For many of the people I meet, unfortunately, this is a daily practice. A practice that affects our happiness, and our ability to live the life that we want. Why do we do this?

Well, I can speak for myself on this front because I have suffered from 'people pleaser syndrome' for years, and I'm slowly skilling in the art of more 'no'. Why? Because I have experienced first-hand how saying 'no' more often creates the space for me to realise my dreams quicker, and have a greater impact on the lives of others.

Every 'yes' you give away unconsciously and without due consideration is like adding bricks to an invisible wall between you and your aspirations. Remember to embrace the JOMO we discussed in chapter 4? Learning to love saying no, and using it effectively, is a super power that frees up your time and enables you to move from Destruction-based activity to Deliberate!

Now, I'm not suggesting you can say 'no' to everything. We all know that there are some things we may not like doing that we have to do. That's life. I'm here to challenge you to consider where you could experiment with using no more often; where are you giving yeses too freely, but to the detriment of your focus on the things that matter to you?

Practising your no means that you will have to accept that you will let people down (albeit with kindness). That is the reality of using no more often. People pleasing is exhausting and time consuming and, in my experience, often comes at the expense of your own happiness. It's like the oxygen mask rule on planes. You have to apply your own first before you can help others; happiness is the same. You have to focus on your own happiness first before you can make others happy.

Learning to love a no starts with getting clear on what we will say no to and why.

We want to learn how to be wise with our time and create a practice that enables us to be confident in our delivery of a 'no' when an opportunity does not fit with where we want to focus our energy for long-term happiness. This is where the No Selection Criteria come in.

Simply put, it's a short list of criteria or questions that you create for yourself that must be met in order for you to say 'yes' to an opportunity. When we are clear on what we want it enables us to be clear (and confident) on what action we take. The No Selection Criteria are intended to make the delivery of a no a little easier because it acts in support of creating the space for higher impact, higher value activities.

If an opportunity doesn't tick the boxes of your No Selection Criteria, you gift yourself permission to practise the delivery of your 'no'. Now, not all noes will land as you expect, but the more you practise the easier it gets.

Here's an example of my No Selection Criteria. When an opportunity presents, I ask myself:

- Does it positively affect the lives of others and have the potential to help them hack happiness?
- Does it enable skill building in Intentional Adaptability for myself, others or both?
- Will it enable me to still spend quality time with my son?
- Will it be fun, and are the requestors value aligned?
- Will it involve human connection?
- Will it make my business more sustainable or provide access to a new growth market?

If the answer isn't 'yes' to at least three of these criteria, then I know it's a 'no' for me.

> The important thing to remember is that creating the space to focus is all about trade-offs—every yes you give to someone else could very well be a no to you and your happiness.

HAPPINESS HACK

Using your Thinkology practice, carve out 30 minutes to focus on the creation of your No Selection Criteria. Write down three to six criteria that you will use to assess opportunities. Keep them handy and experiment with them over the coming week and see what happens.

PRACTISE NO

As you practise saying no, you will discover this two-letter word is really hard to deliver! We all want to be liked and don't enjoy letting others down. But learning to be effective at delivering a no and doing it with kindness and confidence can not only garner respect, but also equally inspire those around you to do the same.

Starting is the hardest part, and, like with anything new, it's the practice that enables the skill to be built. You will feel more comfortable over time.

So how do you deliver an intentional no and do your best not to piss people off or look like a pain in the arse?

1. Acknowledge

Start with acknowledging the person's request. Show them you have listened and that they have been heard, for example, 'I understand that you are asking me to…' Paraphrase what you heard them say and ask them to confirm that what you understood is correct.

2. Own it

Be honest in your response, for example, 'I'm on a mission to achieve X which means I need to be single-minded in my focus, to create the space to realise the impact I seek. Unfortunately, this opportunity is not a fit with my priorities at this point in time, but thank you for considering me'.

If you are saying 'no' to someone you work for, because you have too much on your plate, try this: 'These are the top three priorities I am focusing on at the moment…If you feel this is a higher priority, can you please advise which of the other three priorities you would like me to put on the backburner, to create the space for your request?' Now, while this is not a direct 'no', it demonstrates you can prioritise and puts your boss in a position to decide what is most important for the business at that point in time. It also helps clarify your priorities and enables you to be more confident in a difficult conversation. If you continually don't like the priorities agreed and it's affecting your happiness, then you have a bigger decision to make (we pick up on this later in skill 2 – Courage).

If you're saying 'no' because you feel ethically or morally compromised by what you are being asked to do, consider stepping into vulnerability and putting your 'why' on the table, for example, 'I am not comfortable accepting this request because

I feel it is not aligned with my values, which are ... and this is why'. This is a powerful way to demonstrate what you believe in, which can often connect with others in unexpected ways.

3. Say 'no'

Plain and simply state it (remember the language you use will determine your ability to make change and this is a lived example!). For example, 'Therefore, at this point in time I will need to say no' or 'I will have to decline your offer' or 'I can't commit to that right now'.

4. Consider connecting

Consider how else you might be able to help this person. Is there someone else you can connect them to who may be able to help? Is there a resource you are aware of that might assist them? If there is then tell them.

5. Don't apologise

Be unapologetic in your delivery of a no. So often I hear people apologise for their no, but here's the thing: you don't need to be sorry for giving yourself permission to focus on what matters to you. You should be doing the complete opposite, and high-fiving yourself. So, be firm but kind in the language you use and confident in your no. Trust me, every no you deliver moves you closer to where you want to be and makes the next no a little easier.

HAPPINESS HACK

Pick one no you would like to deliver in the coming week. Work it through the above framework so that you feel prepared. You may even want to role play it with a friend. Then get out there and experiment!

PRACTISE WHAT YOU PREACH

We have only just scratched the surface when it comes to amplifying your ability to focus in order to be more intentionally adaptable. Building your focus muscle is about committing the time to practise daily, and the best way I've discovered to do that is to time block my Thinkology.

It's about prioritising thinking over distraction and setting up your week to enable that. At the end of each week, for example, I get clear on what I want to give my focus to in the week ahead and then I time block one- to two-hour sessions throughout the week where I turn all of my distractions off and I sit and work on that single thing. (I'm doing it right now!)

The more I do this, the less I actually use the distractions that I used to be attached to. It:

- enables you to make significant progress
- improves your ability to problem solve
- builds your resilience
- increases your productivity
- provides higher levels of fulfilment.

Consistently practising working on one thing reprograms your neural pathways to enhance your ability to be rather than do.

Part of practising also means reflecting on what is working and what is not.

For example, every second Friday morning I carve out just 15 minutes to reflect on how I've invested my time and how focused I have been.

I ask myself three simple questions so that I can ensure my focus remains a focus:

1. What worked?
2. What didn't?
3. What am I going to do differently next time?

This simple practice keeps me connected to what I am trying to achieve and what is within my control to make happen.

Your journey from doing to being is unique because how we each choose to experiment with the concept of Intentional Adaptability is different. Some things will work now, some later and others never, and that is exactly how it should be. You just won't know how it will play out until you try.

So ask yourself, what is the cost of not trying?

HAPPINESS HACK

Schedule a recurring meeting in your diary to reflect on your week and then do it. Answer these three simple questions during that allocated time to better understand how you can evolve your practice: what worked, what didn't, and what am I going to do differently next week?

LIFT OFF!

Before we close this chapter, I'd like to share with you a story about Pete and how his Intentional Adaptability practice evolved. Pete was a participant in one of the first Busy = Bullshit programs. His journey over the 12 months that followed that workshop was fascinating.

The focus experiments we ran through in the program created the space for Pete and his colleagues to talk about who was really in control of their time; many of them felt it was not them when we first met. Pete said it was in that conversation that he realised:

> I am the only one who can control my time; how I use it for my joy comes down to me. I'm in a work culture of yes. Yes is the expected answer to opportunities because there are so many great ones available. But continual yeses can be exhausting and mentally unsustainable.

Not long after this program Pete took time out, realising he was in a job that no longer brought joy. He said:

> I felt conflicted because the job I had was a great job but the way I was operating was unsustainable. I didn't quit, I wasn't sure that was the right answer. I felt I needed space to work through what was going on. It took a couple of weeks of stillness to feel normal again and then at about the five-week mark I got my head together. I came to the realisation that boundaries in terms of mental health and rest were just as important as boundaries around my time.

Pete created space by making little changes like notifications in his diary to tell him to go home each day. Bit by bit, he reprioritised his life, stopped *saying* 'X is important to me' and actually *made* X important by giving it oxygen. Pete says:

> When I returned to work I didn't know how it would play out but I chose to experiment with new ways of using my time. I just wanted to have fun in my job again and I found a way to make that happen. I let go of the guilt and shame around whether I'd chosen the right path and started to practise gratitude, which enabled me to make a mindset shift.
>
> What's interesting is the environment hasn't changed, I have. I don't let it get to me anymore because I'm comfortable now in what's important to me. I say 'no' to things a lot and actively choose the things I will enjoy. I just stopped giving a fuck about the repercussions of saying 'no' to things that didn't light me up because I knew that they came at a cost long term.
>
> Interestingly I've now triggered a number of conversations in my workplace that would not have occurred 12 months ago because of the visible choices I've made and the behaviour I'm employing. My journey has also helped me tune into making sure others are okay.

Now, Pete's changes didn't happen in a one-day workshop. He had to move through the pain to learn how to come out the other side. Hence, your focus experiments are not an end point; they are a launching pad for the amplification of your skill in Intentional Adaptability and more happiness.

EXPERIMENT NOW

The Doing to Being Action Plan (outlined below step by step) is designed to help you create more space and then do something intentional and focused with it.

1. Disable a distraction

Pick one distraction habit you would like to change and work it through the following process.

* What habit hack would you like to experiment with to set yourself up for success? (Refer to the Habit Hacking section on pages 86–89.)

* What new habit could enable you to disable your distraction habit? (You may want to refer back to the list I shared on pages 87–89 or come up with a new one.)

* How will you track your progress?

____

____

* When will you review your progress?

____

____

2. Deliver a no

The only way to get better at delivering a no is to do it!

* What one no would you like to deliver in the coming week?
* Set yourself up for success by using the No Delivery Framework. Map out a plan by working through how you will...
    * Acknowledge the request so that the person feels heard. Write down your script for how you will do that.
    * Frame the delivery of your no. Write down exactly what you want to say but ensure you come from a place of kindness.
    * Is there an offer you can make to connect the person to someone else or another resource that might be able to help them? If yes write down your ideas.
    * Set a time and place to connect with the person you need to deliver the no to, ideally in a neutral and comfortable environment.
* Reflect on how it went using the Reflection Questions:
    * What worked well?
    * What didn't?
    * What will I do differently next week?

3. Plan your Thinkology

Set up your coming week by creating the space to focus on one thing and go deep on it. Choose something you would love to learn more about or a problem you would like to solve and work it through the Thinkology Plan.

Once you've mapped out your plan make sure you go to your calendar and block out the time.

Thinkology Plan

Week starting	*For example, 1st Nov*
Goal for the week (hours)	*How many hours are you committing to your practice for the week?*
Actual hours for the week	*How many hours did you do? (I track these as I go here.)*
Area of focus	*What will you focus on in the time allocated?*
Outcomes desired	*What would you like to achieve in the time allocated?*
Star rating	*At the end of the week reflect on how it went and give yourself a star rating out of 5.*

REFLECT AND REMEMBER

* There is no quick or easy route to Intentional Adaptability; you must take the hard route, the route with no guarantee of a set outcome other than unlearning, growth and greater being.
* You're not seeking to be busy; you're seeking to be deliberate, considered and giving of your attention to just one thing at a time.
* The more you understand what habits are not serving you and what triggers your behaviour, the more opportunity you have to change.
* Thinkology builds our focus, which enhances our ability to be fully present. In today's world that's an advantage as the quality of your thinking, and your ability to problem solve and innovate is significantly amplified.
* How do you value your time? Assess your Distracted and Destructive activities and create a plan for more Do It and Deliberate ones.
* The more often you say 'no' to others, the more often you say 'yes' to yourself.
* Plan how you intend to deliver your 'no' and practise to build your focus over time.

SHARE THE HAPPY

Take your exploration of what it means to be human one step further and apply the Thinkology practice to ask others 'Who are you as a human being?' You may be surprised at how others choose to define themselves, how that highlights the roles they play in life and the things that challenge them and bring them joy. What's also interesting is how your answer to this question evolves over time. Enjoy!

IAQ Skill 2 — Courage

How to use fear and failure to shape the change you seek.

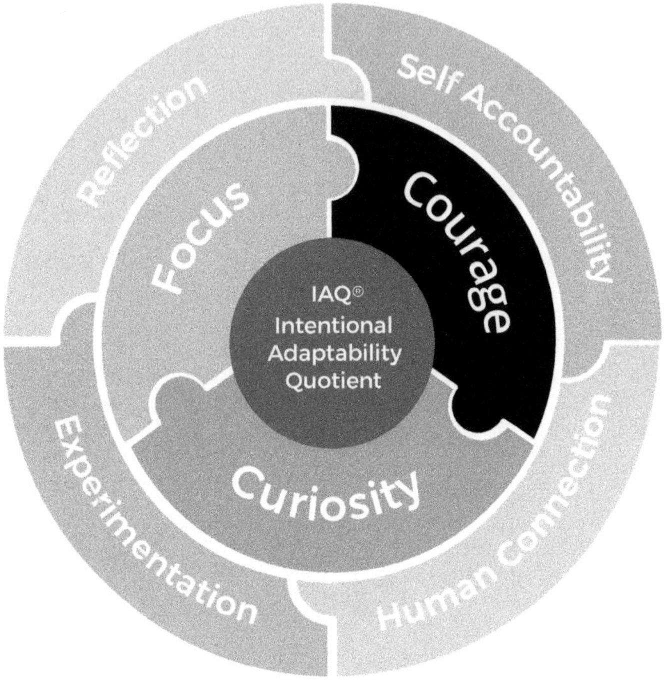

CHAPTER 6

Courage: Fear is your future

In 2017, I was approached to speak at the Level Up Conference in Melbourne to share my perspectives on 'tactics for happy change'. The audience would be 120 professional women seeking to level up their careers. I accepted the opportunity with gusto. I was comfortable in front of large audiences and I was well progressed on my journey toward hacking my own happiness – it seemed like an easy task.

Yet as I started to plan my keynote, I realised that I had a few challenges to address if I was going to have an impact on the women in that room. Firstly, the speaker line-up for the conference was a group of rockstar women who would be bringing their A games; how would I stand out and ensure that I didn't get lost in a sea of speakers? Secondly, I had the graveyard shift. I was on at 2 pm and they were serving wine at lunch – how would I ensure I kept the audience awake?

I felt I needed to push the boundaries somehow, that the status quo talk wouldn't cut it. In that moment I came to a profound realisation: one of the greatest levers you have available to you in realising happiness is fear. The one thing that we seem to so actively avoid holds the key to unlocking greater happiness.

Opportunity lies on the other side of the things that scare us most.

Every change I had made on my journey thus far had required me to lean into fear in a way I had never done before and certainly would never have done when I was in my past life. If I wasn't scared or uncomfortable I wasn't propelling myself forward.

This insight hit me like a lightning bolt. I knew that I had a responsibility to the women who would listen to me in that room; a responsibility to move them in a way that enabled them to literally experience and feel the fear of happy change. I wanted to give them permission to act on their fear and understand that, no matter what the outcome, it would carry them closer to where they wanted to be.

Four weeks out from my talk, I woke in the middle of the night with perhaps the craziest idea I've ever had and it terrified me. The next morning, I called my 75-year-old father (one of my biggest supporters) and told him what I thought I needed to do to make my point. I knew that if he agreed then I was on the right path. Sure enough, Dad told me the idea was brilliant and that was it. I gave myself no choice but to launch into fear at a whole new level in order to demonstrate to others the power of leaning into what scares us most.

The day arrived. I walked out on that stage literally shaking. With a body built for comfort, not modelling, I untied my bohemian wrap-around dress, dropped it to the floor and stood there in my one-piece bathing suit. After a moment, I said:

> Love me or hate me you will not forget me, and if there is only one thing that you take away from today, it's that happy change is found when you learn to get comfortable in discomfort.
>
> I can honestly tell you that it doesn't get any more fucking uncomfortable than this.

There was a short, stunned silence and then the audience cheered and applauded. While what I'd done was crazy (I think I might very well be the first keynote speaker in the world to do this) there was method to my madness. I had married two of life's big fears: public speaking and doing it half naked.

While I was terrified of dropping my dress, I understood that there are few women in the world who do not suffer from body image issues. I knew everyone there would relate to how uncomfortable and scary that moment was for me. They felt the fear with me as I exposed my vulnerability and they saw with their own eyes that stepping into fear could move others in unexpected ways.

My mission to have an impact on the women in that room was accomplished. Many of them approached me after my talk, sharing that I had just given them permission to step into fear in a way they had never considered. I had given them a way to measure their fear by helping them realise that what they were afraid of was nowhere near as scary as standing on a stage in your bathing suit.

Shortly after, the moment was shared on social media, published in newspapers and magazines globally and went viral, with over 70 000 views on LinkedIn. It created a global movement called 'Naked For Change'. Random strangers around the world messaged, telling me that, after seeing what I'd done, they had been propelled to act on their fear. Perhaps most surprising, though, was how it changed me.

When I stood on that stage at the age of 41 with no clothes to hide my imperfections, something changed; I felt empowered. I realised that I no longer cared about the judgement of others. The only judgement I needed in life was my own. As long as I was true to myself and to the impact I sought to have on the lives of others, things would always work out.

That realisation was a game changer. It enabled me to trust my fear in a way I had never considered and use it as a lever to shape my happiness.

Here's what I know to be true: you have no idea what you are truly capable of in life and unless you are willing to trust your fear and dance with it daily you will leave opportunity and unlived happiness on the table.

FEAR NOT

It's all good to talk about using fear as a lever for change, but how? Where does one even begin? Let's start by unpacking the word 'fear' and how it can affect our ability to grab hold of possibilities.

Close your eyes and think about the word 'fear'. What words come to mind?

When I pose this question in my Fear(less) Masterclass, more often than not the words that participants call out are negative, all doom and gloom. This is not surprising, given that most dictionaries describe fear as 'a distressing emotion aroused by impending danger, evil, pain, whether the threat is real or imagined'.

Well, that certainly is not a selling proposition is it? It's hardly saying, 'here I am, use me to your advantage'. The reality is that the pervasive negative language we associate with fear is a barrier. We've been conditioned to believe that fear should be used as an alarm bell to run away rather than lean into possibility. Authority figures, politicians and especially the media use fear as a way to influence and control our behaviour and thinking.

But ask yourself where would we be if Elon Musk hadn't leaned into fear? Arguably not as far ahead on the electric vehicle, driverless car or space front, and certainly not looking at ways to build underground tunnels that could solve Los Angeles traffic congestion with a concept that looks like it was born out of a sci-fi movie, right?

What about Greta Thunberg? Where would she be if she decided to let her fear and negative self-talk take over, especially when publicly criticised by the likes of Donald Trump?

Or Jacinda Ardern in dealing with the Christchurch mass shooting in 2019 or fully locking down New Zealand when COVID-19 hit—what if she'd decided it was too scary to show vulnerability as the leader of New Zealand, too scary not to temper her opinions and be completely honest? We wouldn't have a role model of what a genuine government leader could look like for the future.

Trailblazing alongside fear is tough, and it can be lonely—but it paves the way for us to see what's possible and realise that there can be a better way, even if it makes us extremely uncomfortable.

The reality is that fear is everywhere; we live in uncertain and unprecedented times. Fear is literally all around us as I write these words, with a new normal being formed thanks to COVID-19. Toilet paper is flying off the shelves (if it even makes it to the shelves), in the United States there is a run on gun buying, alcohol sales have gone through the roof...we are completely fearful of what's next. The only certainty in the future is change, and it's only going to get faster and even more disorientating. That in itself is enough to make you feel fearful! I get it. But fear is one of the greatest levers you have to realise the life you always wanted.

Fear is your future. We have a choice to either embrace it or exhaust ourselves avoiding it.

HAPPINESS HACK

The first step to embracing fear is changing your language around it. For every negative word you associate with fear there is an equally positive one; we are just skewed with negativity bias. So brain dump all the positive words you can associate with fear. For example:

* growth
* learning
* challenge
* opportunity...

I guarantee the list is long, and it's powerful if you use those words to switch your mindset from negative to positive when fear presents. It's amazing how you can reprogram your subconscious over time by swapping out negative words for positive words. Try it, I dare you!

WHAT ARE YOU WIRED FOR?

I recently heard someone say that fear is having your mobile phone with one battery bar left and no charger. It made me laugh out loud, but it equally made me a little sad (I bet you can feel the angst just at the thought of this).

Let's take it one step further to understand how our internal wiring works when fear shows up. Imagine you reach into your pocket only to discover your mobile phone is not flat; it's not there at all. Your brain registers a risk, a potential threat, and fear kicks in. This is what psychologist Daniel Goleman calls an 'amygdala hijack'.

Your amygdala is a small, almond-shaped part of your brain that enacts an instinctive response to fear otherwise known as fight, flight or freeze. When you feel fear, your amygdala activates a physical response. So even though it's only a mobile phone, your body responds in the same way as it would if you were faced with a man-eating bear. Your heart starts to beat faster and the stress hormones adrenaline and cortisol start to surge. Understandably, in a life-threatening situation (like being faced with a bear) this automated activation serves us; but in the modern world (like with the phone example), it more often than not doesn't.

The amygdala is hijacking the rational part of the brain when faced with fear and kicking you into irrational behaviour. You might panic, freak out, scream an obscenity, start ransacking your desk and every bit of furniture around you to find your missing phone. (You've been there, right?)

So fear is a natural part of how we are wired as human beings. Our very survival as a species is dependent on minimising risk and maximising reward. Our brains are constantly seeking certainty to help us feel safe and when the unknown presents, our fear kicks in to protect us even when we don't necessarily need protecting.

Fortunately, in our modern life we don't need to run from beasts on a daily basis. The fear we are tackling in relation to our happiness is not the life-threatening fear that can result in our death.

> Nowadays, fear of the unknown is what stands between us and our happiness, because opportunity lives in the unknown.

Irrational behaviour and often unhappiness are fuelled by the feelings of overwhelm and angst connected to the most commonly held fears such as fear of missing out, fear of failure, or fear of being judged. More often than not, these fears play out in our heads like in figure 6.1, and the longer we internalise them without taking action to process them constructively the bigger they grow.

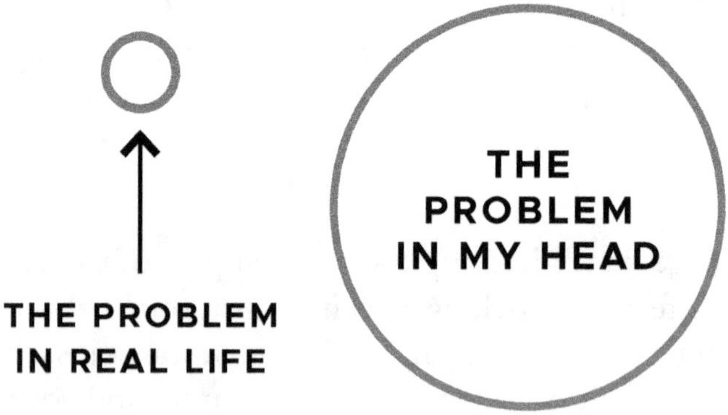

Figure 6.1: the problem with problems
Source: Modified from a meme originally posted on Instagram by @Affirmationsforlife

As Roman philosopher Seneca once said, 'We suffer more often in imagination than in reality'. Just because we feel fear, it doesn't mean it is real or rational.

Remember the earlier definition of fear? 'A distressing emotion aroused by impending danger, evil, pain, *whether the threat is real or imagined*'. Notice how it clearly states that we feel fear regardless of whether the threat is real or not. How often are our fears imagined and not realised? They just stand between us and possibility.

I have observed through my work that many of us will sit in the misery of the known rather than step into the discomfort of the unknown even though we know it could make us happier.

A perfect case in point is a beautiful friend of mine, Lee. Lee is one of those people you would look at and say she has it all: a career as a leader in a tech giant, a family, loving partner, beautiful homes, money in the bank ... However, she is not immune to fear and its ability to block her happiness. As she told me:

> I have Type A fear. It includes fear of not meeting my own expectations of utility, earning potential and social prominence. This is my addiction cycle. When I please others I get rewarded, when I meet external expectations I get rewarded. I have a perfect track record for high performance, earning tonnes of money, getting amazing roles. Yet the more I excel, the more I feel like shit.
>
> Society tells me I should be happy, I should be grateful… but I feel dead inside. I wonder what's wrong with me; everyone's telling me how amazing it all is, but I've come to realise I'm making a living at the cost of having a life. I'm embarrassed but the hamster wheel is so reinforcing. The world is set up to feed my ego beast. It isn't set up to grow the part of me that feeds my soul.
>
> My family and partner are not getting the best of me, my time or my energy. I have a great ROI model for assessing opportunities but I don't factor in a variable for me and my self-care, wellbeing and happiness. The cost of inaction is real, it is great and I'm underestimating that.
>
> Fear for me is the stuff that gets in the way of doing what you truly want to do. It's the internal tension between the things I perceive are expected of me versus the things that I need to do for me. The challenge is that I feel at odds with the choice. I have a long history of pleasing people, which is fed by my fear of the implications of not pleasing people. I've made this much bigger in my head due to the time that has passed and the lack of data I have on what will happen if I let others down.

The learning here is that we fear the unknown and allow that fear to stop us from experimenting in ways that may support us in realising our happiness. Simple experiments such as using language to shift our ability to act can enable unprecedented change. Here's the thing: if you continue to feed your brain negative inputs when fear presents, like 'I can't', 'it's impossible', 'it's all too hard', then your brain will create its very own invisible barrier to progress. If, however, you start to feed your brain positive inputs when non-life-threatening fear presents, starting with words like 'I can do this', 'I can try and experiment', 'I may not have done this before but I will learn when a fearful situation presents', then you start to build neural pathways that reinforce a positive mindset and behaviours.

FROM THREAT TO REWARD

Remember, our brains constantly scan the environment for both risk and reward. When presented with risk often our fear is triggered and kicks us into that fight, flight or freeze mode we considered earlier. David Rock, in his paper 'SCARF: a brain-based model for collaborating with and influencing others', has used neuroscience to help us better understand what activates the risk–reward responses in our brain with a focus on social situations. While his focus is on uncertainty triggered in social situations, it can equally apply to what triggers us outside of those situations. The SCARF model provides a basis for us to better understand what's truly sitting behind many of our fears, enabling us to unpack how we might intercept them.

As you read this list, notice which ones you feel a stronger connection to, and ask yourself why.

- *Status*. This is our ego. Fear can be triggered when we feel our level of importance is compromised.
- *Certainty*. Uncertainty is the mother of fear. Our inability to accurately predict the future can not only distract us, but it can also trigger fear.
- *Autonomy*. Fear can surface when we feel we do not have control over the outcome.
- *Relatedness*. Brené Brown famously said, 'We are wired for belonging'. So we can be triggered when we don't feel connected or included by others.
- *Fairness*. We can experience fear when we feel we are being treated differently from others in the same or similar situations.

Once you understand these triggers, you can start to hack your way from feeling threatened to in control of how you respond when fear presents.

We have an opportunity when fear presents itself to name what is triggering it, identifying what it is that makes us feel at risk, and what our brain is telling us is being compromised. This provides a basis to reflect on our attitude toward fear and how that may be holding us back. We then have a choice to reframe our fear using simple techniques that ground us back in the moment and activate our rational brain to take charge of how we respond.

The more we practise the following four trigger reset skills, the better we get at moving from a destructive place to a constructive space when dealing with fear.

1. Three deep breaths

If you find yourself in a meeting where your ego is compromised, or perhaps in an unfair situation, when the fear starts to bubble up, simply take three deep breaths. It doesn't have to be so deep that it is obvious to others. It's about connecting your mind to your breath and bringing you back into the moment, activating your rational brain to take hold.

I often find taking a pause, a moment to collect oneself rather than speaking, can fundamentally shift how we respond. Equally, silence can be golden and command more respect, as it makes a response sound more considered. It's like when one of those emails hits your inbox and makes you a little mad. You go to fire back, but collect yourself and allow 24 hours to pass before you respond. Choosing to not respond in the moment and allowing the space for rational thought to kick in is a powerful way to shift your behaviour and, over time, your neural programming.

2. What is, rather than what if

I was once running a Fear(less) Masterclass at a large energy company. A courageous soul felt so moved by the safe space we'd created that she shared how she had suffered with debilitating anxiety for the past two years to the point where she couldn't even drive her car. She went on to explain to us that a simple question practised frequently enabled her to overcome her anxiety and step back into daily activities that many of us take for granted. Every time anxiety presented she would say to herself, 'What is, rather than what if?' This would bring her back into the present moment, the reality of the situation, and challenge her to stop over-analysing what could happen at the compromise of being.

We have somewhere between 50 000 and 70 000 thoughts a day, depending on which research you choose to believe. (How you measure this I don't know, but I think we can all agree the number is a lot!) So of those thousands of thoughts that we have daily, how many are 'what if' thoughts? Given we are wired to assess every situation for risk and reward I would argue the majority.

Professor of Psychology Robert Leahy's 2005 research uncovered that 85 per cent of what we worry about never happens. That's a lot of brain power invested in worry that could be redirected to being and activating more joy in each day. Agree?

3. Name it and reframe it

Awareness enables action and the opportunity to challenge behaviour that is not serving us when presented with feelings of fear or discomfort. Naming a feeling and reframing how you sit with it enables you to take back control and shift a negative towards a positive experience. The process is simple:

Name the feeling, for example, 'I feel ______.'

Write it down. Get it out of your head and onto paper. This in itself can provide relief, as leaving feelings undealt with in your head only makes them bigger over time.

Ask yourself, 'Why do I feel this way; what triggered me?'

Consider one action you can take to feel better. What is within your control to influence how you feel? Don't try and get rid of negative feelings; create the space to allow yourself to sit with them for a period of time to really explore and understand the feeling. I find allowing myself to feel negative feelings, but putting an end point on how long I let that go on for, is helpful. For example, I may want to wallow a little in self-pity if something doesn't go my way, but I say to myself, 'You have 24 hours to sit in it but after that it's time to consider what small steps you can start to take to move on'.

4. Excited, not anxious

Did you know that anxiety and excitement are extremely similar emotions in terms of how the brain and the body responds? According to Harvard professor Alison Wood Brooks, who studied this phenomenon, the only difference between the two emotions is that anxiety focuses on the outcome being negative. That means it takes this one simple question to hack and shift your fear: Am I excited or am I anxious?

This question was brought to my attention by a Fear(less) Masterclass workshop participant who moonlighted as a rally car driver. He said to me that he had become aware of a concept called 'anxiety reappraisal', a practical way to quickly reframe a fearful mind. When he was behind the wheel of his rally car and he felt a surge of anxiety coming on, he would simply ask himself: am I anxious or excited? That single question would enable him to take his feelings of fear and channel them into positive action through the frame of excitement.

I myself recently undertook my first skydive from 15 000 feet – jumping out over the ocean with the intent of landing safely on the beach. As the plane rose higher and higher toward my plunge destination I asked myself, 'Am I excited or anxious?' I told myself that it was definitely excitement and I launched into freefall with any trace of anxious fear a distant memory.

It might sound too good to be true, but it has been scientifically proven to work. Try it and see.

HAPPINESS HACK

The next time you're afraid, name what triggered the fear. What was it that made you feel that way? Then try one of the trigger reset skills – three deep breaths, what is rather than what if, name it and reframe it, or excited, not anxious – to help you make a positive shift.

A SAFE SPACE FOR FEAR

What would happen if we started talking more openly about the things that scare us most? What if we created a safe space for fear to be shared on a daily basis? I have spent weeks with thousands of people in professional environments doing exactly that and what happens may surprise you.

> When we create a safe space for people to talk about what is really going on in their lives and in their heads, we normalise fear; we remove the taboo.

Let me demonstrate with a quick exercise.

Let's pretend for a moment I'm your fairy godmother and I have waved a magic wand and made fear disappear. It no longer exists as a concept within your mind. (Stay with me here.)

What one change (within your control) would you make right now, that you know could make you happier?

The change you seek is likely to be something you have longed for, but not stepped into because fear is standing between you and action. What is the fear that's blocking you? Is it fear of failure, the judgement of others, financial instability or is it something else?

When I do this exercise with people I get some very interesting insights. In workshops, I ask participants to write what has held them back from the change they long for on a sticky note and place it on a wall in the classroom so that it's visible to everyone. Together, we then group the fears. This actually creates that safe space for fear because people are surprised to observe that most of our fears are shared and fall into similar buckets!

Table 6.1 shows you the top six fears, covering 82 per cent of what people say hold them back from the change they've longed for. Where do your fears fit in?

Table 6.1: top six fears

Fear of...	*% of participants*
Financial instability	*31%*
Failure	*15%*
Not being good enough	*10%*
The judgement of others	*9%*
The unknown	*9%*
Letting others down	*8%*

When I ask people how they feel when they see this list, they often say 'sad'. The reason is that so many of us are walking through life feeling alone with our fears, like we're the only one in the world that this is happening to – but it's just not the case!

Keeping our fears inside creates a world of pain and angst and it doesn't have to. We are part of one big human family and we are not as different as we like to think.

> Fear is normal and we need to embrace it and help each other to do the same so that we can come out the other side a little better than before.

Creating a safe space for fear helps us realise that the person sitting next to us, more often than not, shares the same fear or has experienced that fear at some point in time. We remove judgement, we seek to understand one another, we empathise with each other. Most importantly we start to reduce the overwhelm and angst that fear drives, and we start to open the door to possibility, innovation, creativity and greater happiness. Now, who doesn't want that?

A beautiful case in point is a response I formulated two weeks into the COVID-19 pandemic. I had decided to act intentionally slow during the onset as I was observing so much reactionary behaviour and I wanted to ensure that whatever action I took was intentional and met people where they were at. So many were struggling to get through the next 24 hours, let alone the next month. Not surprisingly, the level of fear for people at this time was through the roof—and fear, when left to fester, can be toxic and destructive, especially when the uncertainty has no end. I decided to look at how I could use technology to help provide a safe space for random strangers to share their fear. We started running free online Fear(less) Masterclasses for people to openly share what they were afraid of with random strangers, to help them understand the fear, what was triggering it and how they could use themselves and their environment to navigate their fear as a basis for growth. The results thus far have been heartwarming and impactful for all involved. A safe space for fear was considered 'an amazing gift, that released me from fear's grip', or, as another observed, 'who would have thought coming together with a handful of strangers, talking about our fears and what makes us human could have such a profound impact – it was a refreshing change to be grounded in a noisy world'.

My experience tells me that most of us, sadly, are afraid of the repercussions of being real and showing these kinds of vulnerabilities; it's why so many of us put on the mask before we head into the office each day. We hide ourselves, our opinions, our craziness in order to conform and hopefully be accepted. Trying to be someone else or tempering ourselves in this way is hard work – it's exhausting – but many of us do it out of fear. After all, we just want to belong, right?

Yet belonging doesn't mean we have to all be the same; it's about understanding and connecting with one another. So while there is a big push to tell people (especially leaders) to be more authentic, perhaps we need to look at what in the environment is making people feel unsafe to do so.

> Creating a safe space for fear to be shared provides a foundation for us to show up as we really are and for organisations to harness the diversity and potential of the people they employ.

FEARING LESS

Mike Cannon-Brookes is one of the cofounders of Atlassian. He has created a billion-dollar company with his best mate, and he stands up and fights for what he believes is right by putting his money where his mouth is (especially around environmental issues). For example, a couple of tweets to Elon Musk actually saw the billionaires sort out a major power crisis in one of Australia's capital cities (serious).

One could assume that, with the power that this man has at his fingertips, he must be totally fearless, right? I mean, he can do anything! But you wouldn't be further from the truth.

In 2017, Mike took to the stage of TEDx Sydney and delivered a stellar talk on how he has and still does suffer from imposter syndrome: a common fear of being caught out as a fraud when the reality is you are more than capable of doing the job you're in.

After seeing this talk and doing some research of my own, I have come to the conclusion that we should not seek to be fearless; that's not realistic nor helpful. Our aim should be to fear less.

People like Mike are not immune to fear; they allow themselves to be vulnerable and uncomfortable and use fear as a green light to lean into possibility. They understand that while you can't control when fear presents, you can control how you allow it to affect you and how you respond. They trust the fear and know that by stepping into it they will come out the other side just a little better than before, even if it doesn't play out as planned. They accept that growth will occur in the discomfort.

In my experience those who are fear less:

- own vulnerability
- make decisions in imperfection
- trust internal discomfort
- persist in adversity
- embrace failure
- act on curiosity
- thrive in uncertainty
- make it safe for others to act courageously.

Fear(lessness) builds resilience, and resilience is the foundation for bouncing back and having more happy moments.

Fear(less) people practise courage daily. As Mark Twain famously said, 'Courage is resistance to fear, mastery of fear—not absence of fear'.

EXPERIMENT NOW

Let's work your fear through a little process to help you unpack it, and look at it through a different lens.

* Ask yourself: if fear didn't exist, what one change (within your control) would you make right now that you know could make you happier? Take your time, be honest with yourself, really think it through and write your answer here.

* Now I want you to ask yourself: what fear has stopped you from making that change? Write your answer in the row of the table overleaf labelled 'What am I afraid of?'
* Next ask yourself: what is the impact or the worst thing that could happen if your fear is realised? Note it down in the space provided in the table.
* What is the best thing that could happen if you make the change and the fear is not realised? Note it down in the space provided in the table.

- Now let's look at what you can do. Ask yourself what one thing can you do (it can be anything) that could help you minimise the likelihood of your fear being realised. Note it down in the space provided in the table.
- Write down when you will take your action by and get after it!

What am I afraid of?	
What is the impact/ worst thing that could happen?	
What's the best thing that could happen?	
What can I do to minimise the likelihood of the fear being realised?	
What date will I take action by?	

REFLECT AND REMEMBER

- We've been conditioned to believe that fear is an alarm bell to run away from, rather than an opportunity to lean into possibility.
- Our brains seek certainty, and the unknown is often where fear can be found. Fear of the unknown is what stands between many of us and our happiness.
- We have an opportunity when fear presents itself, to name the trigger and reframe it using simple techniques that ground us back in the moment and kick in our rational brain, allowing us to take charge of how we respond.

* We are part of one big human family and we are not as different as we like to think.
* Fear is normal and we need to embrace it as such and help each other to do the same.
* Fear(lessness) is about trusting fear and knowing that by stepping into it you will come out the other side just a little better than before, even if it doesn't play out as planned.

SHARE THE HAPPY

Perhaps one of your fears is sharing your fear—so why not find someone you trust and work through the fear together using this chapter's Experiment Now? The more you share an idea the more it grows, so working with a friend can help you explore your fear in a way you hadn't considered. It's totally possible your friend may have experienced or be experiencing the same fear and you can work out how to lean in together.

CHAPTER 7

Courage: Brave discomfort to shape change

While out walking my dog one morning, I noticed a building near my home with smoke billowing out of it. A neighbour was knocking on a third storey door to see whether there was anyone inside. Something didn't feel right when I looked at the situation, so I walked closer to where the smoke was coming from only to notice that the apartment on fire was on the ground floor and not the one my neighbour was knocking on. I yelled to the neighbour, 'You're at the wrong apartment!'

I ran to the only access point I could find and pulled off the fragile courtyard gate to gain access to the living room window of the smoking unit. By then my neighbour was beside me, and another, noticing the commotion, had joined us. I looked to the ground to see what I could use to smash the window, found a metal outdoor umbrella stand and together we lifted it and launched it at the glass window. The smoke billowed out through the broken window, and the flames furiously crackled inside. My heart was pounding. I started calling, 'Is there anyone in there?'

Suddenly a faint voice came from within what looked like an inferno. It was extremely distressed and disorientated, calling back, 'I'm here, I can't see you, I can't get out'. It felt like a scene from a movie. I called to her, 'Listen to my voice, follow my voice!' then a hand magically appeared through the smoke. I grabbed it and pulled as my neighbours found some clothing from the nearby clothesline and threw it across the broken glass that covered the base of the window frame. Together the three of us lifted her out of the apartment and onto the footpath just as the ambulance and fire brigade arrived. She was barely conscious.

The adrenaline was pumping through my veins; once I knew she was safe and being treated, I had to walk to the park with my dog for 10 minutes to collect myself from the shock of the situation. On my way back the fire brigade leader was walking towards me. I thought to myself, 'Oh shit, I'm going to get into trouble for smashing the window and not waiting for them to arrive'. To my surprise it was the opposite. He shared that what I and my neighbours had done had saved the woman's life. We had acted courageously. He explained that based on the severity of the fire she would not have made it if we had waited for them to arrive.

Acts of courage are born from one of two places: choice or crisis, and life will give you opportunities to experience both. In fact, my story is a combination of the two. The reality is I had a choice even in a crisis; I could have walked away or just called emergency services and waited. My hand wasn't forced – I *chose* to intervene.

We can't afford to wait for a crisis in order to practise our courage; if we do we are living our life avoiding our fears and leaving happiness on the table. We have to learn to experiment with acts of courage in the everyday, not only when reacting to crises.

> Acts of courage born out of the proactive choice to lean into our fears build the confidence and resilience to lean into bigger change over time, realising greater possibility in our lives.

Equally they build a solid foundation to behave more rationally and courageously when crisis presents. When COVID-19 hit I woke up to a new reality. I had spent the last five years of my life as an entrepreneur building my dream business. Then overnight it felt like the world had pulled the rug out from underneath me.

My cash flow stopped, I had just $20 000 in my business bank account, I had an amazing assistant whose livelihood depended on me, my boyfriend lost his job, my best friend and flatmate packed up and fled the country back to New Zealand before the borders shut, my son's school closed, making me a first-time school teacher, and my country went into lockdown... and this was just week one of the pandemic. Now the irony is this should have felt like a crisis – a moment to crawl into a foetal position, let fear take hold and fall apart. But instead, if I'm honest, it felt like a gift, a gift of epic proportions, not just for me but for humanity. I felt a wave of calm amidst the chaos, a feeling that I was exactly where I was meant to be, which enabled me to take rational action in uncertainty.

Crises often do not afford us the privilege of time to consider how we respond; it's more reactive. Yet if you lean into fear daily, you may be surprised at the resilience you build and how it can serve you when you need it most.

IT'S UP TO YOU

Of the people I have studied who have turned their lives upside down in pursuit of greater happiness, one insight is surprising. More often than not they have longed for the change they seek before acting courageously. They have picked apart every aspect of the change in their head, the risks, the rewards, usually over a period of three to four years before leaning into the fear.

Take Jagoda, for example, who I met during a workshop at Microsoft. When I reconnected with her five months later, she was packing up her home after eight years in Australia, leaving a great job and moving to the French Alps with her partner. (Serious.)

Together they had made an intentional choice to realise a dream: to live in nature, closer to her homeland of Poland and her family. It was not an easy choice; there was no safety net of another job in the Alps, no friends were based there, and they'd never even lived in France.

Jagoda shared that this choice had been four years in the making, and it didn't come without fear and guilt.

> I had a fear of it not working out and then regretting having taken the step when we perceptually 'had it all' before. I'm in a position of privilege, having worked at Google and Microsoft most of my career. The positions I've had are those that others dream of, and I was acutely aware of this. It weighed heavily on my decision as I felt for a long time that perhaps I was ungrateful for wanting a different life.

This feeling of guilt has presented in many of the stories I've heard from those who have had successful careers but desire a simpler, more connected life. Many of us only dream of the change; we rarely act on it because we allow our fear to own our dreams. When I asked Jagoda how she found the courage to choose change she shared:

> I sat on it for such a long time. I started to ask myself, are these feelings, these thoughts, these fears really true? Is the situation I'm in really the best thing that could happen to me or could life be better? I realised I was grateful for the opportunities I had, they were what had led me to this point, they helped me build the skills and platform to now take the next step and realise my dream. I started to visualise what life could be like if we moved to France: in my mind I could see the Alps, smell the air, see myself drinking my coffee on the step of my home looking out at the mountains.

> Courage is the ability to do something that frightens you, to act in times of adversity; it's showing strength when things are uncomfortable or painful.

Demonstrating courage by proactive choice isn't easy, but waiting for someone else to pull the rug out from underneath you can often be even harder (for example, losing a job you despise rather than choosing to leave intentionally and doing something fundamentally different). It's why we so admire and are inspired by those who demonstrate it and do so often.

The point as we progress is not to judge your level of courage – it's to understand where it shows up, why it shows up and how you can bring more of it into how you live your life.

HAPPINESS HACK

Hold up the mirror to your courage in order to understand where there are opportunities to bring more of it into your everyday. Write a list of three or four courageous things you've done (e.g. asking for a promotion, initiating a break-up, calling someone out on discriminatory behaviour) then ask yourself: did you choose to proactively lean into your fear or did you do it because it was a crisis? If you're more heavily weighted towards courage in crisis, ask yourself what one small courageous act could you undertake tomorrow that will activate the practice of proactive courage in the everyday. Now get out there and experiment with your small courageous act!

A COURAGEOUS MINDSET

Henry Ford once said 'whether you think you can or think you can't you are right'...and, as it turns out, he was scientifically correct.

Your brain is like a muscle, and how you exercise it will affect how it responds in the future. Neuroplasticity is the scientific term given to our brain's ability to adapt to our environment and our behaviours. You can strengthen your neuroplasticity over time through brain training. The inputs will determine the outputs. If you feed your brain with positive inputs when faced with non-life-threatening fear, you are building neural pathways that will reinforce a positive mindset and behaviours when similar situations arise. As my good friend, behavioural scientist Milo-Arne Wilkinson, once shared with me, our words (be they positive or negative) become our feelings and our feelings drive our behaviour.

Dr Carol Dweck's life work has been centred around the concept of a 'growth mindset', which links to neuroplasticity and the brain being malleable enough to change over time with focus and practice.

A growth mindset is the belief that your ability can grow through commitment and hard work. Dweck explains, 'Brains and talent are just the starting point. This view creates a love of learning and a resilience that is essential for great accomplishment'. Her research on students uncovered that when we believe we can improve and understand that consistent effort makes us stronger, we are likely to commit more time and effort—which leads to higher achievement.

Psychologists have been helping people in this domain for years using what's known as Cognitive Behavioural Therapy (CBT). CBT is using one's understanding of one's own thoughts to intentionally shift how one responds and behaves. While you can't control the random events of life (the crises we've been alluding to), it is proven that you have the ability to choose how you respond.

We all have the ability to be courageous, but we must cultivate a growth mindset first; we have to *believe* we can, and make small acts of courage part of our everyday.

> The mindset you cultivate, through the language you use, will influence your actions and determine your ability to proactively enable change over time.

Celebrate failure

Part of this courageous mindset is the ability to embrace, and even celebrate, failure. It's ironic because even the mere thought of failing at something, for many, is a barrier to courageous action.

Back in the day when I worked in my corporate role, for example, failure was not an option! It certainly was not shared, let alone celebrated. It was swept under the rug, and actively seeking it out could very well prove to be career limiting.

My mindset was one of 'avoid failure at all costs', which meant that I would often over plan, over consult and avoid action until I was as comfortable as I could be. What I now realise is that this mindset and approach just slowed me down and stopped me from trying many things that I would have liked to out of fear of the repercussions.

When I began my entrepreneurial journey, however, I was dumbfounded. I started to spend time with other entrepreneurs only to realise their mindset was one where failure means you're trying, you're willing to take risks, willing to surf the edge of discomfort and work it out as you go. When investing in a startup, many venture capitalists actively seek out founders who have failed at least two or three times before, because it proves they have the resilience to keep trying.

I read about X Development (formerly Google X), otherwise known as the 'Moonshot Factory', the semi-secret research and development facility founded by Google to solve some of the biggest challenges in the world. It was the job of the people in this business to fail – which may sound crazy, but if they didn't have that mindset they would never attempt to try and solve what are perceived as unsolvable problems. In the words of Astro Teller, the director of X Development:

> We spend most of our time breaking things and trying to prove that we're wrong. That's it. That's the secret. Run at all the hardest parts of the problem first. Get excited and cheer. Hey, how are we going to kill our project today?

What a beautiful example of how focusing on what others are avoiding and challenging your belief system in the process can be your greatest opportunity. In his TED talk, Teller shares how at X Development they created a culture that makes it safe to fail and one of the key ways they do that is by bonusing failure. You read that right: they give bonuses to staff who fail trying to solve big problems, and they also promote them. Imagine what you would be willing to try if you decided to reward yourself for failure rather than beat yourself up for things not working out?

Sounds crazy right? Crazy is only crazy until it's proven possible, so with the complexity of the challenges we face, we need a lot more crazy in the world!

When I first attended Singularity University at the NASA Research Center in Silicon Valley to learn from some of the top technologists and artificial intelligence experts in the world, one thing struck me as I listened to each one of them speak about the problems they had solved. Many of them shared that they were told they were crazy (more than once!), what they wanted to do was impossible, they would fail, but they each made the 'choice' to be proactively courageous, progress into the fear and do it anyway. The results of taking this approach meant unprecedented breakthroughs were realised (often off the back of failure) and the quality of many lives improved as a result.

If you need any more evidence that failure is your friend in the context of amplifying your Intentional Adaptability, look to the scientists from the University of Arizona who believe they have uncovered the 'Goldilocks zone' for learning—those who fail

15 per cent of the time learn the fastest. Basically, a good dose of failure is a differentiator and will enable you to speed up your ability to take on new knowledge and solve bigger problems over time.

> If you're not failing on a regular basis, then maybe you are not being courageous enough, leaving possibility unexplored?

PILOT IT

So how do we actually embrace the prospect of failure and reframe our mindset towards it being a growth opportunity? How do we become more willing to experiment and try new things?

A well-known practice for testing the development of a new product in the startup world is what's known as a business model canvas. The intent is to map out what a Minimal Viable Product (MVP) would look like to test whether the product has a market and if there is demand. How could we invest a minimal amount to develop a prototype to see whether this could work – or if not, fail fast, learn and move on?

When I attempt to make a change in my life that I have not done before or learn something new, I say to myself, 'This is a pilot; I'm testing a hypothesis'.

This positive language shift means that my focus is on the learning that will come from trying, not on whether the outcome will go according to plan or potentially fail. The magic in this approach is that the more I do it the more I realise that things not going according to plan can often deliver in unexpected ways for the better.

It's taken around five years (of consistent and persistent practice) but I have learned to love failure. This simple hack has provided the courage to lean into the unknown and do it often. I now see failure as a stepping stone to where I'm meant to be.

So the next time you want to make a change and it scares you, try reframing it in this way. How does it feel to view that change as a test, a pilot? What might happen as a result?

Failure is only failure if you don't learn from it.

HAPPINESS HACK

If you need a little more inspiration around the power of failure consider attending a Fuck Up night (fuckupnights.com). These meet-ups are now run around the world and feature successful entrepreneurs sitting on a stage, unfiltered and sharing their greatest fails in the spirit of showing that without failure success is elusive. I highly recommend it!

CHALLENGE YOUR CHATTER

Have you ever considered how your internal chatter may be affecting your ability to act courageously? How much of your internal chatter is negative? I have asked this question of my Fear(less) Masterclass participants and been astounded to find that on average it's around 60 per cent—and for many women it can be higher.

Let's take Kim, a professional who took the leap to start her own company a few years back. She shared with me her challenges around negative self-talk and how it has affected her self-belief and at times her mental health.

When we last spoke, however, her courage to experiment had improved significantly. When I asked her why she explained:

> I learned to become a watcher of my thoughts. I used to get caught up in them, I believed that if I'm thinking them they must be true. I started to challenge myself around feeling

versus fact. It helped me hone the skill of being aware of my negative thoughts rather than allowing them to influence my actions. I've enabled myself to label them, air them and allow them to pass rather than change my course of action. It's a practice—I still have self-doubt—but I now call it out and hold myself to account.

My beautiful mum passed a number of years ago and in self-doubt I still turn to her and ask myself, 'What would Mum say?' This simple question has given me the personal mantra of 'Just keep going. Just take the next little step', which is what she used to tell me. When I ask myself this question my courage returns. It helps me realise that I've got this, and it's helped me reach a new point in my journey and pushed me further along than I had dreamed.

> It takes courage combined with hard work to shift your internal chatter, but it is absolutely something we have to commit to if we are to embrace fear and failure to enable meaningful change.

A participant once shared with me that when her negative self-talk creeps in she asks herself 'How would I talk to Donald Trump if he spoke to me like this?' Not only does this make her and everyone I share it with chuckle a little, it quickly kicks the rational brain into saying, 'If I wouldn't allow someone else to talk to me like this, why should I allow myself?'

HAPPINESS HACK

Think about something new you've wanted to try but have been too afraid to because you might fail. Rather than focus on failing, ask yourself: what would it look like if I tested whether I could do this? What would a pilot look like? How could I step into trying this in a small way to build my courage and confidence?

100 DAYS OF MICRO BRAVERY

Eleanor Roosevelt once said:

> You gain strength, courage and confidence by every experience in which you really stop to look fear in the face. You must do the thing you think you cannot do.

Choosing to act courageously can be challenging but the benefits can blow you away. If you had told me back in 2014 when I left my corporate career that I would have had the opportunities I have had as an entrepreneur, that my path would see me being accepted as a member of faculty at Singularity University or publishing this very book, I would have said you were crazy. This was not my plan back then – I had no idea what I was capable of.

Why? Because I had never used fear and courage to their fullest potential in order to realise what was possible. I wasn't skilled in acts of courage by proactive choice – until I discovered the concept of 100 Days of Rejection by Jia Jiang.

Like many migrants Jia Jiang arrived in the United States seeking the great American dream, but realising he was starting from scratch. He knew it was going to be a challenge to succeed, and that rejection was going to come thick and fast as he attempted to seek out opportunities. So, he and his friend did something unique: they set themselves a challenge to achieve 100 Days of Rejection.

In Jia's TED talk, which is now tipping 6 million views, he shares that his goal 'was to desensitise myself from the pain of rejection and overcome my fear'.

Basically, Jia and his friend set themselves a list of 100 'asks' that they would request of others, one per day, ranging from trying to borrow $100 from a stranger to planting a flower in a stranger's backyard. Each ask was set up with the intent of being rejected.

The concept of desensitising oneself to failure was explored earlier by Jason Comely: he developed it to overcome his fear of being rejected after his partner left him. Jason went on to create the Rejection Therapy game, a self-help tool where being rejected by another person or group is the sole winning condition.

Jason and Jia learned that getting yeses to what you want in life is a numbers game. You can't get yeses unless you are willing to actively seek out and embrace noes. And the only way to get noes often is to step into fear and discomfort... daily.

Small acts of courage over time, like the crazy asks Jia and Jason undertook, built the confidence to lean into bigger acts of courage. This is how you push yourself and your potential to places you never even imagined.

These small acts are termed 'micro bravery'; it's doing little things every day that scare you, with the realisation that over time the impact can be profound! Acts of micro bravery are relative to you because everyone's courage baseline is different. But everyone has the potential to grow. It can be as simple as:

- emailing someone you've admired from afar and asking them out to coffee
- introducing yourself to a stranger at the bus stop
- joining an art class when you've never painted in your life.

The intent is simple: it's a practice in surfing the edge of your comfort zone. It's how you practically immerse yourself in and get comfortable with discomfort, and it provides the basis to act more courageously by proactive choice not only in crisis.

HAPPINESS HACK

Try an act of micro bravery right now. What one small thing could you do in this moment that makes you feel uncomfortable, but could move you closer to being your most courageous self? Put this book down and go and do it!

THE COST OF INACTION

Still struggling to act courageously? I want you to consider the story of hugely successful entrepreneur Tim Ferriss. He is the best-selling author of *The 4-Hour Workweek*, and *The Tim Ferriss Show* is one of the most listened-to podcasts globally. But it wasn't always this way.

A while back Tim suffered from severe depression and found himself couch surfing with no permanent address. Tim turned his life around and credits 'fear-setting' as one of the key tools to do that. Rather than set goals each quarter, Tim unpacks his biggest fears and plans strategies around how to tackle them, which is what continues to propel him to new heights and build his courageous mindset.

One question I love that Tim uses to amplify his courage is 'What is the cost of inaction?' If you do nothing and sit with the longing, not acting constructively on the fear, what is the cost? In a year from now what will be the cost of doing nothing on your mental health, your physical health, in terms of your relationships, your happiness? What is the cost of not leaning into the fear that stands between you and taking action on something that you know could make you happier?

So I ask you, is the cost of inaction worth it?

Let me share with you a little story that may help you decide the answer to that.

Bronnie Ware was a palliative care nurse in Sydney. She spent 15 years with the dying. Conversations with her patients were often a distraction from the inevitable, but one day Ware decided to change the course of the conversations by asking 'What are your regrets in life?'

Over time, Ware started to observe themes in how her patients responded and decided to write a blog titled the 'The Top Five Regrets of Dying'. The blog went viral, with a book deal not long after and numerous speaking opportunities for Ware to share her insights. According to Ware the number one regret of the dying is: 'I wished I'd had the courage to live a life true to myself, not the life others expected of me'.

I ask you: could this be you? Do you want this to be you? If the answer is 'hell no' then there is no time like now. It's time to make fear your future and courage your choice. And if you still need a little more push, then Guillaume Apollinaire might help:

'Come to the edge,' he said.

'We can't, we're afraid!' they responded.

'Come to the edge,' he said.

'We can't, We will fall!' they responded.

'Come to the edge,' he said.

And so they came.

And he pushed them.

And they flew.

EXPERIMENT NOW

A peer and I were once talking about the fears associated with our respective entrepreneurial journeys. She referred me to a concept called 100 No's (similar to Jia's 100 rejections) and suggested I take a closer look. While there are multiple references to variations on Google, its origins are hard to trace. Nonetheless, the concept made logical sense to me so I dived in and created my own 100 No's Challenge (overleaf). The results of which have led me to where I am today.

Your goal is to get out there and get 100 No's. You must seek one per day. Every no you get is a win, as you get to tick it off your 100 No's challenge and it moves you closer to your goal of 100.

100 NOs

NO	NO	NO	NO	NO	NO	NO	NO	NO	NO
NO	NO	NO	NO	**15** *High fives*	NO	NO	NO	NO	NO
NO	NO	NO	NO	NO	NO	NO	NO	NO	**30** *Reward yourself*
NO	NO	NO	NO	NO	NO	NO	NO	NO	NO
NO	NO	NO	NO	**45** *Time to reflect*	NO	NO	NO	NO	NO
NO	NO	NO	NO	NO	NO	NO	NO	NO	**60** *Share your experience*
NO	NO	NO	NO	NO	NO	NO	NO	NO	NO
NO	NO	NO	NO	**75** *Almost there*	NO	NO	NO	NO	NO
NO	NO	NO	NO	NO	NO	NO	NO	NO	**90** *You Got This!*
NO	NO	NO	NO	NO	NO	NO	NO	NO	**100** *Resiliant rockstar*

YOUR YESs

Write down every time you receive a Yes instead of a No

________________ ________________

________________ ________________

________________ ________________

________________ ________________

But it's actually harder than you might think, because every no you get moves you closer to a yes. So it's likely you will get more yeses than you expected. Some of the yeses I have had since I started using this tool have blown my mind. Make sure you write down your unexpected yeses in the space provided so that you can track them.

It's time to get out there and practise your micro bravery. Start asking for all the things you've ever wanted but been too afraid to ask for.

REFLECT AND REMEMBER

* Acts of courage born out of the proactive choice to lean into our fears enable us to build confidence and resilience.
* The mindset you cultivate and how you allow your thoughts to influence your actions will determine your ability to change over time in service of your happiness.
* When a thought presents that holds you back, ask yourself, 'Can I influence the outcome, is it within my control to change this?'
* Getting yeses to what you want in life is a numbers game. You can't get yeses unless you are willing to actively seek out no's. The only way to get no's often is to step into fear and discomfort, daily.
* Failure is only failure if you don't learn from it. If you're not failing regularly then maybe you are not being as courageous as you could be.

SHARE THE HAPPY

Take on the 100 No's Challenge with your friends and build your love of no together. Each week share what you observe and how this simple practice is affecting your ability to use fear as a lever for the change you seek.

IAQ Skill 3 — Curiosity

How to use curiosity as a state of being, not something you do in your spare time (of which people say they have none).

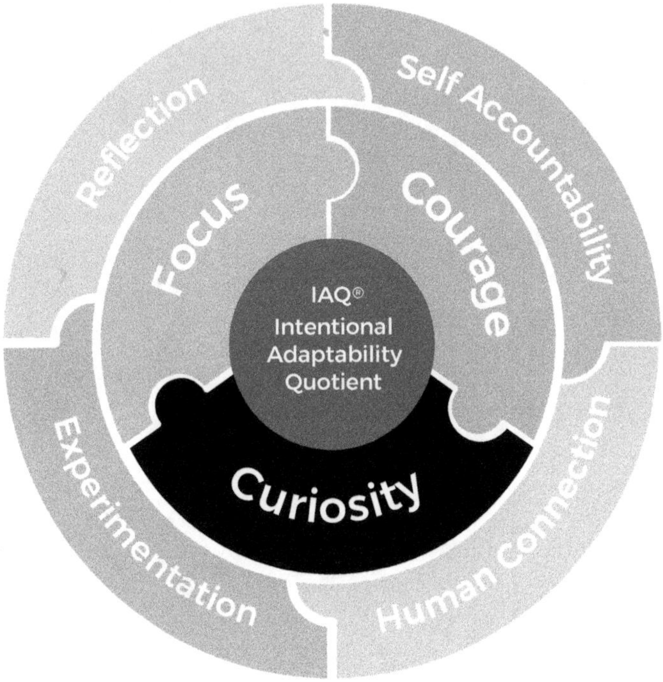

CHAPTER 8

Curiosity: Embrace the unknown

Harry is a curious young man who comes from what he describes as a 'privileged background'. Up until the age of 22, he'd ticked all the boxes he was meant to by way of education. Then he quickly found himself asking, 'Now what?' Where was that elusive roadmap that would guide him towards what it was he was meant to 'do with his life'?

Like many of us when we finish school or university and enter our twenties, Harry found himself backpacking around the world in search of something he 'couldn't quite put his finger on'. He started pondering, 'What's life about and how can I discover the answer in order to work out where to from here?'

Harry's curiosity led him to start asking people this very question. He soon came to realise that there was no right answer—everyone is different—but it started his quest to find out what was right for him. This spawned the idea to create a YouTube series titled 'What's Life About?'

For the series, he actively sought out culturally, spiritually and generationally diverse people who looked at the world through a different lens. He asked them the same question – 'What's life about?' – and recorded their answers in the hope of challenging his and others' perspectives. Harry's goal through the YouTube series is to help himself and others remember what's important to them and why. He believes that asking people this simple question enables them to connect with what gives them meaning and hopefully bring more of it into their everyday. His intent is to now ensure that every person in Australia has at least once heard the question 'What's life about?'

Curiosity is born out of an innate desire to know more, and questions provide the platform to launch into the unknown, to challenge what we think we know to be true or to discover something we had no idea existed. Harry's question is a perfect case in point: his desire to know more provided the itch that curiosity could help scratch.

His story encapsulates the magic of curiosity and how, when partnered with skill in focus and courage, it can propel our learning, our development, and our ability to intentionally adapt in unexpected and joyful ways.

As Albert Einstein once put it:

> The important thing is not to stop questioning. Curiosity has its own reason for existing. One cannot help but be in awe when he contemplates the mysteries of eternity, of life, of the marvelous structure of reality.

CURIOUS ABOUT CURIOSITY

Years ago, when I worked in my corporate job, I prided myself on how much I knew about my industry and the breadth of the connections I had created. Yet when I stepped out into the entrepreneurial world, I realised that what I knew was a lot less than what I'd thought!

> My perceived success had become the enemy of my curiosity; I'd grown comfortable with my fat pay cheque and internal opportunities and in turn it had made me unconsciously insular and, in many ways, narrow in my behaviour.

We are very good at talking to each other, for example—the same industries watch each other, attend the same events, build the same connections—but when we're all the same then we don't actually see differently, let alone learn to *be* different.

When I stepped out of that world after 20 years, the realisations came thick and fast: what got me here won't get me to where I'm going. I had no idea what I needed to know or who I needed to know it from. It was quite literally like going back to being a university graduate.

The only way I could work out what was next was to become curious about curiosity and how I could use it as a basis for reinvention.

In 1899 philosopher and psychologist William James described curiosity as 'the impulse towards better cognition'. In other words, it's the innate motivation to use one's brain power through thinking, immersing oneself in experiences and stimulating the senses to acquire new knowledge and understanding.

When I ask participants in my Curiosity Challenge program to define what curiosity means to them they use words and statements such as:

- an openness and desire to learn
- inquisitiveness

- the discovery of new things
- an interest in why things are the way they are
- learning through questions.

In the context of building skill in Intentional Adaptability, curiosity is an interest and openness to the world, other people and yourself.

GREAT MINDS

If we look back through history at the change makers who have fundamentally altered the progress of our society or those who have shifted the foundations of their own lives towards greater meaning, their breakthroughs have been born from curiosity. Thomas Oppong shared in his article '5 Things The World's Most Original Thinkers Have in Common' that 'there is no single path to extraordinary success but there are some common attributes of great minds' and one of those is that 'they are insanely curious'.

Take Percy Spencer, the inventor of the first microwave, for example. He was working on a radar-related project testing a vacuum tube when he noticed the chocolate bar in his pocket had melted very quickly. He thought that was unusual and started experimenting with pointing the vacuum tube at things such as eggs and popcorn. He realised that the food items were heating from what he termed 'microwave energy'. Not long after, the company he worked for at the time filed the first microwave patent and the rest is history.

Cal Newport shares in his bestselling book *Deep Work* that curiosity is one of our greatest levers for differentiating ourselves from technology. Computers are great at processing data and learning patterns, but they are not curious. Our curiosity is what sets us apart from the technology that is permeating every corner of the world. In Cal's words, 'If you can create something useful its potential is limitless. To make that happen you have to produce your best work' – and that requires focus, courage and a healthy dose of curiosity.

> Curiosity takes shape in the desire to solve the seemingly unsolvable, to explore the unexplored, to feel like you've never felt before.

Not only that, but unleashing our curiosity is scientifically proven to make us happier. In their paper titled 'Curiosity and Exploration: Facilitating positive subjective experiences and personal growth opportunities', researchers Todd Kashdan and others showed that curiosity is linked with 'higher levels of positive emotions, lower levels of anxiety, greater life satisfaction and enhanced psychological well-being'.

Furthermore, studies have shown that curious people who have a habit of lifelong reading and writing have a rate of cognitive decline in old age that is 30 per cent less than if they just undertook average mental activity.

It's a fact when we are curious we feel more connected to ourselves, others and the world around us. It propels self-accountability, self-guided action and cultivates a perpetual learning mindset. Curiosity holds the key to self-disruption, adapting and thriving. It is also a skill that is increasing in demand with future-focused employers.

The reality is that companies need to continuously and proactively disrupt themselves in order to remain relevant. The best way to do that is by employing and incentivising curiosity.

Australian-born billion-dollar software success Atlassian is an excellent case in point. It creates the space and incentive for its people to spend 20 per cent of their time on their own ideas.

They call this space 'Shipit Days'. This focus on curiosity has not only benefitted the employees' development, but it has also delivered a range of new product development features for Atlassian's software.

> The shape of the future belongs to the curious.

HAPPINESS HACK

Reflect on a time when you find you are most curious. How are you feeling, what are you doing, where are you doing it, who are you with, what behaviours are you displaying? By observing when you are at your most curious you can identify the conditions that make you curious, and then you can enable those conditions more often in each day.

THE CHALLENGE TO BE CURIOUS

Anyone who has ever taken the time to observe and engage with children can see that curiosity is just a part of how we are wired from birth. It's fundamental to our physical and mental development. Babies point to show where their curiosity lies well before they can talk (interestingly, research has shown if their pointing goes un-attended to, they soon stop pointing. As adults we also seem to have learned to stop pointing…).

The real issue is that as we progress into adulthood, the inclination for deep curiosity – the type that takes time to explore with no guaranteed outcome or benefit – dissipates without us even realising it. Why? How is it that such an innate, important skill diminishes as time goes on?

This shift has a clear connection to the conformity constructs we push our children through as they progress into adulthood.

We teach children through education how to answer questions, not ask them, and condition them to conform by providing exhaustive constraints around expected behaviour and ensuring that those who don't comply are labelled disruptors. Those who follow the rules, who don't challenge the status quo, are rewarded for good behaviour. Seth Godin explains this brilliantly:

> We often forget to teach kids to be curious. A student who has no perceived math ability, or illegible handwriting or the inability to sit still for five minutes gets immediate and escalating attention. The student with no curiosity, on the other hand, is no problem at all.

Same thing is true for most of the people we hire. We'd like them to follow instructions, not ask a constant stream of questions or challenge the status quo.

Yet, without 'why?' there can be no, 'here's how to make it better'.

Fast forward from school and university and we find that the traditional workforce applies similar rules around conformity. Partner those rules with the 'busy' mindset we spoke about earlier, and there is little room for curiosity, the source of creativity and innovation.

Too many people have told me that when they come into the workplace 'I leave my curiosity at the door'. (Seriously.) Curiosity is seen as a luxury, a leisure activity, a hobby or something that happens in your 'spare time' – of which you have none, remember?!

The irony of these insights is that Hacking Happy Assessment results from the participants on our programs show that most people believe themselves to be much more curious than perhaps they are. They rate themselves highly when asked the question 'How curious would you say you are?' Yet when we follow up with behavioural questions such as 'How often do you surprise yourself?' or 'How often do you find yourself having curious conversations?' or 'How often do you surround yourself with unlike minds – people who challenge you to look at the world through a different lens?' they say … sometimes or rarely.

Our belief and our behaviour don't match up.

I've seen this play out beautifully, even more ironically, in a program we ran called the Curiosity Challenge, where teachers and students were together in the same classroom. I went into this program as a facilitator believing that this group would be the most curious I'd ever met, especially the school teachers. My belief was and still is that a teacher's role is like a curiosity coach; it's about helping students expand their thinking, teaching them how to ask good questions, experiment, problem solve in new and innovative ways, experience new things. It doesn't get more curious than that does it?

There were a few teachers in that classroom who told me when I arrived, 'We are the most curious people you will ever meet, it's our job to be curious!' Unfortunately, their behaviours in the classroom didn't quite match their self assessment.

What I soon realised was believing you are highly curious is a limiting belief, a barrier to full curious expansion. If one believes they are already at the top of the curiosity mountain, what room does this leave to really push the limits and realise the full potential of curiosity?

A hallmark of some of the most curious beings in history is that they attest to how their curiosity practice reveals how little they know. In the words of Greek philosopher Socrates, 'I know that I know nothing'; and Einstein once said 'the more I learn, the more I realize how much I don't know'.

This is the curious mindset, the perpetual learner who seeks to constantly challenge what they believe and consider the uncomfortable question: what if I am wrong or I just don't know?

NOVELTY VERSUS KNOWLEDGE

When I first started teaching the Curiosity Challenge to professionals an unexpected conundrum presented itself. Our objective was to create the space and the skill for people to work out what they were curious about and how to explore it.

As we facilitated the process within the classroom, educated, well-paid professionals had a look of fear and confusion on their faces. They started asking:

- 'What is it that I should be curious about?'
- 'I don't want to invest my limited time on a whim unless it's going to benefit me.'
- 'How do I make sure my curiosity is efficient and that I don't go down a rabbit hole that doesn't work out?'

This line of questioning reinforced my belief that our current efficiency culture stifles curiosity and drives limiting behaviours. We have created a desire to be told what to do rather than to seek our own way, and a fear that without direction from others we won't get it right and that will cost us time. If there is one thing I know to be true it's that your internal motivation to stay curious about something you are told to be curious about is likely to wane, and quickly.

> The reality is curiosity is unruly. It's not meant to be efficient—exploration rarely is—and it doesn't sit well alongside order and control.

Is this very statement making you feel uncomfortable? Great! That's exactly where you need to be. Curiosity requires risk taking (this is where your courage comes in), it requires trust and a lifelong commitment to its practice (that's why you need focus) to realise its beautiful and unexpected benefits.

Harnessing your curiosity for greater happiness isn't an easy task, but it's a worthy one. While there are no silver bullets, and I certainly will not tell you what to be curious about (that's up to you!) you can improve how you channel your curiosity. The best place to start is through awareness of the types of curiosity that help you to thrive versus the type that distracts you and takes you off course.

Novelty Curiosity

Renowned psychologist and philosopher Daniel Berlyne is known as the forefather of curiosity research. He dedicated 25 years of his life seeking to better understand the phenomenon of curiosity. 'Diversive Curiosity' was the term Berlyne coined for the type of curiosity that has the potential to distract us (if used in the wrong way). This is the desire to seek out novelty, so let's call it 'Novelty Curiosity' to make things easier to remember.

Novelty Curiosity is linked to our hard wiring to seek stimulation in a range of different ways. Animals equally partake in this type of curiosity; it's the driver behind their exploratory behaviour. In a modern day context, this might show up as jumping into Instagram or LinkedIn to see 'what's going on' or binge watching a Netflix series.

Now don't get me wrong; Novelty Curiosity has its place in life, and it can be helpful to use to unwind without having to draw on too much brain power. The point is to become aware of when Novelty Curiosity is at play, and the time and space it's occupying. Awareness allows it to exist with intention, rather than it becoming an unconscious habit that pervades every free moment of your time (which is the distraction space covered in chapter 5).

Novelty Curiosity, when understood and intentionally channelled, can be a powerful way to kick start your curiosity into closing a knowledge gap or learning something completely new.

Knowledge Curiosity

The ideal way to harness our curiosity is to channel it for our development as opposed to for distraction. We want to combine our desire for novelty with our ability to solve problems, and this is where Knowledge Curiosity comes in. It's focused on closing knowledge gaps, to answer a question or set of questions that enable us to take on new learning.

It's different from Novelty Curiosity in that it is not about the act of seeking stimulation to solve, as Berlyne put it, 'an in the moment uncertainty' such as how old Kim Kardashian is; it's about 'the acquisition of new knowledge'. This type of curiosity, according to Berlyne, is mainly applicable to human beings, thus it differentiates our curiosity from that of other animals. We have the ability to not just undertake the quick fix through novelty, but to grow ourselves and our brains if we choose to focus our curiosity towards closing bigger gaps that interest us.

Knowledge Curiosity is where the hard work and long-term benefits of curiosity come into play as we seek to deepen our understanding of a subject in a quest to take on new information.

Knowledge Curiosity can be partnered with Novelty Curiosity for greater benefit. An example might be that you jump into Instagram and stumble across a post from a friend who has been to see an improv show (Novelty Curiosity). Your curiosity about improv is sparked; you've often wondered how improv might help you with your presentation skills at work and with your confidence (this is the question/new knowledge to acquire), so you decide to dig deeper. You look up local classes, sign up for a beginner's program and turn up to learn a new skill and close that gap.

Who knows where that may take you? (If you're curious, then make sure you read the next chapter because it digs into a true example of this from my own life.)

HAPPINESS HACK

Spend a day observing your curiosity and see how much of it is in the space of Novelty versus Knowledge. Challenge yourself to shift the pendulum towards a little more Knowledge Curiosity. Where could this take you?

THE SWEET SPOT OF CURIOSITY

Now that we understand which types of curiosity are available to us, how do we use this to enhance our curiosity skills?

On the surface, it seems like we would be most curious about things that we know little to nothing about, but this is not the case. We actually need to know a little something on a topic in order to generate an awareness of a gap in our knowledge. The awareness of this gap is what creates positive tension; it motivates us to want to learn more. If we have too little knowledge on the topic it may seem overwhelming to the point of anxiety because we just don't know where to begin.

On the other hand, too much knowledge creates the reverse problem, because nothing kills curiosity faster than certainty. And nothing ignites it quicker than surprise. It's the incongruity, a mismatch between what we expect and our reality, that invites our attention and excites our curiosity. Too little surprise and it's boring. Too much surprise and we're beyond our capacity to embrace.

Curiosity researchers Celeste Kidd and Benjamin Y. Hayden put it so eloquently when they explained that curiosity's 'diminution is a symptom of depression, and its overexpression contributes to distractibility'.

Just as importantly, we need to anticipate a benefit for our curiosity to be kindled. If we care too little about finding an answer, our curiosity can be extinguished by our apathy. If we care too much, the topic can become a source of anxiety – and no-one learns much when they are scared. So we need to find our sweet spot, as figure 8.1 shows.

Figure 8.1: the curiosity sweet spot

The 'future of work' is a great example of how this sweet spot played out for me. In 2016 I started to hear this term frequently in business conversations and TED talks, and I'd read about it in many journals. I felt the nature of my work provided me with some insight into what the future of work could look like (a little knowledge), I cared about the direction it took because it affected me and many of my friends, family and peers (a little care) and I felt I was continuously surprised by how technology was affecting how the future of work would look (a little surprise).

I used this sweet spot to direct my curiosity towards my:

- self-development
- business development
- product development.

I spent a significant amount of time in the years that followed reading, reaching out to people I saw as subject matter experts, attending talks, sharing my perspectives, creating my own talks and workshops and obtaining feedback from others on the topic.

Fast forward to now, and this curiosity about the world has grown into business opportunities I would never have imagined. I am fortunate enough to now share my personal perspectives on this topic on panels, stages and in articles around the world.

> This is an example of the power that is at play when you use your curiosity to your advantage.

So now it's time to turn the tables on you.

What are you curious about? Where could that lead you? How might that add to your everyday happiness?

When you start to challenge your mindset and behaviours, you step into the magic of curiosity as a practice in the everyday. This is how you become your most curious being; this is how you realise more joy more often.

EXPERIMENT NOW

Let's turn your insights into action and have a little fun using your curiosity.

You're going to create a curiosity list by writing down all the things you are curious about that would close a knowledge gap for you.

This is not about getting an instant answer from Google (Novelty Curiosity); we're talking the type of curiosity that leads you down a path of exploration, problem solving and greater learning.

Remember our curious definition: In the context of building skill in Intentional Adaptability, curiosity is an interest and openness to the world, other people and yourself.

Use the prompts below as a guide to channel your curious themes into creating a curiosity list.

My Curiosity List

What I am curious about in the context of myself

1

2

3

What I am curious about in the context of others

1

2

3

What I am curious about in the context of the world

1

2

3

Done? Highlight the one curiosity that speaks loudest to you in each of the three sections. Consider the remaining curiosities like a parking lot for you to come back to in the future. We will tap into your chosen curiosities as we move into the next chapter.

Note: This little experiment can be used time and time again. You may choose a curiosity to explore and find it doesn't excite you as much as you thought. That's totally okay; it happens when we uncover new information. You can come back to this experiment, run through it again and find something new. The only warning I will give is that chopping and changing your curiosity topic all the time may prove to be a distraction in itself. If you find that is the case, perhaps use your curiosity to explore why. What is driving your loss of interest? This may prove helpful in how you approach the next pursuit from your curiosity list.

REFLECT AND REMEMBER

* Curiosity is an interest and openness to the world, other people and yourself.
* The curious mindset is one that cultivates a perpetual learner who seeks to constantly challenge what they believe and consider the uncomfortable question: 'What if I am wrong or I just don't know?'
* The reality is curiosity is unruly. It's not meant to be efficient—exploration rarely is—and it doesn't sit well alongside order and control.

* Knowledge Curiosity is where we seek to deepen our understanding of a subject in a quest to take on new information and store it in our long-term memory bank.
* There is a sweet spot for curiosity: we need to know a little about the topic to generate awareness of a gap in our knowledge, but not too little as it may seem overwhelming, and not too much, as it can create apathy.
* Nothing kills curiosity faster than certainty, and nothing ignites it quicker than surprise.

SHARE THE HAPPY

If you work as part of a team, why not hold a curiosity party in one of your team meetings? (You could also do this with your friends.) Get everyone to write a curiosity list and then each share one curiosity with the group you would like to explore and one action you will take to make that happen. You may find others share your curiosity and want to partner with you to explore it further.

Reconnect in a few weeks' time and share what you learned. It's a fun way to get to know your peers better and learn something new in the process.

CHAPTER 9
Curiosity: To be, not to do

In 2016, CJ had a dream job running luxury travel conferences in exotic locations for thousands of people around the world – that was, until he had a breakdown from exhaustion.

CJ explains,

> I was half a world away from the family I loved and felt I couldn't face another cold dark winter living in London. I knew I had to change but had no idea how. I decided to start applying for industry-related jobs closer to my family in New Zealand, but with each application, something still just didn't feel right.

It was after an unexpected conversation with a peer, who was also a referee on his resume, that something clicked. CJ says,

> I shared with him honestly how I was feeling and he said to me, 'Why don't you take all that you've learned and create your own event here in Australia?'

CJ thought about all the events and conferences he had been involved in or attended outside of the travel industry in the past. One particular conference stood out in his memory – and not for good reason.

'In 2015, I was attending what looked like the sexiest conference on paper,' he says.

> The venue was awesome and it was complemented by a line-up of 16 CEOs from the coolest hotel brands around the globe. Sadly, it turned out to be yet another echo chamber, talking about 'trends' that had been around for longer than I had worked in the travel industry! It was at that point that my curiosity really started to take hold. I asked myself, what if we shifted these events from 'talking about trends' to 'inspiring trends'? That simple question was the catalyst for me to explore possibility.

That was the spark CJ needed to pack up his home in London and move to Australia with just one connection in his back pocket. A rather influential connection, as it turns out: multi-award winning advertising gun, brand strategist and founder of Thinkerbell, Adam Ferrier. Adam believed in CJ and his potential and agreed to help him get his idea off the ground. (Fulbright Scholar Holly Ransom joined the fold shortly after, making it an unlikely trio driving a unique change in Australian conferencing.)

CJ explains,

> When I landed in Australia, I wanted to create something bespoke. I wanted to build on the concept that had been born from my curiosity around the intersectoral cross-pollination of ideas. I hit the ground running and continued to attend as many different conferences as I could and quickly identified a 'cookie-cutter' model. The consistent traits of Australian conferences were:
>
> 1. They were in a big city.
> 2. They were in conventional event spaces (dark rooms, no natural light, with freezing air conditioning).
> 3. They did little to disconnect people from their day-to-day (i.e. people sat on their phones all day and didn't engage with the content or other attendees).
> 4. They were generally one industry looking inwards on themselves.
> 5. They all embraced a broadcast model of speaker and audience rather than a dialogue.

Let's just stop there and reflect – because I bet you have attended at least one such event in your time. You know exactly what he's talking about, right?

CJ goes on,

> I never set out to be an entrepreneur, nor did I seek to disrupt for the sake of it. But in my (very fortunate) adventure to so many different events all over the world, I identified how to create a unique experience that could change lives and industry paths for the better.

That meant events had to have the following attributes, which were in opposition to the way things were currently run. They needed to:

- *be immersive*. People need and deserve to be fully engaged, which means a break from typical routine, away from the big city where most delegates live. A connection with nature is even better. (IAQ skill enabled: focus)
- *have a festival vibe*. Which sounds more fun: festival or conference? Which would you rather attend? Exactly! So let's deliver thought leadership in a more engaging environment. (IAQ skill leveraged: curiosity)
- *go offline*. In a world of constant distraction, people are *desperate* to be given permission to put their phones down. (IAQ skill leveraged: the courage to step away from the norm, sprinkled with a little focus)
- *enable cross-pollination*. In the past, when CJ attended events he was the 'outsider' and often learned more from an engaged conversation with someone than from a keynote presentation. He explains, 'It was this that gave me the insight, "What does the person sitting next to you know that you don't know?" And vice versa.' (IAQ skill enabled: curiosity)
- *allow you to choose your own adventure*. If you can gain valuable insight and learnings from the people sitting

> next to you at a conference, then why not move away from the speaker and audience model and have a deconstructed content format where everybody is on the same 'level'? There is no division between speaker and audience, and every guest must contribute to the content and/or experience. (IAQ skill enabled: the courage to be different).

CJ continues,

> These insights were born from my curiosity and the desire to truly connect people around the ideas that matter to them—this launched me into s p a c e, quite literally.

In May 2018 in the beautiful town of Byron Bay, the first space event (nicknamed 'Burning Man for Business') was held with over 200 unlike minds from across Australia. These people came together with one intention: to create a more ambitious Australia.

As a space cadet myself (and a keynote speaker who is all too familiar with speaking in windowless rooms to large audiences) I was completely blown away by the experience, the human connection cultivated, the quality of meaningful conversation and the community that was born from CJ's leap of faith … and I was not the only one!

Interestingly, every aspect of CJ's curious journey to reinvention had leveraged a component of Intentional Adaptability (as highlighted in the previous list). Once he had an initial insight, he honed his *focus* to learn more, he used *courage* to challenge the status quo, to financially invest in himself and leap into the unknown area of entrepreneurship, and leveraged *curiosity* to determine what elements would make for a truly unique experience. Equally, he cultivated an opportunity for others to practise their Intentional Adaptability through the environmental elements of s p a c e.

CJ's story is his own, and I'm not by any means suggesting that you use your curiosity to turn your life upside down and move halfway across the world.

What I hope you have felt is the possibility that can unfold when you allow yourself to become a 'curious being'; someone who lives and breathes curiosity in the everyday.

THE PRACTICE OF A CURIOUS BEING

So just how do we cultivate the practice of a curious being? The word 'practice' is perhaps the most critical component of that question.

Your ability to amplify your curiosity comes from practising daily behaviours that enable you to be open to the unexpected, and to the element of surprise when it comes to yourself, others and the world around you.

I've spent quite some time now being curious about curious beings, and through experimentation and research I have discovered that there are seven common practices curious beings employ that make them unique.

Let's walk through each one so you can consider how you might leverage them in your everyday.

Practice 1—Ask, 'What if I was wrong about that and how would I go about proving it?'

Mark Twain once said, 'It ain't what you don't know that gets you into trouble. It's what you know for sure that just ain't so'.

As human beings we are wired to seek out the most efficient way to process information, and in the realm of harnessing our curiosity to its fullest potential that doesn't always work in our favour. Confirmation bias is the psychological phenomenon that explains our natural tendency to seek out and process information that reinforces our existing beliefs.

Sadly, often we don't even realise we are doing it and the pitfall of this unconscious reinforcement (of potentially false beliefs) means that we ignore or don't give due consideration to anything that may go towards proving we are wrong.

You may recall I mentioned earlier that: your belief system is built on a sample size of one. It's based on *your* experiences, *your* environment, *your* feelings. If you overlaid a research lens across this fact, you would quickly realise that a sample size of one is not statistically sound. (I use this analogy all the time to challenge myself to consider new paths, especially as a parent!)

Let me share an example of how confirmation bias plays out. It relates to the outbreak of COVID-19 in 2020. In a conversation with my father about the outbreak, he shared how frightening it all was and said 'none of us are safe'. I asked him why he felt that way and he said, 'The world has gone mad. People are fighting over toilet paper in the supermarket, to the point where a supermarket worker was stabbed. There is a run on guns in the USA and alcohol restrictions are needed to curb the run on booze in Western Australia'.

Now, yes, for many it was a scary time, I'm not disputing that. But my dad chooses to actively seek out media on a daily basis that confirms his unconscious bias (which he has held for a long time) that the world is falling apart and dangerous. Now, this is not a dig at my dad, whom I love dearly and consider to be an intelligent man (at the age of 77 he knows how to operate an iPhone better than many under 30). However, his love of traditional news sources (which I *am* having a dig at) consistently reinforces his confirmation bias that the world is getting worse, and chaos is everywhere.

My dad and I often chuckle about how he has called the wrong person – i.e. me – when he wants to talk about how terrible the world is. The irony is I have my own unconscious bias. I believe that the world is wonderful and that most people are generally good, with kindness at their core. So when COVID-19 hit I made a choice to actively seek out good news stories that confirmed *my* bias. I even took it one step further and committed to my social media and email supporters that I would only share good news and random acts of kindness with them during a time of uncertainty.

I try to avoid the news as much as possible as I feel that it often instils only one feeling in society – FEAR – and I don't want to allow one-sided negativity into my everyday. (That's another happiness hack you may want to consider!)

There's an old saying in the context of a good news story: 'if it bleeds it leads'. It reinforces beautifully a majority-held unconscious bias that the world is self-destructing – and it helps sell news!

> We can actually enjoy our confirmation bias as it makes us feel safe and comfortable and enables us to avoid the hard work that comes with unlearning.

F. Scott Fitzgerald, a great American novelist, once said, 'The test of a first-rate intelligence is the ability to hold two opposing ideas in mind at the same time and still retain the ability to function'.

This is exactly what curious beings do. Like our friend CJ, they actively seek out diverse and opposing views around the questions they have and create the space to provide due consideration to both.

When I asked CJ how he continued to stay curious he shared:

> I love to seek to understand and detest sweeping generalisations. No matter what the topic or issue I like to

look at all sides and make a call once I feel confident I can back it up. Sometimes it means I might look like a fence-sitter, but in the polarising world in which we live, considering all sides to a story is more important to me than fitting in with any one group. I consume all manner of news media, on different political skews, and from different global sources. I love seeing how the same story is reported differently by different media outlets.

A curious person is not afraid to prove themselves wrong about a previously held belief; in fact, they consider it a win because it provides a growth in their knowledge base; it's how we build skill in unlearning.

HAPPINESS HACK

Take something you think you know to be true (it can be anything) and then ask yourself: What if I was wrong, how would I go about proving that?

For example, I once thought the biggest challenge with supporting people who are homeless was finding them adequate housing. So I actively spoke to people with lived experience of homelessness and those who work with people who are homeless. What I learned is that often the idea of four walls for someone can reconnect them with significant trauma. Many who have experienced a home have suffered within that environment, which means a house alone is not the solution. I learned that people who are homeless want integrated support services that enable them to navigate the fundamentals of life, feel safe and be mentally well.

This simple practice is a great way to get you to actively look at the world through a different lens and seek out a more diverse set of resources to do that. How will you prove yourself wrong?

Practice 2—Make time for deep conversation and questions

Remember Harry, our YouTuber in chapter 8? His curiosity was focused around asking the question 'What's life about?' Harry shared with me early in our conversations that, while his curiosity started with a single question, that question led to the generation of even *more* questions. For example, during interviews he would find himself in his own head asking, 'How many more pages are there in the book of this person? How does their story help me fill my own gaps?'

In the digitally connected world, we invest less and less time talking to each other face to face and going into deep, unplanned, serendipitous conversations, such as Harry's. In the interests of efficiency, we consciously avoid conversation with those we know in order to save time. It's worse with random strangers; we avoid eye contact as we walk down the street and we stand at the bus stop entranced by our hand-held devices, not noticing who might be standing right next to us.

We are less curious about our fellow human beings than ever before, and without intervention this behaviour will only continue to diminish as we allow new technologies to replace what was once a human experience.

I have learned that opportunity lies at the other end of human connection, so I do something your parents always told you not to... I actively talk to random strangers. Yep, I am *that* person. But for every one person who doesn't want to talk to me, there are many more who do. These conversations, these strangers, continue to surprise and delight me with stories, new knowledge and a refreshed sense of curiosity.

When COVID-19 hit I realised that we finally had an intervention that would show us the importance of human connection. Physical distancing and self-isolation made people quickly realise how critical it is to our mental wellbeing and our happiness. I decided in this moment to support those longing for human connection around the world and show them the benefit of connecting with random strangers. I created humanhour.co a simple movement where I scheduled regular Zoom calls for groups of random strangers to connect with one another for an hour using exercises that are scientifically proven to make us happier. The response to date has been amazing, and the conversations deep. The idea has been so well received we've created toolkits for businesses to roll this out across their remote workforces during self-isolation and also for individuals to do the same with their friends, family or peers. Why not challenge yourself to talk to one random stranger a day for a week and observe what happens? Or, better still, set up your own human hour and promote it on social media and see who joins. I dare you!

Questions and human connection are the gateway to exploring the unknown, to reshaping our beliefs and changing our behaviour.

Curious questions + curious connection = knowledge currency.

According to Professor Michael J. Marquardt, author of *Leading with Questions: How leaders find the right solutions by knowing what to ask*, many of us suppress our question-asking ability for four main reasons:

1. *We're too busy*. Well, no surprises here! Asking questions takes time and sometimes we might not like the answer and it may create more questions.

2. *We're fearful*. Our natural tendency to protect ourselves can stop us from questioning. What a great opportunity to practise your courage!

3. *We lack the skill*. The less we ask questions, the less skill we build in how to structure them. Equally, when we are not trained in how to ask questions this affects our practice.

4. *We don't reward it.* Some cultures, and often business cultures, don't incentivise questioning as they don't want the status quo challenged or the productivity machine slowed down.

> Curious conversations enhance our level of connection, our relationships, our feelings of belonging, our skill in understanding one another, our ability to have difficult conversations, our problem solving, our capacity to innovate and our resilience.

And the best part is, this is all free! The opportunity to ask questions is something we can do every day to enhance our curious being and build all of those highly relevant skills that clearly link to our ability to thrive. So simple, but what a game changer when practised consistently!

HAPPINESS HACK

Become aware of your question-asking ratio: in your next meeting or conversation, observe and note down how many questions you ask in comparison to how many you answer. At the end of the conversation or meeting, calculate the results and transfer them into percentages. Set a target to shift the balance in your next meeting or conversation to increase the percentage of questions you ask and decrease your opinions. Observe what happens.

Practice 3—Surround yourself with unlike minds

CJ's story provides a basis for so many facets of curiosity to be explored. One of the most powerful objectives CJ had when he created space was to connect 'unlike minds in unlikely conversations', thus weaving the magic of surprise together with perspectives that challenge individuals to look at the world through not only a different but an often unconsidered lens. What better way to challenge your thinking!

Curious people actively seek out unlike minds – not once in a while, but daily. They take their ideas across the office floor and find the person who is likely to challenge their thinking. They accept it can be uncomfortable and may require more work, but they equally understand that the more you share an idea the more it grows.

What's fascinating is that seeking out unlike minds requires effort. Professor Lauren Rivera of the Kellogg School of Management discovered in her research on hiring as cultural matching that 'employers sought candidates who were not only competent but culturally similar to themselves'. We have an unconscious bias towards wanting to surround ourselves with people who are like us. Being agreed with makes life a lot more comfortable.

On the flip side, it is highly problematic because it cultivates groupthink, where we all just reinforce each other's beliefs, creating an echo chamber. Surrounding yourself with unlike minds is like saying, 'hey I want to actively seek out conflict'. Conflict doesn't have to be destructive; it can be constructive. It doesn't need to be an argument; it can be a debate.

Intentional constructive conflict is a powerful tool that curious beings leverage to amplify their knowledge.

When I think of the term 'constructive conflict' I think of an unlike mind I challenged back when I worked at Shell. Pete was a young, highly intelligent executive working as the right-hand man to the country chair. It was an extremely high-pressure position; his role was to be across everything and ensure that the country chair was briefed on what they needed to know before every meeting she had.

I had to work with Pete in order to progress an initiative that the country chair was passionate about. Having access to her was critical to the success of my work and Pete was the gatekeeper. Every time I made a request for time or information from Pete it felt like he'd blow me off. He was short and sharp and didn't give me a feeling of wanting to help. We were very different people. We challenged each other on many things. I decided that I had to confront him about how he was making me feel and how it was affecting my ability to get what I needed done.

So I scheduled a meeting in a relaxed, informal setting. When we sat down I started by sharing that I appreciated his position was a challenging one with many demands for his time from people of seniority. I explained that I wanted to understand what I could do to make his life easier. After all, we both needed to deliver our work and I wanted to ensure that when I made requests of his time or knowledge that I did it in a way that worked for him, and didn't annoy him. I explained to him that I had felt that my previous requests had frustrated him and perhaps there was a better way for me to work with him.

Pete was gobsmacked! His whole demeanour towards me changed and he immediately apologised because he had no idea that he was making me feel that way. He was so caught up in what he was doing, he was just trying to move quickly. He gave me some advice around how I could help him progress my requests in future and then turned around and offered to coach me on some areas that I really needed help with. He became an unlike mind that I continued to reach out to, and we developed a mutual respect because we now understood each other better.

So who is your Pete? How might you take this learning into your own life, right now?

Write down the top three people in your life who have made you feel uncomfortable because they haven't agreed with your perspective on something (not in a mean way, but just because they view the world differently). Consider what it was about the conversation that made you feel uncomfortable.

Now consider how you can actively seek out a couple of people who you can add to your network who fit the mould of an unlike mind, are willing to have constructive conflict and challenge you on potential blind spots.

Practice 4—Listen more often than you speak

> A wise old owl lived in an oak,
>
> The more he saw the less he spoke
>
> The less he spoke the more he heard.
>
> Why can't we all be like that wise old bird?
>
> Unknown author

Ann Pickard was a smart, assertive woman who had climbed the ranks of an oil and gas company (Shell) at a time when there were few women at the top. She showed many of us what was possible and her presence commanded respect. One day while in a meeting with her and her team of vice presidents she said something that has stuck with me forever: 'You have two ears and one mouth, and you should use them in that proportion'.

Think of the most curious person you know. It's highly likely that when you are in conversation with them, they make you feel like the only person in the room because they are truly listening to what you are saying. The more frequently we practise listening, the more it supports our ability to process information and close knowledge gaps, thus strengthening our curiosity. So why is it then that we find just listening so hard?

We spend our listening time thinking about what we will say next, or, worse, thumbing a device, which distracts us from absorbing what is really being said and noticing the nuances of body language that may signal something we'd otherwise miss. Thus, the practice of listening not only activates our curiosity, but it also requires our focus muscle, doubling the effort required but also the benefit it can deliver in building skill in Intentional Adaptability.

Curious beings thrive on listening deeply in conversation.

In a curious conversation the single goal is to fully understand the perspective of the person or persons you are talking to. This skill requires you to ask questions, and provide your undistracted attention so that you can reaffirm what you think you understood back to the listener. This ensures you are processing the information in the way it was intended to be received, and is called 'active listening'.

Active listening as a concept was developed by Carl Rogers and Richard Farson and published in their paper of the same name in 1957. They articulate that this concept is a critical tool for evolving personal change:

> Despite the popular notion that listening is a passive approach, clinical and research evidence clearly shows that sensitive listening is a most effective agent for individual personality change and group development. Listening brings about changes in people's attitudes toward themselves and others; it also brings about changes in their basic values and personal philosophy. People who have been listened to in this new and special way become more emotionally mature, more open to their experiences, less defensive, more democratic, and less authoritarian.

The practice of active listening involves five techniques that, when used in combination over time, can enable not only curiosity but equally our propensity to intentionally adapt:

1. *Activate your focus muscle*. Remove all distractions and give the person you are actively listening to your undivided attention. Note: Having your phone on or in your line of sight won't support this technique.

2. *Show me you're listening*. Use your body language to let the other person know you hear them. Nod or smile occasionally, look them in the eye and keep your arms open (crossed arms indicate that you are closed).

3. *Tell me you're listening*. Paraphrase what you thought you heard the person say, ask them questions to clarify your understanding.

4. *Leave your judgement at the door*. Put yourself in the other person's shoes to understand their perspective, even if it is fundamentally different from yours – it doesn't mean it's wrong. Don't jump in with your opinions; let them get out what they're trying to say.

5. *Yes and…* Consider constructively adding to the conversation by using the practice of 'Yes and…' instead of saying 'but'. There is a saying that 'everything that goes before "but" is bullshit'. So when you say 'Yes but…' you are diminishing the perspectives of the other person.

HAPPINESS HACK

Practise a curious conversation using the active listening techniques and see where it takes you. Set yourself up for success by removing all distractions and allowing the time to explore the perspectives of the other person.

Practice 5—Avoid relying on Google as the only source of answers to questions

How often do you look to resources *outside* of Google to enhance your curiosity? (Chapter 4 also covers this.) Remarkably, only 40 per cent of the people who have undertaken our Hacking Happy Assessment state that they do this sometimes if ever.

Now, don't get me wrong: I use Google, and often. It can be a great resource for the quick fix to your Novelty Curiosity (which is covered in Chapter 8). It is helpful for finding a new dinner recipe, online shopping, and so on.... However, how curious are we if we are using Google to get the answers we need to *every* question we have? How do you think this quick fix approach over a long period of time affects our brain's ability to process problems, retain knowledge or create the space to think and connect the dots?

There is a term that researchers have coined called 'cognitive offloading'. It's basically our willingness to outsource our memory and our thinking to the internet. Nicholas Carr, author of *The Shallows: What the internet is doing to our brains,* believes that our dependence on the internet is affecting our ability to move the facts we come across daily into our long-term memory, which he says is

> essential to the creation of knowledge and wisdom. Dozens of studies by psychologists, neurobiologists and educators point to the same conclusion: when we go online, we enter an environment that promotes cursory reading, hurried and distracted thinking, and superficial learning.

What is equally fascinating are the studies that have demonstrated that those who read linear text in any form are more likely to understand, retain and learn more than someone who reads text that is sprinkled with hyperlinks. This might explain why the highly curious Bill Gates carries a bag of over 15 books around with him pretty much everywhere he goes.

I recently stood in a lift chatting with one of the most renowned robotics professors in Australia. He shared with me that he does not use a smart phone as he chooses not to give his data freely to technology companies. I asked him how he builds his knowledge outside of technology. He smiled at me and opened what looked like a very heavy backpack filled with books and said, 'I prefer old-school methods'.

'Information Obesity' is a term coined by my friend, introduced in chapter 5, work futurist Dom Price. This obesity is driven by the bombardment of information coming at us and our inability to self-regulate our behaviour with technology. Sadly, the research indicates that information overwhelm is not transferring into improved intelligence, as our short-term memory is operating in what is termed 'cognitive overload'. When our short-term memory is full it can't take in any more and is unable to transfer new information into our long-term memory, which is what helps expand our knowledge and wisdom.

One could argue that cognitive overload is directly linked to cognitive offloading, in that when our brains are so full it is likely that we are more inclined to outsource our memory and thinking to the internet. It's self-perpetuating!

> It is imperative we use a diverse set of learning mediums because a quick answer does not always result in a quality one.

Have you ever actually considered what happens when you do that Google search? How that first answer, the seemingly 'correct' one, got to the top? It's what's paid for and what's popular, with a filter of what they know about you from your past searches, that comes to the top of your Google search. So if I search 'curiosity' on Google and ask you to do the same, what comes to the top of your search is likely to be very different from mine.

The algorithmic smarts built into the technology (and it's not only Google) are creating what is termed a 'narrowcast'; it's narrowing our view of the world based on what it thinks we want to see. One might also argue that this narrowcast is more likely to reinforce our confirmation bias. So next time you Google something, try checking out page 10 instead of what comes to the top of page one. The answer might be more factually correct and from a more reliable source, and it might provoke your curiosity in a different way!

HAPPINESS HACK

Revisit the curiosity list that you developed in the Experiment at the end of chapter 8. Select one of the curiosities you highlighted and start exploring it without the help of Google!

You may like to draw on some of the following ideas:

* Read a book. You may even want to spend an afternoon exploring the quiet of your local library and unpacking what resources they have on the topic.
* Listen to a podcast.
* Seek out someone with lived experience or who is considered an expert and have a conversation.
* Watch a documentary or a TED talk.
* Sit in a co-working space for a day and connect with a couple of random strangers and ask their perspectives.
* Attend an unlikely event.
* Complete a free course online.
* Try an experiment that enables you to apply your curiosity and observe how it plays out.

Practice 6 — Surprise yourself, often

I find it odd that life is considered a journey, an experiment, an exploration… and yet at around the age of 16 we start pressuring children to try and determine a career path. In a world where, according to the World Economic Forum, 65 per cent of children entering primary school today will work in jobs that don't even exist yet, how can we know which path is the right one when we don't even know what the options are?

When I speak to children of high school age about their 'future', there is an innate fear of choosing the wrong path. But is there really a wrong choice? What if you just make a start and try something? Isn't trying when we surprise ourselves? Isn't it more important to try something and get it wrong than not trying due to decision paralysis?

It would seem wiser to me that we ask the next generation, 'What experiment would you like to undertake to start your journey into the unknown?' What a great basis to amplify curiosity and weave the element of surprise into your everyday, not to mention practise courage. There could be a thousand right paths for you — even more — and it's likely you don't even know many of them exist.

If we don't learn, or teach others, from an early age how to be open to the discomfort of uncertainty, how to surprise ourselves and do it often, we may never unlock the door to true fulfilment.

Tania Luna, co-author of *Surprise: Embrace the unpredictable and engineer the unexpected* shares:

> we feel most comfortable when things are certain, but we feel most alive when they're not… Welcoming surprise is just asking yourself, 'How alive do I want to feel?'

Curious beings love the element of surprise and they seek it out by trying new things, talking to strangers, putting themselves in unfamiliar situations or posing questions they've never asked before.

In the previous chapter, we talked through an example of being curious about improv acting. This is something I had on my own curiosity list for some time. So in December 2019, I attended a four-day Level 1 improv intensive program. I wanted to understand whether improv could make me a better speaker, and whether it would improve my ability to connect with audiences. I could have gone and booked a speaking coach to improve my skills, but that seemed like an easy and less fun option. The idea of improv made me feel uncomfortable and extremely vulnerable, which is why I just knew I *had* to do it (remember, fear is the green light to lean in).

Improv surprised me. It was more challenging than I anticipated, and it took me down an unexpected path. It turned out to be a class in how to be curious about yourself and others, how to reconnect with how we feel in the moment and use those feelings to evolve a scene. It was not about thinking, it was about building skill in being completely and utterly in the moment with the other person on stage. It wasn't about acting, it was about trying to respond like we do in real life, which seems easy, but damn, it's hard! It was about having the courage to remove the filter and say what you really think even if it sounds crazy. It was not about trying to fix the problem that presented in the scene, but supporting your fellow actor to explore how it makes them feel. Imagine if we employed these skills in the everyday!

Quite frankly, improv was a lesson in how to look in hard places within yourself and equally within others to unlock surprise. It required listening and observation skills that should be innate but sadly are lacking. My improv class didn't just make me a better speaker; it helped me become a better human.

Unpacking your curiosity by looking in hard places can deliver magical and unexpected results.

To challenge your perspective, and put your listening skills into action at the same time, pick one of your curiosities from your curiosity list and go ask a child or a senior in the community their perspective on your topic. You may be very surprised at what you learn!

Practice 7—Invest in your curiosity

Call it courage or call it curiosity—or perhaps it's a combination of the two—but curious beings are willing to invest their money, as well as time, in expanding their Knowledge Curiosity because they trust that it will provide a stepping stone to where they are meant to be.

The most powerful time to invest in your curiosity is when you are in transition and yet many of us tighten our purse strings out of fear.

When I left my corporate job with no idea of where to next, I had some savings in the bank. I realised it had taken me 16 years and a lot of money invested in my development by my previous employer to climb the corporate ladder and achieve success. I couldn't step out of that and expect to reinvent myself overnight. It was going to take time, experimentation and, equally, an investment. I decided for the first time in my life to carve out some of my savings and call it my 'development fund'. This money was for me to invest in the things that I was curious about that might help me navigate a path forward. Let me be clear: there were no immediate paybacks on that money, nor were there any guarantees, but what it did was provide a platform for long-term exploration.

The first thing I did was buy myself a ticket to the Conscious Capitalism Conference in Sydney. That investment was well worth it; I learned so much about creating a company that could make the world a better place while turning a profit. I met people outside of my circle who I still connect with today and it ignited a flame inside me to leave the world just a little better than when I arrived. I have never regretted that investment.

Just the other day my friend told me she had always been curious about writing a fiction novel, so I encouraged her to invest in her ability to do it. Two hours later, I received a text saying she had signed up to a beginner creative writing class. I know that brought joy into her day, and it certainly put a smile on my face! Where could your investment in you lead?

HAPPINESS HACK

What is one thing you've always been curious about doing? (It may be on your curiosity list.) Why not go and do it now? Give yourself permission to invest in your curiosity.

INNATELY BEING

At first, you may need to work a little harder to amplify your curious being. But over time, the skills you build through consistent practice will become more natural and innate.

We want to get to a stage where you don't have to think, 'I need to be curious now'; your brain will just go to autopilot and take you there. To make that happen, you've got to work on your habits (explored in chapter 5), which is something my good friend Aden is great at.

Aden wanted to create a new practice that made curiosity top of mind and intentional, so he decided he would write down at least one question every day that he would like to find an answer to. It could be anything at all – whatever came to him in the moment.

He wanted to ensure that this practice became a part of his usual routine, not something he just did when he could squeeze in time, so every morning when Aden would make his bed, he would also place his notebook of curious questions, with his pen, on top of the covers. When he went to bed each night, he had to pick up the book to get into bed, so it prompted him to spend a couple of minutes writing down his curious questions. He actually would have to go out of his way NOT to practise his curiosity because his setup was so on point.

This practice is now part of Aden's new norm, which he tracks using a habit tracker. This motivates him to continue as it makes him feel good.

Make curiosity a habit, and you'll make your happiness a habit, too.

EXPERIMENT NOW

It's time to develop a curious plan to enable your practice of curious being.

First, pick something from your curiosity list (chapter 8), or something else you might be curious about. Write in the space provided what you are curious about. For example, 'I'm curious about developing a highly engaging online program to teach hacking happiness'.

I am curious about

____

____

Often having a question or a hypothesis around our curiosity helps us direct where we begin our exploration. What question or hypothesis do you have on your topic right now? Using my example above, the question I might ask is, 'What would a highly engaging online program look like from a customer experience perspective?'

My curious question or hypothesis is

____

____

Now let's leverage the list of curious being practices we worked through in this chapter to enable you to explore your curious question or prove or disprove your hypothesis. Use the table (overleaf) to guide your thinking. I've added examples to help you. Remember to keep it simple. Small, focused, consistent action builds the skill to step into bigger change over time. Make sure what you write down is realistic but with a stretch.

This simple tool can be used time and time again as you seek to explore new curiosities and hone your skill in your curious being.

List two curious practices you would like to experiment with.	*1.* *2.* *For example, the practice I would like to embed is Curious Conversations.*
List two actions per curious practice you will undertake to explore your curiosity. Keep them simple and specific.	*1.* *2.* *For example, two actions I will undertake to embed this practice are:* * *Schedule one curious conversation a day with a customer or prospective customer.* * *Create a set of curious interview questions and practise active listening in each interview.*
Write down how you will track your practice frequency.	*For example, I will track my progress daily using the Habit-Bull app to track how many curious conversations I have in a week.*
Commit to when you will reflect on your practice to review what's working, what's not and what you would like to do differently as a result.	*For example, I will reflect on my practice on Friday at 9 am each week.*

REFLECT AND REMEMBER

* Confirmation bias is our natural tendency to seek out information that reinforces our existing beliefs.
* A curious person is not afraid to prove themselves wrong about a previously held belief; in fact, they consider it a win because it provides a growth in their knowledge base.
* Questions and human connection are the gateway to exploring the unknown, to reshaping our beliefs and changing our behaviour.
* Curious conversations enhance our level of connection, our relationships, our feelings of belonging, our skill in understanding one another, our ability to problem solve, our capacity to innovate and be resilient.
* A quick answer does not always result in a quality one. Try avoiding Googling the answer to your next question and seek out an alternative, old-school source!
* Curious beings love the element of surprise in their everyday and they seek ways to try new things, talk to strangers, or put themselves in unfamiliar situations.
* Make curiosity a habit. How can you link an existing habit to a new curiosity habit?

SHARE THE HAPPY

Share the concept of active listening with your team or a friend and practise building your skill together through curious conversations. You may be surprised at where it takes you!

PERFECTION DOESN'T LIVE HERE, PRACTICE DOES

'Know that if I die tomorrow, I die completely happy.'

I remember saying these words to my mum and truly meaning them. 'Yes, there is always more I could do if I had more time, but I truly feel I am living my best life and for that I am grateful,' I said.

It took me 44 years to land in a place where happiness was my state of being. These words, this statement, was only possible after I redefined success on my own terms and prioritised my happiness over my ego and material worth. This feeling, this joy, was a by-product of experimentation, failure and all the practices from this book that I had employed in my everyday, which enabled me to be the person I am today – imperfect, flawed and loving every minute of it.

I let go of seeking to be perfect and embraced the powerful practice of being human and I want to encourage you to do the same.

Hacking happiness is messy, challenging and uncomfortable, and equally mind blowing if you allow your practice to be persistent, consistent and sprinkled with imperfection.

I don't profess to have all the answers and I am far from perfect. I am my own Intentional Adaptability experiment, which means I too am a work in progress. I created this book to demonstrate that, in the realm of happiness, perfection does not live here, practice does.

My intention has never been to tell you what to do; it's been to act in your service by supporting you to work out for yourself what's right for you, through the practice of Intentional Adaptability. I hope I have encouraged you to look at the world through a different lens, to challenge your definition of success and shine a spotlight on what you've been avoiding.

According to Professor Felice Leonardo Buscaglia, the ancient Egyptians believed that upon death they would be asked two questions and their answers would determine whether they could continue their journey into the afterlife. The first question was, 'Did you bring joy?' The second was, 'Did you find joy?'

While I can find no historical evidence to support this as truth, it still struck a chord. What a beautiful and simple way to measure the daily joy in one's life in this very moment. I now use these two simple questions as a guidepost at the end of each day to check in on my happiness and keep myself accountable to my practice of Intentional Adaptability.

Maybe you'd like to do the same?

> Now is the time to ask yourself honestly, did you find joy today, did you bring joy to others? If not, how can you tweak your practice to find more joy tomorrow?

Your happiness is not an end state; it's a choice, a way of *being* and its realisation is your responsibility.

Your practice does not end; your exploration and experimentation is really just beginning!

You have the compass, the experiments and everything you need within you right now to stop reacting, start intentionally adapting and be happy.

Go forth and get after it!

CONTINUE YOUR HACKING HAPPINESS JOURNEY

Thank you for inviting me into your world and allowing me the opportunity to share what I know to help you bring a little more happy into your everyday.

I hope that you have found your journey to be constructive and your experiments challenging yet rewarding.

If you would like to find out more about hacking happiness using Intentional Adaptability, or how you can work directly with me and my team, please visit:

HackingHappy.co

RESOURCES

CHAPTER 1

Seligman, M. (2002). *Authentic Happiness*. Free Press.

Sachs, J. (2018). *World happiness report, America's health crisis and the Easterlin Paradox*. Retrieved from https://s3.amazonaws.com/happiness-report/2018/CH7-WHR-lr.pdf

Kahneman, D. & Deaton, A. (2010). 'High income improves evaluation of life but not emotional well-being.' Princeton University, Proceedings of the National Academy of Sciences of the United States of America. Retrieved from https://www.princeton.edu/˜deaton/downloads/deaton_kahneman_high_income_improves_evaluation_August2010.pdf

Rice-Oxley, M. (2019). 'Mental illness: is there really a global epidemic?' *The Guardian*.

Fottrell, Q. (2018). 'Nearly half of Americans report feeling alone.' *Market Watch*.

Australian Psychological Society, Swinburne University of Technology (2018). *Australian Loneliness Report*. Retrieved from https://psychweek.org.au/wp/wp-content/uploads/2018/11/Psychology-Week-2018-Australian-Loneliness-Report.pdf

Diamandis, P. (2012). 'Abundance is our future.' Retrieved from https://www.ted.com/talks/peter_diamandis_abundance_is_our_future

Duffy, B. (2018). *The Perils of Perception: Why we're wrong about nearly everything*. Atlantic Books.

Rose, C. (2017). 'How well are you investing your time.' Retrieved from https://youtu.be/nH5K0yo-o1A

Whillans, A. (2019). 'Time for happiness.' *Harvard Business Review*.

CHAPTER 2

Grisold, T., Kaiser, A. & Hafner, J. (2017). 'Unlearning before creating new knowledge: A cognitive process.' Conference paper, Hawaii International Conference on System Sciences.

Lyubomirsky, S. (2008) *The How of Happiness: A new approach to getting the life you want.* Penguin Books.

Quoidbach, J., Mikolajczak, M., Kotsou, I., Gruber, J., Kogan, A. & Norton, M. (2014). 'Emodiversity and the emotional ecosystem.' *Journal of Experimental Psychology: General,* vol. 143, no. 6, 2057-2066. Retrieved from https://www.hbs.edu/faculty/Publication%20Files/quoidbach%20et%20al%202014_9105d828-db78-49eb-b434-23f53cdba042.pdf

CHAPTER 3

Reives, M. & Deimler, M. (2011). 'Adaptability: The new competitive advantage.' *Harvard Business Review.*

CHAPTER 4

Tottle, S. (2019). 'Burnout is on the rise, and it's contagious. This is what we need to do about it.' *Business Insider.*

Greenwood, K., Bapat, V. & Maughan, M. (2019). 'Research: People want their employers to talk about mental health.' *Harvard Business Review.*

McKee, A. (2015) 'How to free your innate creativity.' *Harvard Business Review.*

DiNardi, G. (2019). 'Why you should work less and spend more time on hobbies.' *Harvard Business Review.*

Lino, C. (2019). 'Broaden-and-Build Theory of positive emotions.' *Positive Psychology.*

Achor, S. (2011). *The Happiness Advantage: The seven principles that fuel success and performance at work.* Currency.

Rice-Oxley, M. (2019). 'Mental illness: Is there really a global epidemic?' *The Guardian.*

World Health Organization (2001). 'Mental disorders affect one in four people.' Retrieved from https://www.who.int/whr/2001/media_centre/press_release/en/

Udemy Research (2018). 'Udemy in depth: 2018 workplace distraction report.' Retrieved from https://research.udemy.com/research_report/udemy-depth-2018-workplace-distraction-report/

Raphael, R. (2017). 'Netflix CEO Reed Hastings: Sleep is our competition.', *Fast Company*.

Breyer, M. (2013). '10 accidental inventions that changed the world.' Mother Nature Network.

Ballard, J. (2019). 'Millennials are the loneliest generation.' YouGov.

Wikipedia. 'FOMO Fear of missing out.' Wikipedia. Retrieved from https://en.wikipedia.org/wiki/Fear_of_missing_out

Dictionary.com. 'FOMO.' Retrieved from https://www.dictionary.com/e/acronyms/fomo/

McKeown, G. (2014). 'Why we humblebrag about being busy.' *Harvard Business Review*.

CHAPTER 5

Wikipedia. 'Homo sapiens.' Retrieved from https://en.wikipedia.org/wiki/Homo_sapiens

Clear, J. (2018). *Atomic Habits*. Avery.

CHAPTER 6

Rock, D. (2008). 'SCARF: a brain-based model for collaborating with and influencing others.' Retrieved from http://web.archive.org/web/20100705024057/http://www.your-brain-at-work.com/files/NLJ_SCARFUS.pdf

Goewey, D.J. (2017). '85 percent of what we worry about never happens.' Huffington Post.

Khazan, O. (2016). 'Can three words turn anxiety into success?' *The Atlantic*.

CHAPTER 7

Miller, K. (2020). 'CBT explained: An overview and summary of CBT.' *Positive Psychology*.

Weston, P. (2019). 'Failing 15% of the time is the best way to learn, say scientists.' *The Independent*.

Jiang, J. (2015). 'What I learned from 100 days of rejection.' TED talk. Retrieved from https://www.ted.com/talks/jia_jiang_what_i_learned_from_100_days_of_rejection

Spiegel, A. (2015). 'By making a game out of rejection, a man conquers fear.' NPR.

CHAPTER 8

Kidd, C. & Hayden, B.Y. (2015). 'The psychology and neuroscience of curiosity.' *Neuron,* vol. 88, no. 3, 449–460. Retrieved from https://www.ncbi.nlm.nih.gov/pmc/articles/PMC4635443/

Campbell, E. (2015). 'Six surprising benefits of curiosity.' *Greater Good* magazine. Retrieved from www.greatergood.berkeley.edu

Koren, M. (2013). 'Being a lifelong bookworm may keep you sharp in old age.' *Smithsonian Magazine.*

Godin, S. (2010). 'Why ask why?' Seth's blog. Retrieved from https://seths.blog/2010/01/why-ask-why-2/

Kidd, C. & Hayden, B.Y. (2015). 'The psychology and neuroscience of curiosity.' *Neuron*, vol. 88, no. 3, 449–460. Retrieved from https://www.ncbi.nlm.nih.gov/pmc/articles/PMC4635443/

CHAPTER 9

Rivera, L.A. (2012). 'Hiring as cultural matching: The case of elite professional service firms.' *American Sociological Review*, vol. 77, no. 6, 999–1022. Retrieved from https://www.asanet.org/sites/default/files/savvy/journals/ASR/Dec12ASRFeature.pdf

Wikipedia. 'Active listening.' Retrieved from https://en.wikipedia.org/wiki/Active_listening

Carr, N. (2010). 'The web shatters focus, rewires brain.' *Wired.*

World Economic Forum (2016). 'The future of jobs.' Retrieved from http://reports.weforum.org/future-of-jobs-2016/

INDEX

CPSIA information can be obtained
at www.ICGtesting.com
Printed in the USA
FSHW022004290920
74221FS

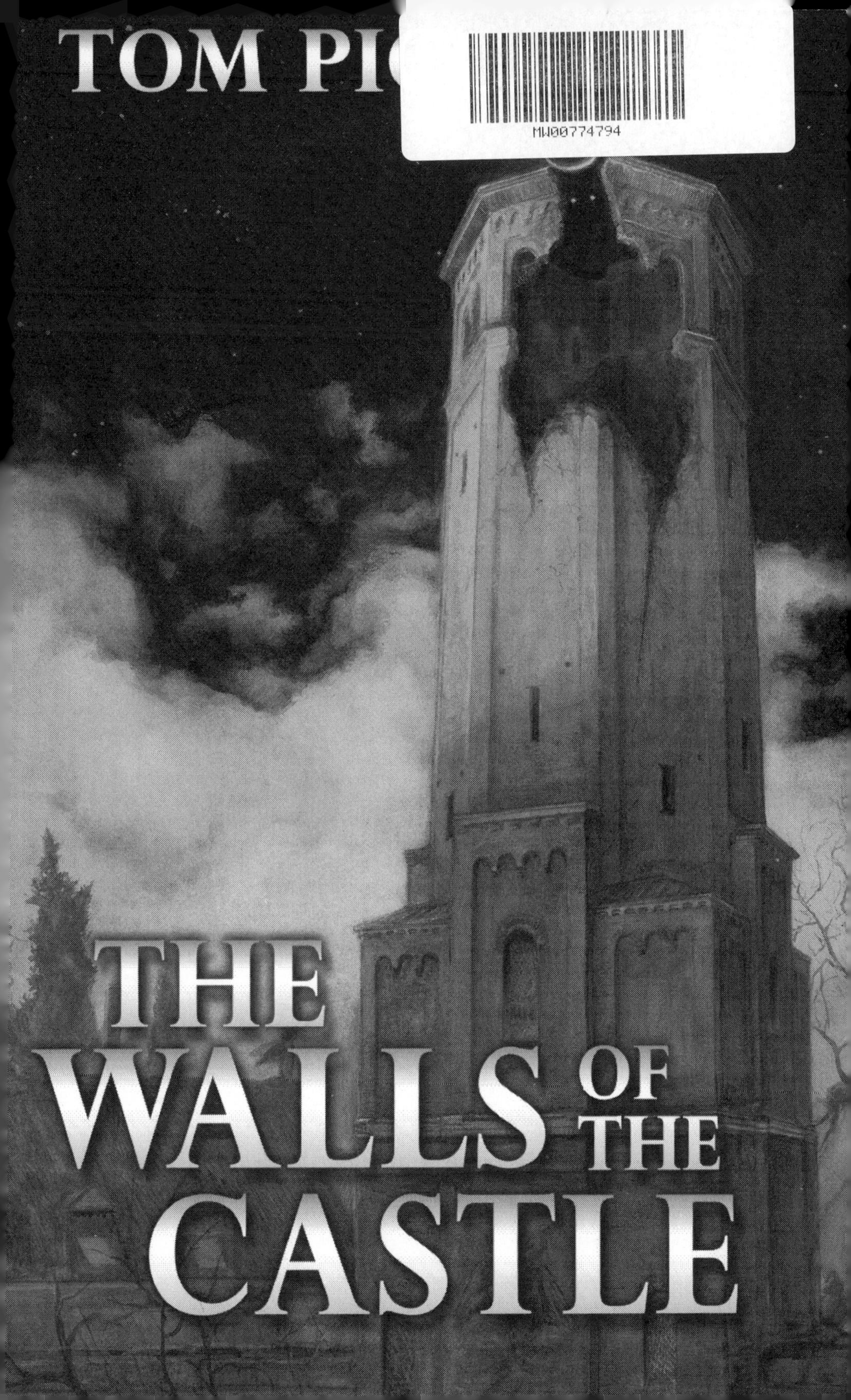
TOM PI
THE
WALLS OF THE
CASTLE

First Limitless Trade Paperback Edition

Cover and interior design by:
David G. Barnett
Fat Cat Graphic Design
fatcatgraphicdesign.com

Editor and Publisher: Chris Morey
www.ChrisMorey.com

Dark Regions Press, LLC
300 E. Hersey St. STE 10A
Ashland, OR, 97520

www.DarkRegions.com

Black Labyrinth Book I
DarkRegions.com/BlackLabyrinth

BlackLabyrinth

Book I

Watch for new releases in the
Black Labyrinth imprint at
DarkRegions.com/BlackLabyrinth

For everyone with a sorrow that can't be set down, a patch of night that owns your heart, a recurring dream that never stops calling, a memory with claws, a treasure stolen from the sand, a slashing regret, a face you no longer recognize, a last meager hope that remains beyond your grasp, THE WALLS OF THE CASTLE is for you—

&

For Thomas Tessier

The Walls of the Castle

His son had been dead for two weeks, in the ground ten days, he was told, and Kasteel was still sitting in the ICU waiting area, spooking the nurses. He was so pale now that the deep old scars hidden by his usually dark olive coloring looked fresh and vicious.

The staff no longer called him sir. They no longer offered to fetch him coffee. They eyed him suspiciously and twice invited him to speak with a grief counselor. They gave him bad directions to the psych wing. He already knew the hospital better than any of them. Kasteel remained polite, talkative, and amicable, but he just wouldn't leave. So the administration sent up two tight-faced, no-neck security guards to throw him the fuck out.

He'd lost a lot of muscle mass eating nothing but cafeteria food the last four months. The incessant crying had left him dehydrated and salt-deprived. The lack of sunlight had given him a Vitamin D deficiency that he was trying to combat with pills stolen from the dispensary. His back was in bad shape from sleeping on waiting room benches and operating theater tables. When they hauled him to his feet his lower vertebrae cracked as loud as a shot from a snub .32.

Their name badges read Conrad and Watkins. They were cut from the same granite as the bulls in Sing. Angry, icy-eyed men who liked to parcel out punishment because it gave their lives momentary purpose, provided definition, and made them feel self-righteous.

They pulled disgusted faces when they caught a whiff of him. Kasteel had been wearing the same ill-fitting clothes for five weeks, stolen from a prostate cancer patient who'd died on the table in September. He smelled like the ass-end of a morgue.

They shoved him along with their truncheons and rapped him hard in the back of the thighs. He held himself in check until they were around the corner from the elevator, and then he fought dirty as hell. He cut loose, letting some of the savage tension go. He hooked Watkins under the heart and threw a couple of tight jabs into Conrad's jaw. Six months ago he could've taken both easily. But he was weak from lost electrolytes and lack of sleep, and they quickly overpowered him. After barely a minute of brawling they clubbed him to his knees and stomped his guts until he vomited bile.

It went too far and they knew it. They were under orders not to make a scene. Kasteel's nose and mouth pulsed blood and his beard was dripping. Watkins said, "Shit," and wiped his hands clean on Kasteel's shirt.

They didn't realize they were so close to the elevators. They discussed alternate routes through the Castle, following the chipped, outdated color coded lines painted on the floors.

They grabbed him under the arms almost gently this time and carried his limp body between them. They walked corridor after corridor, Watkins swiping his key card and shouldering through the fire doors. They were getting anxious and angry again. Kasteel wondered if they were trying to take him to the psych wing. This was the way they sometimes brought the disassociatives, depressives, catatonic cases, the biters, nyctaphobes, narcoleptics, nymphos, multiple personality disorders, paranoiacs, schizoids, and the chronic masturbators.

Instead, they finally reached another set of elevators, hit the button for the ground floor and worked his kidneys for a couple of floors on the way down. It wasn't enough to do anything more than make him piss blood for few days. He'd been kicked around a lot worse in the showers of C-Block at Sing. Funny how many Aryans were queer when Adolph hated the rainbow brigade. Maybe not so funny when you got down to it, but he found himself grinning. He tried not to laugh, but for some reason the need was there. He bit his tongue but a chuckle still floated up from deep inside his chest.

"What are you so happy about, asshole?"

Watkins had punched the wrong button and watched frantically as they continued to descend—3, 2, 1, P5, P4, P3—into the underground parking lots. Watkins let out a small grunt of frustration. They dragged Kasteel through F14, sub-level 3, this particular parking area reserved for visiting cardiologists and pulmonary specialists. There were red arrows all over the place, pointing in every direction. There were no exit signs.

A distant noise made Conrad call, "Hello?"

Kasteel laughed again.

For the next twenty minutes Conrad and Watkins squabbled over directions, growing more and more tense and anxious as they tried to find the outer door. They were nowhere near it. Their lips were tight with confusion and irritation. Kasteel wished he had a cigarette.

The Castle always got people twisted around. The Castle didn't let you go unless it wanted you to go.

They circled and spiraled and tried to follow the red arrows. Conrad kept calling, "Hello? Hello?"

Watkins said, "Who in the fuck are you saying hello to? There's nobody here."

"Somebody's got to be here, look at the cars. We just passed three Mercedes."

"They're not here, they're in the hospital."

"Someone might be walking from here into the hospital or back out again."

"Someone might be except nobody is."

Eventually they got back in the elevator and up to the ground floor. They ushered Kasteel down a few more hallways, past the university clinic for child medicine. Kasteel knew he looked like death but couldn't help waving to the bald, terminal kids through the large plate glass window as they passed by. He thought of his son but he couldn't remember his son's name or face. A few kids waved back.

Watkins said, "Breaks your heart."

"Yeah."

"They ought to lighten the place up some."

"What do you mean?"

"There should be some…I don't know. Board games. These kids would probably enjoy a few board games."

"Some balloons would be nice."

"Yeah, balloons."

Yeah, balloons, Kasteel thought, in a sterile environment with sixty percent oxygen content. One static spark off the surface of a plastic balloon and you'd have an explosion as big as half a pound of C4 blowing out a bank vault door.

They hit the stairwell and went up another level. They dead-ended at a series of locked labs and had to double-back and take the stairs back down. Kasteel thought about his first day in Sing, surrounded by twenty million metric tons of concrete, thousands of cons, bulls, other fish, other strings, pro heisters who'd taken a bad fall, old-time juggers who'd been in the can for fifty years.

They entered an older part of the Castle, where security hadn't been updated to the use of key cards. Lengths of untangled wiring hung from missing ceiling tile squares. Soon the stonework of the original fortress began to show through. The lighting changed. The smell in the corridors grew heavy with mildew and rotting mortar. Kasteel was feeling stronger, walking on his own, the ache in his kidneys only a dull passive discomfort.

Conrad and Watkins snapped and barked at each other. They squared their shoulders and went nose to nose, rattled.

"Where the hell are we?"

"Turn left."

"Why left?"

"Go left."

"I heard you. I'd like to know why."

"Just fucking go left!"

Kasteel knew exactly where they were. They'd gotten turned around and were heading towards the inside court leading to the Fool's Tower.

Twelve stories high, the tower had originally been considered a "praying pavilion" though no religious persuasion was reflected in its construction. Vertical window slits appeared in the brickwork on each of the open floors. At one time you could go in, meditate, and commune with your higher power or just sob your guts out while your loved ones died inside the Castle. On bright days shafts of sunlight would slant within like purifying divine radiance. At night, mercurial silver moonlight would rain down inside.

After World War II it was converted into a transformer station. After Vietnam the remains of the original stone tower were restored as a kind of a memorial, though there were no plaques or statues to tell anyone what kind of memorial it was supposed to be. It became the place where you went and begged the powers that be until you couldn't speak any longer. Over the last ten years there were at least three cases where the bereaved committed suicide by leaping from the top turret into the courtyard gardens below. Another tried but suffered only severe brain damage and spinal injuries. He was still around, a vegetable on life support over on Ward Six for the last eight years. Kasteel visited on occasion.

The administration hastily bricked and cemented the doors up, but the Catholics decided the place was too much like an ancient church and wanted it reopened. The Archbishop even bitched about it in a press conference so Admin was forced to restore it completely even before the south wing that led out to the tower was finished.

Conrad and Watkins were starting to get a little flipped out, bored, tired, and their shift was about to end. They seemed like children that had wandered too far away from their parents, Hansel and Gretel lost in the forest without their gingerbread.

"Okay, this is good enough," Conrad said.

"Good enough?"

"Yeah."

"Good enough for what?" Watkins asked.

"Far enough."

"Far enough for what?"

"To let him go."

"What are you talking about?"

"Shut up!"

They manhandled Kasteel out to the tower and then hurled him through the open arch. He tumbled heavily across the cobblestone floor, trying not to smile. The pain was nearly enjoyable when compared to the fuzzy, warm numbness of the past few months.

He spit blood, climbed to his feet, reached for his cigarettes, and lit one. There was no smoking anywhere on the hospital premises, not even in the two-century old sections of the Castle that hadn't been renovated yet. He snorted smoke and it drifted against their merciless, blunt faces. Conrad wanted to have another go at him, but Watkins held the prick back.

"Enough," he said.

Conrad pointed at Kasteel. "Don't let us see you here again, you crazy son of a bitch. Leave. Go home."

"Sure," Kasteel said. He didn't have a home left to go home to. He already was home.

The no-necks receded into the main building. They were practically skipping when they got to the door. Being outside for a couple of minutes had revitalized them, given them some grounding, focused them. Kasteel held his hand out into a ray of sunshine and let the sunlight fill his palm. He wondered if the Castle was done screwing around with the no-neck guards. Probably not. They were bound to wander around lost for at least another hour or so, maybe longer, maybe forever. He might find their corpses in operating theater #4 a few months from now, the two of them with their hands around each other's throat.

He lay at the base of the wrought-iron spiral stairway and stared up at the mortar of the first floor ceiling. Admin had tried to restore the artwork there but budget cuts canceled the project about halfway through. Now all you saw was a small portion of some gorgeous tableau, a choir of celestial beings that might have been archangels holding swords but without wings, children staring up in awe, a bloated orange hunter's moon being clutched in an enormous deific fist. He was still surprised the Catholics had ever figured this for a church. If anything, he vibed paganism.

The pain in his side made him take short sips of air. He reached into his back pocket and came up with stolen bottles of Percocet, Xanax, Oxycontin, Valium, Codeine, Vicodin, vitamin B, C, D, and zinc. He mixed a handful of pills and tossed them back, dry.

He heard footsteps at the top of the staircase. Someone was coming down.

Chiseled above him across the doorway arch was KASTEEL.

It was the Dutch word for Castle.

He crooked his finger and spelled out names in the dust.

EDDIE.

KATHY.

He started to pray out of instinct. The words had been there since childhood, and they continued to echo down the years, through his time in Sing, at the beginning of Eddie's illness and again at the very end. He'd done so much praying here the past four months that the prayers still wanted to break from him. It was pointless, and he'd always known it was pointless, but you did whatever you could when your boy was dying. You begged and you wept and you performed whatever acts of contrition you thought might pay your debt so the big gun upstairs didn't send an angel with a burning sword to take your firstborn. You cleaned out ten years' worth of cached money and fenced stolen goods to pay for experimental treatments. You huddled with your wife, on your knees, and when your wife told you it was time to go, you let her leave on her own and you groveled there alone.

When she told you that you needed help you went to the "very good doctor" that her friends had suggested. You sat there in the lady shrink's office and you tried to look interested and emphatic and open to changing your behavior. You put on a good show. You nodded and "uh hmmed" your ass off. You held tight to Kathy's hand in a show of solidarity. You answered all the questions about your mother and father and brothers, your months in juvie, being a car thief, a wheelman, a cat burglar, the things you had to do to survive Sing. You told the truth. Kathy knew it all. The doc sucked air between her teeth a few times.

Then the bitch asked, "If the unthinkable happens and your son dies—"

You killed her a hundred times in your head in maybe ten seconds, still holding Kathy's hand. Kath with her chin up, trying to deal with the inevitable, listening to this woman like she would have any answers about how to live without your child, the best thing in your life, the only thing besides Kath that mattered, and yes, his death, though inevitable, was utterly unthinkable. You moved your mind and soul away from it the way you'd back up from someone slashing at you with a shiv. There was nothing else to do.

You stood then, stone still in the middle of her office, and stared at her. Kathy groped for your hand but she couldn't budge it from your side. You have strong hands. Your hands have killed, your hands have done incredible things. Your hands held your boy gently when he was born and you thought that with this child you could live the life you were supposed to live. Straight, normal, without violence, and it had been that way for eight years, until Eddie began to get sick, and your boy began to die in front of your eyes.

The shrink, she couldn't handle staring at you anymore, the expression on your face too blank yet intense for a normal person to handle. Kathy spoke, rattling on and on, and meanwhile you just stood there in the office, wondering what kind of psychiatrist would dare to ask someone what they would do or feel if the unthinkable should happen. How could someone ever know until it happened, until it began to happen, the way it began to happen when the specialists came and stopped by on their way to their golf games, four am, only to find you lying in bed with your arms around your son. And the specialists always put out by finding you there, telling you, "You're not allowed to be here. Visiting hours aren't until—" You knew exactly when visiting hours were, but you were going to stay with your boy no matter what. Security threw you out again and again, but how do you keep out a man who spent most of his life sneaking into warehouses, jewelry stores, and banks. You once killed a man by stuffing a bar of soap down his throat in the showers at Sing. How could any of these people ever hope to understand what you were, what you'd done, what your son meant to you. Even Kathy had no idea until the end.

Kasteel must've passed out for a few minutes in the pool of warm sunlight at the bottom of the Fool's Tower. When he opened his eyes again his cigarette had gone out and Hedgwick was leaning over him.

"Do you have any Percocet?" he asked.

It took Kasteel three tries to find his voice. "I just took the last of them. You want Codeine?"

He reared in disgust. "Christ, no, it reacts badly with the Lithium. And it gives me the runs." He felt around in his pockets. "You running low on cigarettes?"

"Yes."

He handed Kasteel a couple packs of Lucky Strikes. Hedgwick's mother sent him a care package twice a week and he used the contents to barter with, the same way they did it in prison. Kasteel found his lighter and relit his cigarette.

Hedgwick was twenty-five, stood six-one, slim, with waving, wild curly blonde hair that all the young nurses liked. His wide dark eyes glowed like black embers, and when he hit you with his glare full-on you knew this was how zealots or revolutionaries stared into a crowd. He was wearing his thick fluffy red robe and cart wheeling clowns PJs today. He'd traded away his sophisticated leather slippers and now wore purple bunnies. The bunnies suited him better.

His pockets bulged and Kasteel could smell mayonnaise and ham that had gone bad. He had a thing about packing ham sandwiches and never eating them. He sometimes had three or four stuffed in his robe. It had something to do with the way his mother used to make his father lunch every day when Hedgwick was a kid. He'd ask his father for a bite of the sandwich before the man left, and his father would unseal the wax paper and let his son nibble at a corner. His old man worked high steel. One day he took a wrong step and fell sixteen floors into a newly poured section of foundation. There was no way for them to get him out so they let the concrete seal around his corpse and dedicated the building to him.

When Hedgwick got older he used to call in bomb threats to the building and run around naked trying to chase his father's ghost out of the place.

Hedgwick said he still saw and even talked to his father's phantom occasionally. He said his old man looked much the same, hadn't aged, was stuck in time and space, moved very slowly and didn't seem to notice that Hedgwick or anybody else was around. He said the psychiatrists had yet to prove to him that his father's ghost didn't exist. He didn't blame the shrinks for failing in that regard since it was impossible to prove a negative.

He woke screaming some nights gagging and gasping, imagining himself slowly drowning in millions of metric tons of concrete. He told Kasteel that the orderlies in Ward Eight sometimes would stage death matches between the paranoids, the firebugs, chronic masturbators, bi-polars, claustrophobes, walking comatose, the sociopaths, and depressives, and bet on the outcomes. Kasteel doubted a lot of what Hedgwick told him, but he wasn't sure that he doubted that.

Hedgwick lay on the floor beside Kasteel and traced the names in the dust. He spoke them aloud, something Kasteel could no longer do.

"Eddie. Kathy."

Kasteel shut his eyes. Hedgwick ran a hand through Kasteel's gray patch. He had a thing about gray patches because his father had had a gray patch. Kasteel didn't mind it most of the time but now he knocked the kid's hand aside, turned over and spit more blood.

"I...I'm sorry," Hedgwick whispered. "I'm sorry I didn't help you. I was frightened. I followed you through the halls. I saw what they did.

I should have helped. My father would have helped. He was strong. He had big muscles. He helped people."

"It's okay, Hedge. You did the right thing."

"In the ward matches we at least have garbage can lid shields and two-by-fours with nails hammered through them."

"It's time for you to make some new sandwiches. They're going to take those away from you soon."

"I know. Maybe tomorrow Mom will bring more."

Lying on the floor like that, listening to the rhythmic thrum of his breathing reminded Kasteel of the ventilator Eddie had been on, a ten million dollar machine rigged to force air in and out of his small, frail body. A sob tried to work up Kasteel's throat but it died long before it got there.

"Are you going to hurt them?" he asked. "Those prick security guards who beat you? Conrad and Watkins."

Kasteel kept hissing while his bruised ribs clawed at him, scratching deep from the inside. He needed to get them taped up soon.

"Do you think I should?"

"Yes. Those bastards. They're thugs. They've all failed the police psych exam because of violent behavioral tendencies. So they've followed up with the next best job they could get that gives them handcuffs and billy clubs. Admin is hiring the biggest and freshest of them, instead of the kindly grandpa types who have experience working with people. Admin likes to keep a youthful healthy face. The old men remind them too much of the geriatric wing, the stroke victims, the Alzheimer patients who wander around in their shitty diapers." He reached for Kasteel's gray patch again. "They shouldn't bring more pain to a grieving father."

Kasteel could find out where Conrad and Watkins lived. He had access to all the staff files and hospital records. He could visit their homes and creep their bedrooms while they slept and bring the goods to a variety of fences and have his cut sent back to Kathy. He could hurt them. He could rob them. He could scare them. He could prove he was still alive, assuming he was. Sometimes he felt like Hedge's father, stuck out of time and place, moving slowly when he was moving at all.

Maybe tonight.

The Castle let him loose at night. Sometimes.

«««—»»»

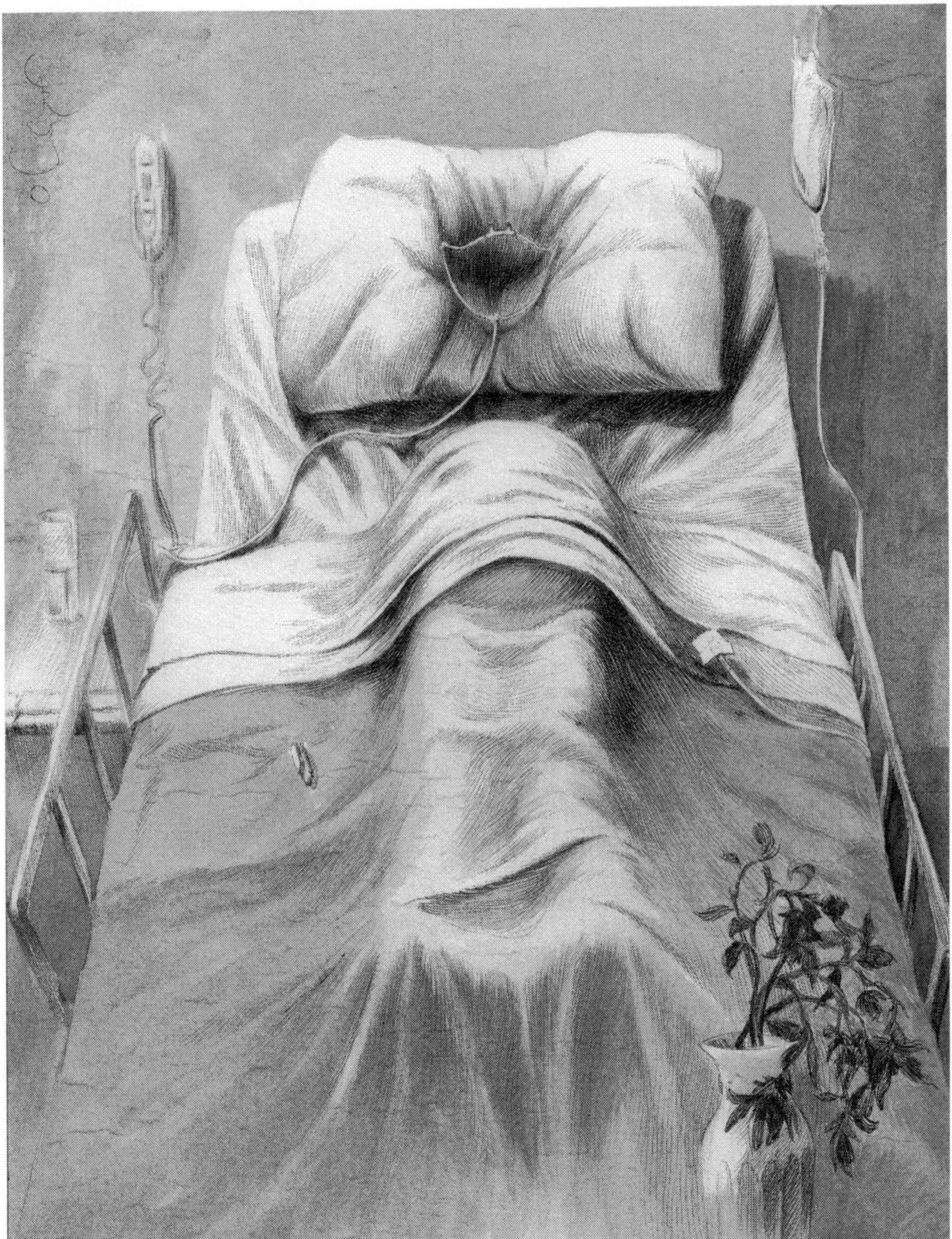

KASTEEL.

Before the American Revolution, the original Castle consisted of five fortress-like circular buildings constructed by the Dutch settlers of the area, who used it as a base stronghold to fight off Indian attacks. It grew into a village and then a town. In its strict geometrical form and simplicity, the original compound was considered a high point of European classicism. A military hospital was established during the war but was soon shifted to being an epidemic hostel during an outbreak of yellow fever.

Soon the emerging small city's primary employer was the hospital. Catering trades and smaller enterprises died off. The Castle had its own bakery, butcher, ironworks, and cemetery. After the worst of the epidemic had passed, disabled soldiers and their families were quartered in the epidemic wards. What had once been nearly two hundred acres of farming tract became the patient yard, student yard, craftsman center, the house supervisor yard, and a mental asylum. Over the last hundred and fifty years the complex had attached to it a medical school, university campus, personnel lodging, child medicine clinics, and the mental scientific institute.

The Castle became a city until unto itself. Currently over nine thousand people were employed at the hospital. Sixteen hundred physicians and forty-five hundred health and nursing workers attended to the patients. The mental wing consisted of fifteen separate wards and kept a rotating staff of about two hundred psychiatrists and therapists. Included among them were dozens of holistic healers in case your emotional disturbances ran in that direction. If your chakras were out of alignment, your chi wasn't flowing right, your crystals were too cloudy.

Annually, nearly a hundred thousand people were treated as in-patients and another half million attend the Castle's outpatient clinics. Along with the parking garages, geriatric facilities, coma wings, gardens, and rehab centers, the Castle compound covered more than two square miles.

You could read all the historical facts off plaques placed along the nature trails threading through the grounds. The hospital had its own station on the TVs in the waiting rooms and clinics. Admin hired a pretty actress who'd never been sick a day in her life to promenade through the place and wave to doctors and show smiling pregnant women up in the maternity wards.

It took Kasteel twenty-five minutes of navigating the inner courtyards and moving from one medical building to the next before he finally made it to the ER.

It was another savage night. Ambulances wheeled past, sirens whining like rampaging children, EMTs shouting, chubby nurses rushing back and forth, swinging their wide hips in uniforms two sizes too small. Heart attack victims were wheeled past

A teenage girl was lying half on the curb, half in the street, clawing at her face, streaks of blood down her cheeks, wailing uncontrollably. She was ten yards from the heart of the ER activity and no one else had seen her yet. Kasteel rushed for the automatic doors wondering if they'd open for him, wondering if he still existed enough in this world to set off the electric eye. He held his breath until he was through and standing outside once again.

He moved through the chill air to her side as she began to choke on her own vomit. Seemed like another OD whose friends had dumped her out in front and then driven off, afraid of being busted. They couldn't even walk her in. They couldn't even get her up out of the gutter.

Kasteel turned her over, cleared her breathing passageway, and called for help over his shoulder. All the ER staff and EMTs were already busy. He shouted louder but no one paid any attention. She began convulsing as he was trying to get her up. She was young but had been doing crank for a while. Several of her teeth were missing and others were black shards. She weighed almost nothing, meth-starved and burned down to ash. With his joints creaking, his muscles like sandbags, his nervous system practically as wrecked as hers, he lifted her over his shoulder and carried her inside the ER. The pain med cocktail was still doing its job, but the come down later was going to be bad.

The girl coughed up and spewed bile down his back. It wasn't going to make him smell much worse. As he clutched her and hauled her forward they were immediately lost in a flood of groaning men, crying children, pregnant ladies, beaten tough guys, the crippled, the feverish, the hobbled, all of them seated, vacant-faced, with eyes like his eyes, like twin slashes made in rotting fruit, waiting patiently while they suffered and went right on dying.

As Kasteel maneuvered among them she whimpered a word, perhaps "Calico…" Sounded like she was calling out to a boyfriend, maybe admonishing him.

"Who's that?" he asked. "Keep talking to me. Who's Calico?"

"Cal…"

"Is he the one who left you?"

"*Cal…!*"

Her body thrashed as she convulsed again. Kasteel started shouting, his tight voice full of centuries of dust, the decimated mortar of the Castle, the cremations in the morgue, the destroyed biological hazards, the dirt scrubbed from the nails of the surgeons after playing the back nine. He shouted and the sound of him raised a wave of noise from the others, tired of sitting, tired of staving off death, tired of following rules. They shouldered their way to the registration desk and started demanding to see a doctor. The fat nurses formed a line, and so did the patients. The lights flashed red out at the curb and the ambulances kept coming in and going out.

By the time he got her onto a free gurney she was barely breathing. The stink of sex and urine wafted through the hall. He kept her mouth clear and muttered to her words of encouragement that he hoped would keep her conscious. Her pitted face began to twitch. Her eyes opened and rolled. Her lips framed the word or name Calico again. Two attendants shoved him aside and wheeled her away while a stern supervisor from Admin asked him for the girl's name and insurance information. He said he didn't know.

Admin didn't like hearing that. Admin needed insurance information.

They could skip your name and address and whether you were allergic to penicillin, but they had to have insurance info. He'd been run up and down the wall by the financial department. His insurance was good. He'd paid extra into it. He figured the way things had gone for him in the world he was as likely to catch a bullet in the back as lung cancer. He'd watched his old man die a long horrible death from lung cancer, the docs taking small pieces of him for months and months until the man was hardly recognizable anymore. Kasteel had been fifteen when the man died. He never should have started smoking. But he did. It was one of his better vices, when you looked at them all together.

He had first-rate insurance, for first-rate machinery, and first-rate care for his boy, but in the end it would've been kinder if the kid hadn't been hooked up to the tubes and ventilators and dialysis and everything else. The boy so weak at the end he couldn't eat, couldn't breathe, couldn't use the bathroom, couldn't speak, couldn't hold his head up, couldn't die.

Admin asked again. "Her insurance?"

"I don't know."

"Your relation to the patient?"

"There is none. I found her on the curb."

"Your name?"

Even check-in had a long line. He watched a hangdog family of five, all of them sick and sullen, the kids not even whining, just wheezing, eyes red and spinning. Each of them waiting their turn, bleeding onto the floor, hacking up virus, swallowing pain.

Admin didn't bother to raise her chin. It was easier for her not to look.

"Your name, sir?" she asked again.

His name, like his son and his marriage and his freedom, had somehow slipped away from him. He didn't remember the old name anymore.

He said, "Kasteel."

She wrote it down, typed it into the computer, and handed him a clipboard without meeting his eyes. She underlined the insurance box with a red pen. "Please fill out this paperwork, including insurance information. When you're done, return it to me. Someone will see you shortly."

"But I don't need a doctor."

"You need a doctor, sir."

He took a half-hearted stab at the paperwork for both the girl and himself, handed the clipboard back to Admin and sat down among the others.

It took five hours. Not bad for the Castle.

The doctor was young, under thirty, with short hair sculpted into place with double handfuls of mousse. Lively brown eyes, a vivid smile, a lot of energy in his face. One of the few ER doctors who could actually interact with you like you were still alive and not already on your way to the morgue. His name was Burroughs. He'd been on duty the night that Eddie was brought in. He didn't recognize Kasteel.

He had a good manner, friendly but not happy, the way some of them get; loud, incessant, beaming, guffawing, telling jokes and talking about Saturday night with the nurses while some kid bleeding from his ears moaned just a few feet away.

Burroughs flashed a penlight in Kasteel's eyes checking for a concussion. He spotted all the meds in there but didn't say anything about them. Kasteel said, "What about the girl?"

"What girl?"

"The girl I brought in. She was left in front of the ER, maybe twenty, looked like she was OD'ing on meth."

"She's stable and resting."

Kasteel just nodded. Sometimes the machinery and the meds and the specialists couldn't do a damn thing, and then there were times when somehow it came out all right. "When you transfer her, move her to Ward Nine. Not Eight."

"Why would you say that?" Burroughs asked.

Kasteel didn't answer. He sat there while Burroughs continued to examine him, noting the billy club bruises, the old knife scars, gunshot grazes, razor slashes, his history written in his flesh.

"Looks like a pretty bad brawl," Burroughs said. "Who'd you have it with?"

"Two assholes."

"Have you reported it to the police?"

"No."

"You need x-rays to makes sure your lung hasn't been punctured. You're breathing heavily and if the lining of the lung has been breached, it could deflate."

An intern wheeled him over to x-ray, where they took a full set of his chest. Then they wheeled him back down again. Burroughs had already moved on to an old Asian lady who was yelling at him in without any accent. She was explaining about the benefits of caterpillar juice. Burroughs listened attentively, the same way he had when Kasteel had carried Eddie in four months ago, his dark eyes utterly focused on the moment. He spoke quickly and sharply, but he was all there, right with you, without any distractions. He wrote out a scrip for the Chinese woman and then turned back to Kasteel.

He checked the results of the x-rays and pursed his lips. "Hairline cracks in four ribs, but at least your lung hasn't been perforated. What are you on?"

Kasteel gave it his best guess. "Prozac, Xanax, Codeine, zinc, assorted vitamins, and Vicodin."

"Are you under a personal doctor's care?"

"What do you think?"

"I think not," he said. "You're malnourished. You need to eat more and eat better. You already know you're suffering from vitamin deficiencies. Pills won't be enough, you need to eat good food. I'm going to tape you up and you probably won't feel much where those bad ribs are concerned, but when the meds wear off you're going to be in a lot of pain."

Burroughs taped him up and he didn't feel much of anything. Then he heard another doc somewhere, one of the loud guffawing ones, and a nurse answering the call like some exotic animal in the brush, squealing, screeching, a laugh that went through your head like the cry of a beast caught in a trap.

"Why aren't you eating or spending any time outdoors?" Burroughs asked.

"Been busy the last few months."

"You work at home?"

"More or less."

"You still need to eat right, get a proper amount of sleep, and spend time out in the fresh air."

"I'll try harder."

The doc stared at Kasteel, going deep, and Kasteel looked back and saw the face of the man who had saved his gasping son's life that first night, the beginning of the end. Kasteel remained impressed with him, but also stabbed by awful memories, Eddie fighting for air, Kasteel holding his boy in his arms, Kathy ahead of them and shoving her way into the ER, Admin asking about insurance. Burroughs coming out, asking questions, Kasteel answering them one after the other, Burroughs shouting to interns, calling out code words and asking for 50ccs of one thing or the other. Eddie terrified but not crying, the kid tough, not wanting to let Kasteel down, not wanting to disappoint.

"I'm not going to give you any scrips without doing blood work first. But I am going to give you three shots of vitamin supplements. It'll help when you come down off the tranqs. And I want you to come down off the tranqs."

"I hear you, doc."

"Do more than hear me. Listen to me."

"Right."

Burroughs had Kasteel drop his pants and Kasteel took the shot in the meaty part of his thigh, almost the same spot where he'd been stabbed with a sharpened toothbrush shank in Sing. In a minute he felt sharper, more present, and alert, everything he didn't want to be.

"Thanks," Kasteel said. Then added, "Remember what I said about the girl and Ward Eight."

He hopped off the examining table and turned his back. He had to get strong again. He knew it. He had to start stealing more food from the cafeteria. He needed to put muscle back on. He needed to keep guys like Conrad and Watkins off his back. He needed to be able to carry twenty-year-old junkie girls over his shoulder.

As he was leaving he passed a cubicle where the privacy drapes were slightly parted. A blonde-headed boy of about ten was sitting up on the table, kicking his heels against the metal side, bored and edgy and scared. The metal drumming, thump, thump, thump, a slow and steady beat. Kasteel's pulse fell in sync with the pounding. The kid's face was white with pain but expressionless except for a shadowed puzzlement in his eyes. The barest hint of a question furrowed his brow.

He was shirtless, well-muscled for a child. His right arm had been pulled from the socket. The intern was having trouble popping it back in, but all of his jostling and pushing just made the boy sweat harder and grow paler. His chest was slathered. His forearm was swollen badly, probably fractured. No matter what they'd given him for the pain it wouldn't be enough. Kasteel could hear bone scraping bone as the boy's shoulder finally snapped back into place. The kid grunted and hissed through his teeth. He handled pain well.

He had almost outgrown four or five faint burn scars on his belly and chest. They were perfectly round, about the size of a quarter. They were from a cigar.

The kid's mother stood beside him and ran her hand through his hair in a kind of nervous tic, the way Hedgwick did it. She looked like she might pass out. She looked like it was her arm that had been jerked so hard it had popped out. Her heavily painted face was in tatters. Her incessant silent tears had washed enough of her foundation away to show abrasions beneath. Without the make-up and the bruises and the cut lip and the swollen jaw she would be pretty.

The kid stared into space. His eyes had narrowed. He was full of rage but it hadn't begun to eat him alive yet. There was still time to save him.

Burroughs would have caught it. Burroughs would've called the cops. Burroughs would have said something to them. The intern was new, fresh, and unsure of what to do about anything that fell outside his direct job description. Maybe he didn't notice. Maybe he was at the end of a twelve hour shift and just wanted to sleep.

Kasteel walked out of the emergency room and through the front automatic doors. He scanned the front parking lot until he found a Coup de Ville with MD tags illegally parked in a handicapped space.

He had his leather case of burglar's tools inside the dead man's jacket pocket and got the car door open with a slim jim in eight seconds. The alarm bleated once before he snipped the wires beneath the dash. Then he got comfortable behind the wheel, lit a cigarette, watched the ER doors, and waited in the darkness, starting to feel alive.

«««—»»»

A half hour later the woman and her son stepped outside and proceeded across the lot. The kid had a cast on his forearm and wore a sling. When they were out of expanse of the bright lights of the ER entrance she began to stagger and then started to sob. She slowly fell to her knees in front of the boy and pulled him to her gently. He placed the side of his face against hers but his eyes were still empty except for the hate. Kasteel lit another cigarette.

They got into a five-year-old Chevy Malibu. The car had been in a lot of recent fender benders and scrapes, but no major accidents. The signs of road rage driving, nervous driving, too many with the fellas from work driving, rushing off in the middle of a rainy night driving.

He followed close behind. There was no need to stay back four car lengths or keep to a different lane, the way he might've shadowed another heister to see if the guy was worth working with on the next job.

He kept right on them as they moved through town. She drove slowly, with trepidation, and didn't run any yellow lights. She drove like she was heading towards her own execution. The passenger seat was too high for Kasteel to see the boy, but he could imagine the kid sitting staunchly, that same anger building in him, the same question tearing at him. It would be there for the rest of his life, through years of therapy and liquor and all his shattered relationships. It would be there when he had his own son. It might destroy him or it might make him a better man in the end.

When they came to a neighborhood in a new development, near a lake, near a park, near everything that helped to make you a happy family, she stopped dead in the middle of the road, gathering herself to continue on. Kasteel dimmed his lights and pulled over to the curb. He watched her as she thought about turning around and running. He knew what was going through her head. He knew what kinds of fantasies spun through your mind when you were faced with a moment of truth.

She tugged the wheel a little too hard to the right and the Chevy angled awkwardly and blocked the road. She started to go into a three-point turn but she was so anxious it turned into a five-point, and then a seven-point, and then she backed up so fast she nearly ran into some garbage cans stacked on the sidewalk and almost took out the front quarter panel of the Coupe. The boy laid the side of his head against the window. His cast and sling were bright white in the darkness of the Chevy.

She continued to turn, nine-point, twelve-point, until she'd completed a 360 degree turn and was again faced the same way she had been when she entered the street. She seemed to think there was no escape, and of course, there wasn't. She tipped down again towards the boy. The kid leaned into her. Kasteel watched it all ahead of him, backlit by dashboard light. They were preparing themselves to meet the enemy.

He didn't blame her at all. He knew what it was like to be cornered, surrounded, to have nowhere to run. You couldn't do anything except put your hands over your head and wait there for them to either kick the shit out of you or, rarely, to show just a touch of mercy.

Finally she straightened out and coaxed the gas, headed home again. A spasm of anxiety must've worked down through her leg because the car jumped, slowed, and jumped again as if she couldn't hold her foot firmly down on the pedal.

Kasteel pulled away from the curb and began to follow again. He could imagine the husband telling his friends that his wife was a shit driver. Kasteel could see her smiling embarrassedly at barbecues and coffee klatches, assuming that she went out anymore, if he allowed her to have friends anymore. Kasteel could see him grinning at her, a world of agony hidden in his charm, pinching her chin, maybe giving her smooches, everybody else thinking, *what a perfect couple, but she's so quiet, so shy, and that kid, that kid always falling down, tripping, uncoordinated, hurting himself.*

The woman pulled in to a new house on a new street in the new development, only a few saplings in the yard, no mature landscaping but lots of flowers bordering the split-rail fence and in front of the small porch. The garage door opened and she pulled in, and she and the kid got out of the car and held each other there for a second in the dim garage lighting. Then the door came down again.

Kasteel parked two houses down on the opposite side of the clean, wide street. All the houses were different but they all seemed the same. Their details appeared to be fluid. He saw them merging and flowing one into the next, like the corridors of the Castle.

He climbed out and crossed the lawn and looked through the front window. The woman was standing in the living room staring flatly at her husband. He was smaller than Kasteel was expecting. Maybe that was a part of it. Short guy syndrome, always had to be right, always had to be up in other people's faces, stewing, stubborn, a resentful little fucker. In prison they were the cutters, the knifers, the stickers. They'd run up and stab someone in the hip two or three times and then run off again. You couldn't just worry about the big bruisers, the bubbas and the giant Aryan skinheads you could see coming from halfway down the cellblock, you had to keep an eye out for those five foot nothing pricks with their hands cupped at their sides.

There were fresh flowers on the kitchen table. He guessed there would be a new toy in the boy's room, something the kid wouldn't even be able to play with because of the broken arm. A new baseball glove, a football, a hockey stick. Something sports-related, probably because the father had always been puny, last chosen for a team at recess. The kid's eyes were rolling with pain and shock. His body practically vibrated like a plucked violin string.

The husband was talking. Kasteel could tell from the guy's body language that the little prick was quickly overcoming his guilt and the anger was already reasserting itself. He touched the kid's head and patted him like he was the family dog. He turned and pointed at the woman, emphasizing certain statements by poking the air. Eventually he would poke her in the guts and in the chest, and then he would pinch and shove and punch. Kasteel could see it as clearly as any score he'd ever planned in his life.

The swinging metal gate at the side of the house slid open smoothly as he slipped past. Laid out on a tarp beside a charcoal barbecue were parts to the exhaust system of a '68 Chevy Nova. His old man used to leave scattered car parts around the yard like this in the garage, on the patio, on the side of the house. His mother was always shouting for somebody to clean the place up. She'd find a half-finished carburetor in the laundry room.

They'd rebuild the cars together and sell them to the racers who met down at the abandoned airport strip. Kasteel was twelve or thirteen, just starting to get into a little trouble, and he'd watch the dragsters flying down the ocean parkways hitting triple digits in 8.8 seconds. His father was always paid in fat wedges of cash. Later, when Kasteel was a driver, a wheelman, he'd be sitting outside of a bank and think of his father and the racers who bought his cars, and hear his mother yelling about the greasy hand prints.

He checked the back door. No alarm system, no deadbolt. He tried the knob. The door was loose in the frame but the lock held. He slipped out his tools and gave himself a countdown of twenty seconds to get through. It took fifteen. He stepped into the house and could feel the tension and bad blood history soaked into the walls.

A pile of mail was on the kitchen table. They were mostly unpaid bills for a Brace Clarke. Kasteel didn't find anything with the woman's name on it.

He felt a flutter of sympathy for the short shit. Bill collectors, the IRS, the endless calls from the credit card agencies, the mortgage company, it could bend you, kill you from the inside, chase you out of your own head. It could make you do a lot of things. It couldn't make you hit your wife. It couldn't make you break the bones of your own boy.

He chewed the name over. Brace. It tasted sour in his mouth. It offended him.

There was no beer in the fridge. Whatever Brace's action was it wasn't too many 40s after work. Kasteel drank half a carton of juice then sat at the kitchen table and listened to Brace Clarke murmuring apologies to his wife. The deep anger underlined all his words, the hate tinged everything he said. It was too much a part of him. It would be there no matter what he said or how he tried to say it. His inflection changed a bit every time he prodded the woman to stress significance.

Kasteel craned his neck and caught a glimpse of her. She looked like a soldier readying herself for a suicide mission. She was too demoralized and detached to even respond to Brace, which only fueled his further contempt.

His voice rose. A plaintive whine worked through it, laced with a hint of hysteria. "What, don't you believe me? I told you, it was the last time, Beth. I'll never do it again. Christ, why can't you believe me? Why can't you show a little faith in me? John believes me. Don't you, John?"

The rage had quickly built up in him again. His ragged breathing filled the house. He couldn't stay in the same spot any longer and started to stomp across the living room, his small feet making the bric-a-brac on the shelves shake. Pictures fell. Candles tipped out of their holders, rolled, and hit the floor. Kasteel heard a repetitive sound like the fine whisper of a hand brushing silk and knew instantly what it was. Brace Clarke was now stroking his son's head.

"I'm going to give him a bath," Beth Clarke said. "And put him to bed."

"I'm not finished yet."

"Finished with what?"

"Speaking to my son."

"John's tired. He's in pain. He needs to rest and heal."

"He needs to listen. He needs to learn."

"You've taught him enough already."

More murmured apologies, this time spoken with a more exacting harshness, icy, slick. He was digging in, finding his comfort zone, the guilt leaving him, his conscience chipping off like shale. No one could hurt him, not even himself. The constant sweep of his hand moving through the boy's hair underscored his buzzing chatter, a deep growl growing in his timbre. The kid kept silent.

Soon there was the rasping sound of wet pecks made by someone who didn't know how to kiss. Kasteel stood back in shadow and checked the living room. The boy hadn't moved an inch, as immutable as stone while his old man held and kissed his cheek. He waited like Isaac for his father to slay him.

Kasteel finished off the orange juice and set the empty carton aside. He found a vegetable medley platter in the fridge with dip and ate it silently while the pressure built within the house. A barometer would be going crazy now, as if a hurricane were about to engulf the place. Kasteel kept eating, feeling a little of the old strength coming back. He opened some bottled water, wet a kitchen towel, and washed his face. As he pressed the cold damp cloth to his eyes he flashed on Kathy tending to his wounds. Stitching up his cuts and burns and grazes, setting his broken fingers, giving him a sponge bath when he couldn't get out of bed.

Finally Brace Clarke was through. He released the kid. Beth was grinding her back teeth together so hard that it sounded like an Apache sharpening a stone dagger. Brace kissed the boy again, sloppy, skeevy, then gave him a swat on the ass. Kasteel wondered if something more than rage was happening here.

"Goodnight, munchkin. I love you."

John didn't seem to know which way to go. His mother took his hand

and led him upstairs. She was still grinding her teeth. Kasteel imagined her molars worn down to nubs, the dentist lecturing her about wearing a night guard. A door shut heavily. A lock was engaged. A moment later, the rumbling groan of rushing water filled the home.

Kasteel stepped out of the kitchen and faced Brace Clarke.

Up close he was a dashing little fucker. Kasteel could see why she'd fallen for him. Strong features with blunted edges, brash blue eyes, boy next door looks. Blonde locks falling perfectly across his forehead, tips of his bangs in his eyes so he could give a little wag of the head and they'd flip so cutely. A couple of old battle wounds, a tiny scar at one at the corner of his mouth, another angling from the corner of his eye, the kind of scars that made women purr. Not like Kasteel's.

He spoke quietly. "Hello, Brace. Let's talk."

«««—»»»

Brace Clarke reared away like a mad dog had snapped at him from the dark. The back of his knees hit the coffee table and he almost went over. He kept his balance and stood there wondering if he should put his hands up, if he should run, if he should cry out to his wife.

"Who the hell are you?"

"Someone who knows the truth about you."

Brace frowned, flipped his curls. "What does that mean?"

"You know what that means."

"Get out. You get out of my house before I call the cops."

He went for his cell and drew it from his pocket. Kasteel snatched it from him. Kasteel wasn't the same man he once was, but he still had fast hands.

"What do you want?"

"Just to talk."

"How did you get in here?"

Kasteel grinned at him. "I don't like your voice."

He shifted his stance and squared his shoulders. He could feel his own eyes growing amused. The pain meds were wearing off but the vitamins and the juice and the veggie platter, all that healthy shit, oxygen, sugar, was rushing through his system. It was like he was back in the yard, aware of everything, afraid of everything and nothing, not wanting trouble but willing to kill if he had to.

Brace sneered. "You fucking her? Is that what this is?" he hissed. "You are, aren't you. Or you want to, you stinking bastard. Is that her smell on you?"

"Don't you know?"

"It is. I know it is."

Brace charged and threw a wild left. Kasteel blocked it easily and chopped him lightly across the throat, sick of that voice, wondering how the woman could have stood it this long, how the boy hadn't shot up a school or jumped off a cliff. A voice like that, hissing, seething, full of venom, could sear you like a face full of kerosene. Brace was sent to his knees. He gagged and hacked and glared. His hate mutilated his features. He showed no fear. His eyes were clear. Brace didn't go in for an indulgence of prescription or recreational drugs. He took a six-count and then threw himself at Kasteel again.

Short guy, and untrained, but with some muscle to him, and a lot of heat. He lashed out and caught Kasteel's bad ribs. Kasteel didn't make a sound but his expression must've shown his pain because Brace went to work on the area. It hurt. Brace threw a lot of short jabs, worked his advantage and started in with tight hooks. More jabs to Kasteel's face. Little prick threw about twenty unanswered shots. It hurt, but it was part of the plan.

Kasteel knew about giving a beating and taking one. You could fight through the pain once you knew how it was easy. You could even learn to like it. The real beating went on inside. When despair set in, when you were cut off from your reserves. Kasteel let Brace keep working away, and then backhanded the short fucker hard enough to split his smoochy lips. Kasteel liked the balance of it, how Brace was now a mirror of his wife. Kasteel moved in and did it again. Brace's eyes flared. There was nothing quite as denigrating as being struck with a backhand. It's the way your old man hit you when you were a kid. The humiliation was genetic, and it went back ten thousand generations.

"That ugly voice of yours has to go, Brace," Kasteel said, his own voice still a little gritty. "Swallow red-hot embers. Suck giant black dick. But get rid of it." Kasteel punched him almost gently in the Adam's apple. Brace thrashed and choked, fell back on the couch, and turned a nice shade of purple. The running water shut off. Kasteel waited until the guy had caught enough breath that he could hear what was about to be said.

He crouched, got in close, let him check out what ugly, real scars looked like. "You've got stress in your life, Brace, I understand that. Frustrations, disappointments, defeats. You've got issues. We all do. Maybe the worst of them has to do with your job. You haven't made your quota lately. You've missed out on a couple of promotions you deserved. You've got a tall boss who smirks at anyone under 5'7", something like that. Maybe your old man used to smack you around. Mom didn't give you enough tit when you were a baby. You've got problems with intimacy. You're impotent. A closet fag."

Count on that to get under his skin. Brace grunted and made a jump. Kasteel slammed the flat of his palm under Brace's chin and enjoyed the hard crack of his jaws slamming together. Brace let loose with a strangled yelp and fell onto the floor.

Kasteel stared down at him.

"Or your older brother died in front of your eyes, run over in the middle of the street during a stickball game. Maybe you got gang-raped by your high school basketball team. Hey, these things happen."

And they did. Kasteel reached down and took hold of the little prick's shoulder and patted his back, the way a proud father does to his son, the way a friend lends support. Brace's eyes spun and hardened. His mouth leaked blood from both corners.

"But listen to this, Brace. I don't care. *Nobody cares*. Not your co-workers, not your neighbors, not your wife or your kid. We don't care.

You haven't been able to live with it, whatever it is. Okay, fair enough, some of us have too great a burden. Some of us can't carry the load. We're tired. We're broken. We're ruined, we're wrecked."

Kasteel hefted Brace to his feet, grabbed him by the scruff, and tossed him over the couch and almost through the front window. Brace managed a short scream of fear and pain, a weird warble almost like a newborn's gasping cry. A vase of flowers smashed and pink petals floated into his hair. Kasteel wanted to keep this quiet but the vitamin shots had made him edgy too. He hadn't spoken this much to anyone besides Hedgwick in months.

The bathroom door opened slowly, tentatively. The groaning sucking swirling glucking sounds of a bathtub draining made their way downstairs. Beth was probably up there with her ear turned to listen. Maybe she thought Bruce was going nuts, throwing things. Maybe she heard Kasteel's voice and wondered if he was another enemy or a potential savior. He wanted to call to her, to tell her it was all right, but she wouldn't trust him. She'd have to make the decision from there, in moderate safety.

Kasteel stepped on Brace's chest and exerted a little pressure, just to keep his attention.

"So this is what you do. You go find yourself a competent shrink. Or a priest or a rabbi or a fucking Buddhist monk who'll listen to you. Or you can start self-medicating. You throw back a couple of six-packs a night. You pop percs, you steal scrips for vikes. You fall asleep in the gutter covered in your vomit. You pick up a hundred dollar a day coke habit. You kick back with a crack pipe. You let meth rot out your teeth while you pick your face apart. You pay whores who'll let you smack them around. You become a barroom brawler. You go find yourself a twink boyfriend."

Kasteel stepped on him harder.

"I don't care what you do, so long as you resolve yourself. You never lift a hand against your wife or boy again."

His lips moved slightly. Kasteel could see exactly what the prick was saying. He knew Brace was telling him to go fuck himself. Brace was someone who had to learn all his lessons the hard way, and no one harder than him had come along for the last little while. Not until now. But Kasteel didn't want to have to do any real damage. He didn't want to sell what was left of his soul. But it looked like it might have to go that way.

"I hate your voice, Brace, but I need a response here. Do you think you can resolve yourself or not?"

The little fucker's tongue jutted and flapped. It seemed like he might jump up and have another go, no matter how stupid that might be. Brace just wasn't listening. He wasn't hearing the message. Sometimes a man couldn't learn. He took it to the wall and then right through the rock. Kasteel had known a lot of guys like him before. He might even be like Brace himself in some ways; incapable of change, incapable of living with some trauma, great or small, that had come to define his life.

Brace's gaze diverted. Kasteel glanced up and she was halfway down the stairs, watching expressionless, watching them. John stood beside her wearing fresh pajamas, his hair wet, wearing his sling. Eddie never could dry his hair either, it seemed impossible for any kid to do a good job. It used to drive Kathy berserk. She'd go and do it for him, rubbing his hair down with a towel, taking her time to comb through his shaggy tow-head. It would look perfect for about ten seconds and then it would be a mess again. The symbols of our lives find us wherever we are, wherever we go.

Kasteel met Beth's eyes. She continued to wait and watch. She wasn't going to scream and come running at him with a frying pan. She wasn't going to wrap her arms around her husband and declare her mad love for him. Everyone knew that it sometimes went down like that. No matter how badly they were treated, the devil they knew was almost always better than starting over again. You saw it happen every day. He was glad it wasn't going to happen now.

Brace glared at her. He still thought maybe she was screwing around. He thought maybe she'd let Kasteel in to do some damage. He tried speaking. "*Beth, what have you done*?"

His voice was hardly there but what was there was pure rage. Kasteel wondered where these kinds of guys found the energy. Being that pissed for that long was wearing. You had to be aware in the yard but always seething, always wanting to hurt somebody, it took a lot out of these guys. They burned up over the years until there was hardly anything left in the end.

"I'm going to put you out now, Brace, while we decide your fate. You'll either wake up and have a limp for the rest of your life or you won't wake up at all."

With that Kasteel stomped his forehead and put the little fucker down in the black.

«««—»»»

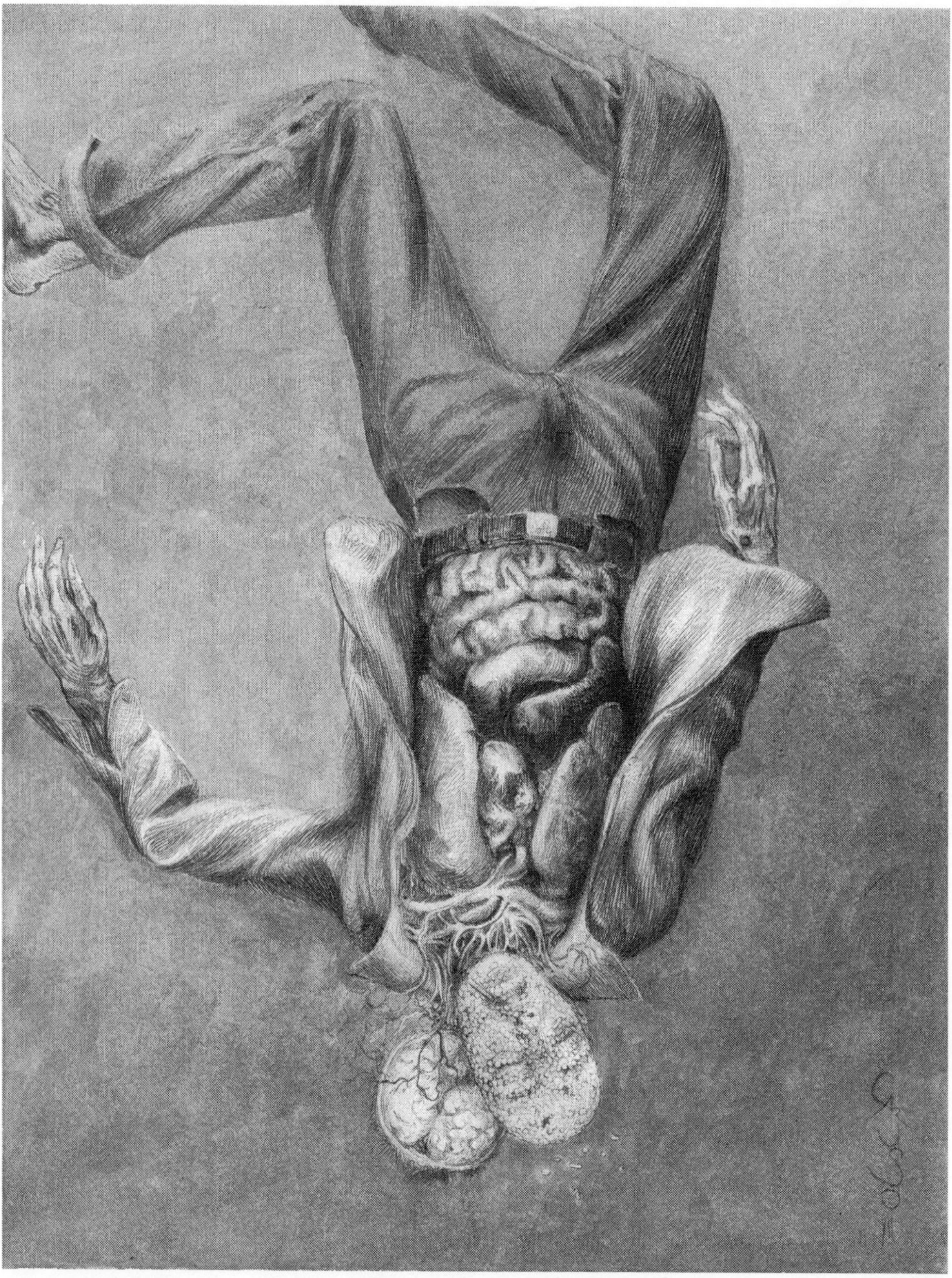

Kasteel hadn't wanted the kid to see that, even though it might be good for him. It wasn't Kasteel's call to make. The woman didn't pull her son's face against her skirt. Kasteel waited for her to say something, ask a question, show some upset, but she didn't bother. She braced herself for whatever might happen next. She was strong. She had to be strong.

The boy looked at his father and then his mother and then at Kasteel. He put his free hand to his cast and scratched at it like he didn't even realize it was there.

Kasteel still hadn't heard the kid speak and suddenly it felt imperative to do exactly that. He had to hear the boy. He wondered if he'd sound anything like Eddie. He wondered if he'd ever see another kid in this world that wouldn't remind him of Eddie. It was one of the things that had spooked the lady shrink. She had a couple kids herself, a boy and a girl, their photos framed on her desk, pointed outward. Why outward? Showing them off to the clients? Hoping to incite feelings, discover dysfunction? It had worked. Kasteel had looked at her boy and asked question after question, thinking of Eddie, until Kathy tugged at his wrist to get him to shut up and the shrink turned the pictures back and eventually put them in her drawer.

"What's your name?" Kasteel asked him.

John didn't respond. And he was a John, not a Johnny, not a JJ or a Jimmy John or a Jackie John. He was a John. Though maybe he wasn't sure about that himself. He seemed to have forgotten his name, or perhaps to have never known it.

"That's okay," Kasteel told him. "Names are overrated. I've had a lot of them. Now I don't have any."

Beth didn't seem to take that to heart, or understand what he meant. She asked, "Who are you?"

Like everybody's, his life had been full of shortcut answers to that question. You tried to compact your response. Nobody had patience for more than a few words. You said, I'm the best two-story man in the tri-state area, which was probably true, or almost true. You said, Prisoner #768259, sir. You choked out, when they asked, I'm a reformed felon.

I'm a husband. I'm a father. You took a knee at your old man's headstone and said, I'm a fuck-up, dad.

He cut through it all and simply responded, "I lost my son. I won't let you lose yours."

Her face began to crimp and fall in on itself as a moan broke from her. She stifled it almost instantly. She put an arm around John and he barely noticed.

"He's already lost."

"There's a chance you can save him."

"Is there?"

"Maybe."

She gestured at her husband. "Are you going to kill him?"

He stared at her. "Do you think I should?"

"I don't know."

"Think carefully."

"Does he owe you money?"

"No."

"Did he do something to you?"

"No."

"Then—"

"I told you already. I'm here for you and John."

At the sound of his name the kid seemed to snap from his trance. He blinked a few times, and yawned, and reached up and touched his wet hair. He looked down at his father and seemed to consider the question.

Are you going to kill him?

You'd think there might be finality to it, but there wasn't. The question and the answer and the action, whatever that action turned out to be, would go on and on forever. The consequences would ripple out across the world and down through your life forever. Kasteel knew it. So did the mother. So did the boy.

Brace lay there unconscious, the fury gone from his face, handsome, snoring softly. Conscience only counts for so much. Fear of prison even less. She cocked her chin as she considered it. He watched her weighing the extent of her own moral imperative. She clenched and unclenched her hands.

"He's going to be worse after this," she said. "A strange man in the house that beats him up? He'll think we're lovers."

"He already made that presumption."

"He's never trusted me, not even when I loved him."

"Some guys are wired wrong."

"Are you?" she asked.

"Yes."

"Did you ever hit your wife or boy?"

"No."

"Then you're not wired wrong."

"Yes, I am. Just not in that way."

"He's going to be worse," she repeated.

"Maybe he won't be. Maybe he'll learn a lesson and come back to his senses. He might change."

"Is anyone capable of real change?"

The easy answer was yes. People changed all the time, for the worse. They got weaker, they got crazier, they got more broken. Kasteel thought about a few guys in the joint who'd managed to turn their lives around. Animals who'd managed to educate themselves behind bars, learn a bit of compassion, find God and their own humanity. He could count them on one hand, but they existed. It seemed possible.

"Would you really kill him if I asked you?" she asked.

"Maybe."

She nodded, thought further on it, her hands squeezing tighter like she was struggling to hold on but was slipping. She glanced at her son. The kid glanced back. He looked at Kasteel, his eyes like you were staring into miles and miles of night.

"I want to watch you hurt him," she said.

"Okay."

Kasteel propped Brace's leg up on the coffee table and then dropped on top of it. The knee snapped and the leg bent back in the wrong direction. He'd limp forever. He'd be in the hospital for months. He'd be in rehab for at least a year. If he wasn't going to change for the better anytime soon, then maybe at the end of the year he'd be a better man.

The agony woke Brace up and he shrieked like a spoiled girl, threw up on himself, and passed out again. The scream had reached into his son and shaken him up a little. The kid looked angrily at his father. Kasteel liked the fire in the kid's eyes. It also reminded him of Eddie when Eddie used to get pissed.

She said, "Is it enough?"

"You tell me."

"He might kill us."

"Give me your cell," he told her.

"I don't have one."

"I'll take his."

"Why?"

"Because I need a phone."

Kasteel had snatched Brace's cell from his hand but where had he put it after that? He couldn't remember. He looked around at the mess in the living room, the overturned coffee table, the broken vase, the shit that had fallen off of shelves. He spotted the phone on the carpet, grabbed and pocketed it.

"If you need me," he said, "for anything, just call his number."

"He'll just cancel it."

"Tell him if he does that I'll break his other knee."

Tears welled again and she let out one yawping sob that came from the center of her body and her soul. She bent and put her face to the boy's hair and cried into it. The kid kept his eyes on Kasteel. They had an understanding now. They were partners in this thing. He wanted Kasteel to know he would honor it.

In a few seconds she was done and her face cleared instantly. She was a woman used to keeping her emotions under wraps, tied firmly, cuffed.

She asked, "How did you lose your son?"

He still didn't know the answer to that. He had listened to the doctors for months and hadn't heard anything they said, none of it had made any sense. They changed the story every few days. First it was this, and then something else, and then they thought it had to do with an infection, and then a genetic illness, and then some kind of trouble with his heart, and it went on and on, surgery after surgery, machine after machine, signature after signature, the financial department calling the insurance company, the insurance company hassling him, until Eddie was alive but unable to speak, unable to see, and finally unresponsive, in a coma for weeks, and then in the ground the last ten days, so he was told.

There was no answer but Kasteel still felt like it was somehow his fault. He knew in his heart that he had caused Eddie's death in some unfathomable, unknowable way.

He said, "I made a mistake."

"I've made a lot of them too. Is that why this is happening?"

"Who knows? But it's over now. Pack up and leave or stay and wait to see what happens. Either way, I'm on the other end of this phone if you need me. I'll be close." Kasteel turned to the kid. "You heard what I said, right?"

John didn't answer or respond with any kind of a gesture, but Kasteel knew he'd heard and that he'd call if he ever needed help.

"You need your sleep. You should hit the sack."

Beth led her son upstairs again. John looked back once as if to ensure himself that the scene was real. He'd be living with it in his head for a long time to come.

Kasteel heard a door shut. He got the kitchen towel he'd been using, ran it under the tap again, got a half glass of water, and returned to the living room. He washed Brace's face down until the little prick began to stir and groan. Kasteel pulled out some bottles of meds, mixed several pills together, fed them to Brace and then let him drink the water. He waited until the painkillers kicked in, helped Brace Clarke to his one good leg, and then drew the guy's arm around his shoulder.

"Come on, Brace. I'll take you to the hospital. I'm headed there anyhow."

«««—»»»

He first heard of Abaddon a couple of weeks later from an old woman with a bad brain.

Her name was Merilee Himes, eighty-two years old, skin dark and wrinkled as a prune, with freckles like a spray of pepper shot burned across her cheeks. She was remarkably healthy for her age. Walked to church six miles from her home twice a week, occasionally walked to the VFW to play Bingo, and had an active social life with many friends spread out across the city as well as a gentleman caller. They picnicked in the park, went dancing, visited museums, and sojourned to four separate cemeteries to visit their deceased spouses. They'd each buried two.

Maybe it was inevitable that some piss-poor driver would come along, on their cell or distracted with the kids or just fumbling around the satellite radio for the perfect song.

Turned out to be a seventeen- year- old girl with a fresh license, texting with her boyfriend. She crossed over onto the shoulder while typing out 2 BLOX AWY, SEE U SOON and ran into Merilee Himes, launching her twenty feet into the air and knocking her into oncoming traffic.

The girl proceeded to text HLY FUK, MY DADS GONNA KLL ME!!!!! even as three more cars proceeded to run over Merilee. All told she lost her left arm, both legs below the knee, her spleen, her right orbital socket, several large pieces of her skull, and about a quarter of her brain.

It was all right there in the police report stapled to the inside back jacket of the chart.

It was either a miracle or a very bad joke that Merilee Himes was still alive. Kasteel went back and forth on which he thought it might be.

Merilee Himes had five children and sixteen grandchildren and forty-three great grandchildren. They visited regularly in great big groups although only two visitors were allowed in the ICU patients' rooms at any given time. They left balloons, plants, cards, children's paintings, candy, and plastic containers of food, all of which were strictly prohibited within the confines of ICU. The nurses collected all the gifts and promised to keep these things safe for Merilee until she awoke. Most of it was thrown away immediately, except for the candy, which was spread out among the staff. The doctors and nurses would flirt, share a piece of chocolate, sometimes make out a little or just go fuck in a maintenance closet or a free room somewhere.

Kasteel ate the food brought by Merilee's family when he could get his hands on it. They had a leaning towards the southern spicy, lots of red peppers, mustard seeds, sausages, ribs, jambalaya, gumbo. The nurses would bring it around to their station and leave it on the counter until the janitor came around to take the food, flowers, cards, and everything else away in their garbage pails. Kasteel would get there first when the nurses weren't around, collect the goods, and go share them with Hedgwick and others.

He'd ripped off a razor and shaving cream and had picked up clippers from brain surgery to trim his hair. He'd been taking more vitamins, sunning himself out in the gardens, and hiking on the nature trails around the Castle. He stole better fitting clothes and changed and showered more often. He worked out in the cardio rehab wing, ran the treadmill, used the free weights, did the stairmaster. He'd put on about ten pounds of muscle, getting back into shape.

Kasteel was washing up in Merilee's room. He had the night nurses' schedules memorized. They came around the floor every three hours for a quick peek and to check all the readings on the machines. They did that up until two am, and then didn't come around again until seven. Merilee's ICU room had a little futon on the other side of the room beneath the window. He managed a couple of hours of sleep at a time and stared at the moon and thought of Kathy.

Just as dawn was beginning to break Merilee Himes said, "*Abaddon*."

She hadn't said a word in the three months since the accident. According to her paperwork she had lost enough of her brain that while she wasn't technically brain dead she had forever lost the power of speech. She could dream and might one day wake up in a partially vegetative state, but her neurological functions were so impaired that she'd had no memory of her life, no recognition of family, and might only have the IQ of a three year old with no capacity for relearning.

He waited. Maybe it was just a muscle spasm in her throat, a murmur that meant nothing. He waited and she slowly turned her head in his direction and looked at him with her only eye. With her only hand she motioned to him. Kasteel leaped off the futon and went to her side. She touched the side of his face and repeated the word. "*Abaddon*."

"What's that, Merilee? What are you saying?"

"Abaddon in shadow."

The intensity in her remaining eye made him catch his breath. He listened very closely. She reached out and clasped his hand in a powerful grip that made him wince. Those who were dying but not yet dead often were stronger than hell.

"What's Abaddon?" he asked.

"The angel of death," she whispered. Even though bandages covered her crushed skull and missing eye, he could feel it staring at him. "The destroyer. He's going to kill me tonight."

"No one's going to kill you. You survived the worst of it. Your chart says you've stablized."

"He'll eat my chart and then he'll eat me."

"I won't let him."

"He told me."

"When did he tell you, Merilee?"

"He comes to me in the night."

"I've been here the last three nights. No one else has been here."

"Before that. He came before that."

Kasteel put his hand to the woman's face. He let her feel the strength and speed in his hand. He let her feel his own scars, minor compared to hers, but still a lifetime of them. "I'll stay again tonight. I'll protect you. No one will touch you."

"He'll eat you too. He's already set the plague upon you."

"Plague?"

"He marked you and murdered your firstborn."

His hand tightened on hers. He stared into the staring eye and said, "Why do you say that, Merilee?" She didn't respond, and soon the eye closed. "How do you know that? Tell me how you know that?"

But she was unresponsive again, back in the warmth of coma, where he couldn't reach her. But could Abaddon?

«««—»»»

Kasteel hunted a deviant candy striper named Tracy who was really only volunteering so she could riffle through patients belongings, take camera phone pictures of sleeping men's penises, torture babies, and satisfy her own sadism. She'd stick pins, needles, and forks in comatose patients, take more photos, and post them to her site VEGETABLE STEW. She'd bite newborns on their bare bottoms, wash the wounds with rubbing alcohol, and take photos before the bite mark faded. She ran another site called TEACH THE LITTLE FUX PAIN. She'd pull back the blankets of heavily sedated male patients, take photos, and then post them to TINY DIX & GIANT COX. Sometimes she would fondle them, sometimes she would use vice grips on their testicles.

Looked like about ten of her friends were also playing the game, but none of them at the Castle. A couple were candy stripers elsewhere, doing similar sport with babies and the unresponsive. They had turned it up a notch and seemed to pick up men at truck stop diners. They'd promise sex for cash, take their money, climb up into the cab, get the guy undressed, bite his johnson hard enough to make him bleed, take a photo, and run off.

Anybody could see that was going to end in tragedy soon.

He tumbled to the whole thing when he caught Tracy biting one of the babies. He thought of hurting her then, doing something to her with his own teeth, but he couldn't become that thing. He owed it to his son. He owed it to himself. He owed it to the Castle.

He'd learned a fair amount about tranquilizers and sedatives in his time here. He knew how to give a shot. He'd given himself plenty.

Kasteel followed her for much of the day and caught Tracy alone just after evening visiting hours while she was fucking around with the catheter stuck in a doped up patient's urethra. The guy had prostate cancer and was receiving chemo and radiation treatments. He'd just gone in for surgery and things hadn't gone too well. He was tranqued out and had a morphine drip giving him max doses.

Kasteel entered the room silently while Tracy was under the bed sheets yanking on the tubing and making the poor bastard's johnson dance around like a marionette, taking pictures the whole time. She had a handful of pins that she was going to send down the catheter and directly into his urethra.

Kasteel said, "You play a nasty game, Tracy."

She glared at him, her expression shifting to terror, but only for a second. She had a tight rein over herself, self-reliant, certain of her strength. "And it interests you."

"Only so far as I'm going to shut you and your friends down."

"Who are you?"

"Someone who doesn't like what you do around here."

"I'm a volunteer. I help out."

"You're a perv and a sadist. Bad enough with the needles and the vice grips, but why the babies?"

She was maybe sixteen, blonde, next-door-girl lovely, and could play innocent like nobody's business. She gave him this confused look that was sexy, manipulative, and extremely crazy when you thought about it. Here she was tugging the guy's tubing, pins right there, camera phone in her hand, and she's playing sincere vestal virgin. "I don't know what you're talking about."

"Of course you do. Why bite the babies?"

"I don't bite babies. I love babies. I spend most of my shift on the pediatric ward."

"I know you do. Why bite the babies?"

"You need help."

"You're right. Why bite the babies?"

Kasteel took a step closer just to look into her eyes in the dim lighting, the guy in the bed still snoring, the morphine drip depressing every few minutes.

"I hate them," Tracy said.

"Why?"

"Why? Why? Why are you asking me why?" she asked. "Why does anybody hate the things that they do? Why do I hate them? They're weak. They're stupid. They cry. All they do is cry."

"They smile and laugh sometimes too."

"No, no never."

"They tend to cry when somebody's torturing them."

"They never shut up!"

Her cell was humming and beeping with texts and calls. Kasteel snatched it from her.

"Give me that!" she cried.

"No," he said.

He appraised her. He studied her. She seethed with her brand of cruelty. He was thankful he'd found her so early on in her cruel studies. Another few nights, another week, and men would be ruptured and hemorrhaging to death all over the wing, and row after row of babies would be turning up with SIDS.

He met her eyes again and she whispered, "What are you going to do?"

"Stop you. Punish you."

It made her laugh. It was the kind of laugh that could kill lonely men in cheap motels all over the world. There was a power to it that would allow her to control boys, sway juries, persuade fate. He closed his eyes and could see it all. Even if she'd been caught, her teeth matching the bite marks, the dead children so clearly killed by her, she would never serve time, she would never go to prison, never come under a psychiatrist's care. She was too lovely for that. As were all her friends.

He opened his eyes and stared at her.

She said, "You don't want to hurt me."

"No, I don't."

She took his hand, his powerful scarred hand, his hand that had not been held in weeks since his son had gotten too weak to grip even his finger. Kasteel almost succumbed to the touch. He weakened. He let loose with a noise that was not the noise of a strong man. She moved closer to him and tried to twist herself in his arms, her lips suddenly at his.

"You would never hurt me."

"Take off your clothes," he said.

"That's more like it, tiger."

"You abuse babies," he said as she smiled carnally at him, still holding the tubing, still making the guy's johnson dance around, presenting herself, the luscious face, the tight body, the perky breasts. Kasteel grabbed her by the back of the hair and pulled gently, as if he was dipping her for a long, swooning kiss, and she draped herself in his arms, and popped the top off the syringe and gave her the needle in the neck. She collapsed and her eyes rolled up, and he carried Tracy to the wheelchair he'd stashed in the rest room, and covered her with two blankets, and wheeled her down the corridor to another corridor to another, until they reached the elevators, and he took them down, down, down past the lobby, the parking garages, the sub-levels of the sub-levels, until they reached the morgue. He texted all her friends.

NOW WE'RE IN THE PLACE OF THE DEAD.

«««—»»»

It took him two hours to set everything up, but once the tableau was finished, it was goddamn disgusting.

It looked like a midnight mass from the blackest church ever built. Ten thousand evil prayers had been said there amongst ten thousand burnt offerings. He dumped her out naked onto one of the icy cold trays and pulled corpses from their vaults and laid naked men beside her with their teeth nipping and their dead tongues lapping. It was a desecration but one that would be forgiven. The dead would understand.

Kasteel threw up twice. Not because this was the worst thing he'd ever done, because it wasn't, not by a longshot mile. But because the smell was everything he remembered about Eddie's last days. He hoped Eddie wasn't watching him now. He hoped that Kathy, alone in their home, wasn't suddenly aware of him, the way we have vivid dreams about someone we no longer see or speak to and just can't reach anymore.

He posed them all in an orgy of rotting flesh and pink beautiful youth. They kissed her nipples, they put their blue hands on her intimate places, their penises sought access and entry. When she came around she started to moan and cry. He liked the sound of it, which said more about him than about her. He took fifty photos and put them up across all her websites. He took a lot of video. He threw the blankets back on top of her. He texted all the brutal awful evidence to the other girls playing the game and wrote:

IT STOPS NOW OR YOU'LL GET WORSE THAN THIS.

He meant it.

The dead watched him.

They meant it too.

«««—»»»

He got back to Merilee's room to watch over her while she slept, the way he had promised. And like she had promised him, she was dead.

The night nurses hadn't even responded yet. Merilee had flatlined less than sixty seconds before. The machinery was redlining, whooping, and squealing. Kasteel had to get out of here. He slipped into the IC unit next door, where another geriatric was on a ventilator. He was awake and scared but couldn't talk with the apparatus affixed to his throat. He stared at Kasteel and held his frail hands up in a plea for mercy.

Nurses and a doctor rushed past. Not so rushed, really, just a quick clip. No one is going to try to save an eighty-two- year -old woman with only about half her head left. They charged the defibrillator, said "clear," hit her with the paddles, turned up the voltage, hit her again, and that was that. One nurse stomped out of the room, frowning. Kasteel was certain it was because she wasn't going to get the good candy anymore.

Kasteel turned to the old guy in the bed, who was still lying there like he was going to be mugged. Kasteel said, "Sorry about this, I didn't mean to cause you any upset."

The guy glanced at the nurse's button but thought better than to push it. Kasteel checked the old man's chart.

He was Chester Milgrom, sixty-two, professor of economics at a local second-rate state university, assorted health problems related to heart disease and diabetes. He'd been in a motel room fornicating with a male graduate student when he suffered a heart attack. The graduate student called 911 and when the university caught wind of what was going on, they immediately allowed Chester to resign before the media whirlwind start. Chester told them to go to hell. He needed his insurance now, he wasn't about to quit. The graduate student was twenty-eight years old, not a kid. He went on record stating that he was a consenting adult and happened to love and admire Chester dearly. It was bad form to ever diddle one of your students, but who was going to be hurt by a media blitz? An openly gay sixty-two-year-old man or a failing state college?

"Good for you, Chester," Kasteel said. "You were a dope for picking your boyfriends from your student roster, but at least you didn't roll over for the board."

Chester's expression shifted just a little. Showed a little embarrassment, a little pride, a little love.

"Has he visited you?"

Chester nodded.

"Good. So it was real. A significant relationship."

Chester nodded.

"You're lucky."

Chester nodded.

"You ever hear of somebody called Abaddon? Somebody who wanders around the Castle?"

The old man, eyes wide with puzzlement, shook his head slowly.

"You see anybody visiting Merilee's unit next door who weren't doctors or her family?"

The old man pointed to Kasteel.

"You saw me prowling around. Anybody else? Night before last?"

The old man shook his head.

"I'm going to be back from time to time, just to check on you."

Chester made a motion like he wanted to write something. Kasteel found a pen affixed to the chart. He took out one of the pages, turned it over, and handed the jacket to the old guy.

Chester wrote: PLEASE DON'T COME BACK.

"I'm not going to mug you, Chester."

PARDON ME FOR WRITING THIS, BUT YOU LOOK LIKE BAD NEWS.

"I am, you're right. But really, you think you're going to get any worse news from me than you've already gotten from your surgeons?"

YOU HAVE A POINT.

"Merilee was talking about someone threatening her. She knew she was going to die."

SHE WAS SEVERELY BRAIN DAMAGED.

"I know, but it still makes me wonder."

ARE YOU A PSYCHIATRIC PATIENT?

"No, I'm not," Kasteel admitted, and the acknowledgment felt like a lie. He paused. "But I probably should be." That's all he wanted to say, but listened to the sound of his own voice continuing, still talking, and he was angry with himself that the truth was seeping out. He knew it had something to do with the fact that Chester couldn't speak, wouldn't ask any shrink questions. "My son died a few weeks ago. I'm out of my head with grief. You know why I can tell you I'm out of my head with grief without breaking down and sobbing?"

BECAUSE YOU'RE OUT OF YOUR HEAD WITH GRIEF.

"See, Chester," Kasteel said, letting out a grin. "I knew you'd understand. Keep an eye open. You got a cell phone?"

The old man nodded.

"Here's my number. You call if you get worried about anything or if you see anything weird. Weirder than a guy like me wandering into your room. Text me or just hit 1-1-1. I'll know it's you and I'll come immediately."

«««—»»»

The next morning Kasteel found Hedgwick in radiology, waiting for a chance to sneak behind the X-Ray machine and dose himself. Hedge had a thing about X-Rays. He thought if he studied pictures of the inside of his head long enough maybe he'd figure out what was wrong with him. Some nugget or walnut clearly shown in his brain, so that he could use a spork and just scoop it out and his father's ghost would be gone, and Hedge could get back to living a life on the outside without any spoiled ham sandwiches.

"You're going to give yourself cancer," Kasteel told him.

"I already have cancer. Cancer of the soul. Cancer of my life."

They sat side by side in the small waiting area outside radiology, where patients were stacked up with various tumors and growths and blooming mold inside of them. The joke was that the doctors didn't give a damn about X-Rays anymore. If they saw something or didn't see something they always said that to get a really good look inside of you they needed to send you down for an MRI. After that it was the CT Scan. You had to go to each one, in order, least expensive to most, no matter what was growing inside of you.

"You know what my father says is the worst part of being dead?"

"Please don't tell me it has anything to do with ham sandwiches."

"No, no of course not. Dad says it's the fact that he knows all the answers to all his questions now, the things that haunted him his entire life, the yearning, the craving, the curiosity. All of that has been sated. And he's thankful for that. He's only sorry that he wasted so much time worrying about all those things. He wishes he knew then what he knows now."

"And he knows everything now."

"Basically."

Kasteel tried to imagine if that would be heaven or hell. To get all the answers to all your questions, to know all the things that went wrong, why and where you and the rest of the world went off track, and to finally understand your own humanity, make sense of your own life, only after you were dead.

They continued to sit there, watching the young and the old, the ones who looked healthy and those clearly dying, the cancer kids and the punks who'd busted their arms in the skate parks, coming and going in endlessly. No one paid any attention to Kasteel or Hedge.

"What do you know about someone in the Castle called Abaddon?" Kasteel asked.

Hedgwick was staring at a bald girl of about seven. The kid beaming, the kid radioactive. As she passed, Hedgwick reached out and ran his palm over the tiny knots on her crown. She flinched and turned to glare at him while her mother, also glowering, opened her mouth to say something.

Then she caught a look of Kasteel there, staring calmly at her, his eyes full of pity, commiseration, and condolences for all she was going to have to endure when the kid was dead, and the woman visibly shivered. She grabbed her daughter's hand and tugged her out of the room.

"You've been talking to someone with a bad brain," Hedge said.

"How do you know that?"

"Only people with bad brains talk about Abaddon."

"Don't you have a bad brain?"

"I've got schizophrenia with a tendency toward psychotic breaks, but I wouldn't necessarily call my brain bad."

Kasteel didn't have a response to that. He waited. He let Hedgwick think it over. Hedgwick clearly knew something. Maybe it would help.

"Abaddon always wins the death matches on the wards."

"He a patient?"

"He is and he isn't."

"What do you mean by that?"

"I mean, he's like you."

Someone who shouldn't be here, but who couldn't leave. The hospital wouldn't let him go either. He was another child of the Castle.

"What's he look like?"

"We don't know."

"Why not?"

"We can't remember. None of us on the wards can remember."

"Explain that."

"We can't remember what Abaddon looks like. The same way you can't remember your name."

"I could remember it, if I wanted to."

"But you don't want to. And we don't want to remember what Abaddon looks like. What he does, who he kills."

"Who does he kill?"

"I just told you I can't remember."

"What do you remember?"

Hedge remembered a lot.

"I know that it's a Hebrew word meaning 'destruction' as in a place of destruction and ruin. In the Book of Revelation an angel called Abaddon is shown as king of an army of locusts, translated as 'which in Greek means the Destroyer.' There's an additional note in the Latin Vulgate not present in the Greek text. 'In Latin Exterminans,' with 'exterminans' being the Latin for 'destroyer.'"

"You remember all that."

"I remember weird things."

"Hedge, why would you know all that about Abaddon?"

"I don't know. The Christian scriptures contain the first known depiction of Abaddon as an individual instead of a place. In Revelation 9:11: *And they had a king over them, which is the angel of the bottomless pit, whose name in the Hebrew tongue is Abaddon, but in the Greek tongue hath his name Apollyon.*"

"Appollyon."

"In Revelation 9:7-11. Abaddon is described as '*the angel of the abyss, and king of a plague of locusts that resemble horses with crowned human faces, women's hair, lions' teeth, wings, and the tail of a scorpion.*'"

Kasteel laid his head back and pictured that. He tried to see the thing eating Merilee Himes' chart, and then later on, devouring her.

"I can see why you wouldn't want to remember that."

"Now you have to forget all of this too. Forget Abaddon like you've forgotten yourself."

"I don't think I can," Kasteel said.

"Of course you can," Hedge said. "You have a bad brain too."

«««—»»»

Kasteel stood at the top of the Fool's Tower, blinded by the glare of the setting sun, and phoned Kathy.

She answered without any kind of a greeting. No hello, no nothing, just the silent waiting. He wondered if it was because she knew it was him or if, like him, she'd begun to lose all the usual social conventions in the wake of Eddie's death.

"It's me," Kasteel said.

Still, the silence.

She'd always been stronger than him. Whenever he had floundered on a job or afterwards, while the take was being split and his own men sometimes got edgy and planned to double-cross him, she'd whisper in his ear the heart and truth of the matter. "He's going to betray you. Watch." And he'd have his eyes on the guy when the rip-off was about to go down, the prick about to shoot up the place with a ludicrous, long-barreled .357, and Kasteel would already have his gun in the other guy's face and say, "No. No. Wrong time, wrong score. Rip off your next partner instead, all right?"

She was intuitive, smart, sharp-eyed, and she'd kept him from killing at least a half-dozen guys over the years, just because she knew when something was going to go down, and him always greedy, thinking about the money, counting the money, excited, heated, instead of keeping cool and keeping watch. Him always in the life and always wanting out of the life, so they could move to the suburbs, start a family.

He wondered what kind of shit the shrink was telling her.

The sun dipped beneath the vanishing point, sparking gold and crimson for a last second before dipping away into darkness. With the night came a cold breeze that worked its way across his throat and down his chest and into him.

"Kath?"

"*Why are you still there*?" she asked. "Better yet, why are you calling? If you don't want to come home then why are you reaching out?"

"To—"

"To hear my voice? Because you want me to tell you about Eddie's funeral? What I chose to bury him in. Who attended? What the weather was like? No, you don't want to hear about that. You didn't want to show up. You left me alone." No anger at all, no rage, no chance of tears, still cool, still sharp. "You're still leaving me all alone. I had to make all the arrangements. I have to deal with circumstances. I have to figure things out by myself. I had to stab a guy in the arm the other night. You want to know why? Because he got it into his head that you've been playing low because you pulled a major score. He wanted to grab a piece for himself. So I stabbed his ass. Let him tell his crew about that instead."

He stepped to the edge of the tower, looking down at the gardens where others had suicided, where the ashes of at least a few hundred cholera victims had to be buried. He wondered if he was just waiting for Abaddon or somebody like Abaddon to sneak up behind him and give him a push.

"Stop it," she said. "I know what you're doing. Just stop it. You don't want to die. You don't want to kill yourself. You don't even want to be there, even though you might think you do. You want to come home. You want to come back to me. But you can't, and you don't know why. But I still have some hope you'll be able to figure it out. And when you do you'll come back. Until then, don't bother calling. Don't ask how I'm doing, I'll make out just fine, you know that. Get better. Get strong. Watch your back. Protect yourself. Fight."

"Yes," he said, and hung up.

«««—»»»

While stealing food from the cafeteria Kasteel ran into a contingent of homeless who were living in the stairwells and pilfering what they could from the trash. He helped where he could. He'd cue distractions and sneak meals out to them. It usually went off like clockwork. But there were several children among them who needed regular meals.

Kasteel slipped into the cafeteria to find that one of the mothers had tried to sneak some milk from the big refrigerators at the back of the kitchen. You had to be really fast to steal from those fridges without being seen. She hadn't made it. One of the cooks went batshit and started chasing the woman around with a spatula. A couple of helpful doctors thought to detain the lady and tried to corral her.

Two pulmonary specialists making five mill a year and a fat cook tipping the scales at maybe three-fifty, six-one, squaring off on a twenty-five-year-old young woman with a toddler in her arms, a couple of small boxes of milk in each hand. She wore worn, thin, stained clothes. The kid was a girl wearing a boy's blue jumper. The kid squealed, laughing, as her mother turned and turned again, stepping away, until she was backed into a corner. The rest of the kitchen staff ignored everybody. They were used to this sort of action, the homeless begging, and snatching fruit and sandwiches off the food line.

The girl giggled some more. The woman glanced left and right, stuck in the corner, finally noticing Kasteel there, knowing he was different, and staring at him plaintively. Kasteel stepped in between the two doctors. As he passed them he tapped each of them on the back of the hand with his forefinger. He smiled at the woman, turned and stood in front of her. He told the doctors, "If you don't back off? First thing I do? I'm going to break your thumbs."

The doctors backed away. It wasn't their fight in the first place. Pulmonary specialists getting involved with some poor lady shoplifting. What The fuck business was it of theirs?

The cook put down the spatula and picked up a meat cleaver. Humongous guy, protecting the milk as if he'd been charged this duty by God. He'd sworn solemn oaths before a dozen cardinals, bowed down on his tubby knee, blessed by the Pope, don't let anyone take the milk.

The woman said, "Wait, I'll put them back. Please, I'm sorry."

"Dirty hippies are always desperate," the cook said, facing off against Kasteel, the cleaver swaying. "Get a job then." He flipped the cleaver and caught it by the handle. One of those guys who practiced maneuvers in the kitchen like he was twirling guns, getting ready for a duel. He'd been waiting for a chance to cut somebody, to chop somebody up, to move up from steak and veal and pork ribs. Killer for morality, murderer for God, vicious for middle class America. Everybody just wanted the self-righteous excuse to maul somebody else, to threaten, to scare somebody else the way they'd been scared their entire lives.

"Please, there's no need for this," the woman said.

"I think there is," the cook responded, glowering, waiting, stepping closer. He kept watching Kasteel, thinking him another homeless wreck, which he was in his way, but not their way.

The woman trembling, the baby smiling, the milk being milk and much more than milk, precious as gold in some circumstances. The rest of her clan hiding in the deep corners and dark pockets of the Castle, running, dying, damned. How ironic was it that a kid could be ill from lack of milk in the largest hospital ever built? The Castle had once had its own dairy.

The cook angled the cleaver towards Kasteel and said, "I don't like the look of you."

"You shouldn't. And you shouldn't try to take on women and babies all alone, fatso. You should call security. Get them down here too."

"I already did."

"Good. They sending Conrad and Watkins?"

"You crazy, smelly bastard."

"I've been using the industrial grade cleansers in the shower, fatty. No stink on me."

That doughy face squeezed into a caricature of real fury. "I don't like the way you talk to me."

"I don't blame you. I'm talking mean to you. Put down the cleaver and go make yourself a stuffed chicken. If you see anybody pilfering some milk or juice or salads or maybe a turkey sandwich, look the other way. There's no skin off your fat ass. Show some generosity. Show some kindness. Show a little mercy. Look, I'll show you how."

Kasteel moved. He jumped the cook, who didn't know how to fight or defend himself at all, and gave him three quick, mean hooks in his tubby belly. Kasteel wanted to do more, wanted to hurt the prick more, but he was good to his promise and showed mercy. The guy's face went purple, then white. He clutched the cleaver more tightly to him, fell over backwards, and rolled to a stop against one of the counters. The rest of the kitchen staff finally perked up and took notice.

Kasteel said, “Go back to your work, you lot. And put less vinegar in the tuna.”

The kid went squeeee and the lady moaned. After a moment she said, “I’m sorry. I didn’t mean for any of this to happen.”

“It’s all right,” he told her. “You didn’t do anything wrong. People are in need. The Castle can provide.”

“No no, now security will come looking for us. They…they use their billy clubs, they’re so cruel…”

“They’re not going to find you. Go on, head out the exit there and go back to your group. Do any of you have a cell phone?”

“No.”

“It doesn’t matter. Use one of the hospital phones. There’s hundreds of them all over.” He said his number aloud and made her repeat it back to him until she had it memorized. “Call if you need any help, for anything.”

“I don’t know what to say.”

“Don’t say anything. What’s your name?”

“Mary.”

“And your little girl?”

“Edie.”

Of course it would be Edie. Of course it would be something close to Eddie, so that the grief would hit him again under the heart and make him that much more certain of why he was here, of what he was doing here. Of course the girl would giggle and reach for him, and he would tickle her under the chin and listen to her guffaw. Of course he would escort them to the exit and Mary would kiss him, trying for his cheek as he turned, her moist lips coming together with kindness and no passion on his throat, under the ear, in the same place where, when Kathy kissed him, threw fuel on his fire.

The fat cook was still down. The kitchen staff had backed off, way off to the other side of the kitchen, some of them watching him, some of them cooking, some of them smoking where they clearly couldn't smoke. Everyone broke the rules. The Pope was just gonna have to tell God about the missing milk, send divine signals up his big Pope hat, "*Jesu, sweet Jesu,* some milk got away today." The cook would have to tithe twice as much this month, stick a chicken leg into the collection plate.

Kasteel backed away, headed down the nearest hall, could feel gravitational and tidal forces carrying him closer and closer, as he sped up his step and turned a corner and there stood Conrad and Watkins with their truncheons already in their hands.

They squeezed a little more drama out of the scene, waiting to beat on some people who had already been beaten down as low as they could go, with no money, no house, no future. All they had to offer now was blood, and they'd willingly trade it for the health of their children.

Watkins said, "Hey, look, it's the happy asshole. And he's still happy."

"And he's still an asshole," Conrad said. "And he's still here. Despite our escorting him out."

Kasteel smiled and said, "Yes, I'm still here."

They were a good team. They knew how to work together. They came at him from two sides, staying clear of each other. Kasteel stood his ground, calm, patient, with only a little anger flowing through him, his heart still full of mercy. The two bitter, icy-eyed guards swung at him in short, tight arcs, going for the sweet spots, the stomach and the ribs. Kasteel dodged and slipped fluidly left and right, almost dancing between them, his fast strong hands fast and strong again, the vitamins rushing through him, the sunlight having ignited health, his now tan skin hiding some of the worst scars so that as they moved down the hall fighting, he saw himself in the reflections of room windows, the shining chrome runners. He saw who he was and who he'd been. He saw himself being beaten by these two men, and saw his blood dripping in his beard, and saw how he'd been without purpose, without any provided definition, with nothing to make him feel self-righteous. He was the same now and he was very different.

They eased down toward the labs where they ran the blood work. Doors open, docs drawing test tubes full of blood, checking cholesterol, triglycerides, glycemic indexes. Obese men worried about their hearts, staring down at their own blood and knowing it would kill them, nobody looking up as Kasteel parried Watkins's truncheon, turned and clipped Conrad on the chin, a short nice nasty chopping blow. It made Conrad's eyes tear up, and the tears made him sneeze.

While his body locked Kasteel snatched his billy club and rapped him hard in the back of each thigh. Conrad cried out and hit the floor like he was dying. Watkins was swinging wildly now, trying to catch Kasteel in the temple. Kasteel parried the truncheon easily, jabbed out and hit Watkins twice in the chest.

Both guards were on the floor, groaning and crawling, shouting, "Help us! Somebody! Help us!"

Kasteel threw the billy club down and followed them both inch by inch, saying, "Nobody can hear you. Nobody heard me when you kicked the shit out of me last time. No one except the Castle."

"You crazy bastard!"

"Listen, when some homeless folks nab a little food here and there, just let them have it, all right?"

"Fuck...you...!"

"Be nice now."

"Fuck..."

What's it going hurt? Just turn a blind eye, leave them alone. In fact, reach out, help them some."

"...you!"

"A little cash, a couple of sandwiches. I think that's what you two should do."

They crawled. They got to their knees and Kasteel beat them back down onto their bellies. They crawled. Not much blood, but a few drops here and there, a little slug trail of their sweaty fear following them along. Conrad tried screaming like a girl and Kasteel smacked him in the back of the head. Watkins tried the same thing, the scream full of dread and fear. Kasteel wondered where such terror came from. Two huge, strong men, well-paid, well-honored out in the world, driven to their knees with a couple of punches, the kind of thing they were probably used to from bar fights, fucking around with the boys, playing football. But in the Castle you could either find yourself or lose yourself. These two, they didn't even seem to know their names anymore. He leaned up against a wall and watched them crawl down the hall, ten, twenty, fifty feet, afraid to stand and hold firm. Afraid to stand and run.

His phone made a noise. He answered and heard three beeps.

1-1-1

«««—»»»

Kasteel ran.

The Castle showed deference and respect, perhaps even love, allowing him clear passage. Locked fire doors were already open, corridors seemed to grow shorter. He hurtled through the halls heading for Chester's room, wondering what had gone wrong now, if the old mute man had been threatened by Abaddon the destroying angel as well. Had Chester's chart been eaten last night?

He sprinted past orderlies, kids in wheelchairs, old folks hobbling along, some of Hedge's friends from the wards wearing trash can lids across their chests, brass pots on their heads, waving PVC piping wrapped in foam and duct tape. Few looked up. Those who did didn't appear to see him. It felt to Kasteel like he was moving between worlds, dimensions, teleporting a few feet at a time, through walls, vibrating through the Castle, the Castle vibrating through him.

Kasteel slipped into Chester's unit and found the old man sitting up in bed.

"Chester, are you all right?"

HE WAS HERE.

"Abaddon?"

WHO KNOWS WHAT HIS NAME IS, BUT HE WAS HERE. I

WAS NAPPING AND AWOKE IN SHADOW TO A WHISPER HISSING IN MY EAR. IT SAID IT WOULD EAT ME JUST AS IT WOULD EAT ALL ITS ENEMIES. IT SAID IT WOULD RELEASE ME. IT SAID I SHOULD THANK IT.

"Any idea if it was a man or a woman? Young or old? Ethnic? Anything?"

NO.

"No idea at all?"

NONE.

Kasteel scanned the floor and the rest of the room for signs of intrusion. He stepped around in the unit, glancing here and there, studying it, looking, searching. He found nothing.

"A friend of mine said Abaddon was someone whose face couldn't be remembered. Who didn't belong here at the Castle but who couldn't leave."

LIKE YOU?

"I suppose so, except I never clipped a brain damaged octogenarian in my life."

IT SAID YOU WERE MARKED.

"Me? How did he mention me?"

HE CALLED YOU THE OTHER ONE. HE SAID YOU WERE MARKED. HE SAID YOU WERE TOUCHED BY PLAGUE.

There it was again. Abaddon claiming Kasteel was marked, and carried a plague that had murdered his firstborn. Abaddon going for the sweet spot, the knife in the wound, breaking him along his greater fractures. Kasteel looked at the door and thought, Where are you, destroyer? When are you going to face me?

THANK YOU FOR COMING.

"I told you I would."

YES YOU DID.

"Same thing as before. If he comes around again, call me."

Chester Milgrom, sixty-two, recuperating from major heart surgery, alone, met Kasteel's eyes. He licked his lips and looked extremely anxious that he couldn't speak. He started to wave his hands angrily at his ventilator tube.

"Don't be so upset, it's keeping you alive, right?"

Chester stared at the paper. He took his time writing. The words formed slowly. Chester had something deep to say and wanted to lengthen the moment so Kasteel would feel it too. So that he'd understand the enormity of what was being written. Kasteel did. He knew what it was going to be. He knew the truth of the matter because the part of him that was still an average family man felt the same way.

I'M SCARED.

«««—»»»

Kasteel and Hedgwick were playing with the cancer kids who were being entertained by a clown named Boffo. Boffo had no balloons but he was juggling rubber balls, bouncing them all over the place, off the walls, off the machinery, off the kids' round bald heads. Some of the homeless kids were in there too, playing the way you had to play with the kids on your block and in your neighborhood. The homeless kids had the cancer kids, and they were all much happier for it.

The homeless mothers of the homeless kids made sure they scrubbed their children extremely well. Just because you had no real roots left after the bank took your house, after the job booted you without your pension or 401k, didn't mean your children had to stand out as dirty, despairing, stupid, or much different at all from the sick kids watching Boffo closely and laughing at his tricks. Boffo had a cane and a top hat he used it as he stumbled along around the kids, sort of dancing, tripping, pretending to fall into the machinery, squeezing his little arooga horn. The children loved him.

"He's not very accomplished," Hedgwick said sadly.

"You're right. He's not very funny."

"Children are so easily pleased."

"Most of them. Sometimes."

"It's a wonder why so many kids are miserable then."

"Not much of a wonder."

"No. But look at them. Terminal cases. Homeless. Hungry. Don't even own a single toy of their own. And they laugh and laugh at a third-rate clown. Boffo doesn't even have big shoes. I always liked clowns with big shoes. Exploding shoes, some of them."

Kasteel had taken Eddie to the circus one time and Eddie had gone nuts for the clowns. None of this, Well, everybody is really afraid of clowns sort of thing with Eddie. The kid had laughed and spun his little blue light and eaten his popcorn and shouted and screamed and clapped like crazy. When the little car pulled up and forty-three clowns climbed out of it Eddie was stunned and thought for sure clowns were magical and could hide in little places. For about a week afterward he checked under the bed, in his dresser drawers, in the cereal cabinet expecting twenty or thirty clowns to parade out. When he started to get sick Kasteel hired clowns to come to the house and entertain the boy and his friends, and most of those guys didn't have big exploding shoes either.

"You're thinking about your son," Hedge said.

"Yes."

"He liked clowns?"

"Yes."

"Think he would've laughed at Boffo here?"

"Probably, he laughed at all the others, and some of them were pretty bad too."

"There's something about this one though."

"I know, I feel it too. Maybe it's just one of the homeless fathers trying to bring a little joy to his kids."

"That cane, he holds it like he wants to break it over their little crowns and shatter their skulls."

"Boffo's got some problems."

"Boffo is definitely unboffo."

More kids piled into the room. The nurses didn't mind. The nurses never minded anything, so far as Kasteel could tell. The woman, Mary, spotted him from across the room and gave a tentative wave. He waved back. Her kid was guffawing again. Mary had gotten her hands on some more milk containers and eased the cardboard spout to the child's mouth every so often.

Just as Boffo started finishing up, doing a little dance, miming some goofy nonsense, Beth and John showed up. Kasteel got to his feet. The children clapped, the nurses clapped, the homeless clapped, Boffo took his bows. Hedgwick spotted his dead father across the room and started crying for his daddy. Beth texted Kasteel. WE CAME TO VISIT BRACE BUT HE'S NOT IN HIS ROOM.

John's arm was out of the sling. Kasteel asked how things were going. Beth said Brace was seeing a hospital therapist. He wanted to work on the troubles in the marriage. She'd gotten herself a lawyer and was seeing how much she could take him for. She wanted out. She wasn't going to take another chance on her little prick husband. She had to protect herself and her son first. But until she could get things going she put a false face on and pretended to be the perfect wife. Anything to keep him happy until she could run.

Kasteel said that he would escort her around if she needed it, in case Brace ever got mean again.

She said he wasn't mean. The ass kicking Kasteel had given him had done the job. He'd changed. He seemed to change.

IT COULD BE AN ACT, he wrote.

I KNOW.

DON'T LEAVE YOUR SON ALONE WITH HIM.

NEVER.

YOU HANDLING THE BILLS OKAY?

WE'RE ON AN INDIGENT PLAN. I WORRY ABOUT LOSING THE HOUSE.

A LITTLE PRICK LIKE BRACE MUST HAVE MONEY TUCKED AWAY. LOOK FOR BANK DEPOSIT BOXES. CHECK THE FLOOR OF YOUR CLOSET. THE SPARE TIRE. HE'LL HAVE SOME CASH HIDDEN. FLASH IS PART OF PRIDE, AND PRIDE IS EVERYTHING TO HIM.

HE HAS NO PRIDE.

PRIDE MEANING 'SHOWING OFF' AND 'NOT BEING EMBARRASSED.'

She stared around at the homeless families, the terror beneath the smiles, the desperation swirling in their eyes, the kids oblivious the way they should be. John didn't smile, grin, laugh, nothing. Boffo did an especially bad job on him. The kid glared. He cocked his head at the people around him, trying to figure them out in relation to himself, wondering who was worse off, who could defend themselves, who was at the mercy of fate. He squeezed and released the fist of his broken arm, doing a series of exercises to keep the arm strong.

Hedge said, "You're being rude, not paying attention."

"I'm paying attention."

"My father says you're not."

"Your father is dead and he's wrong."

"Who are you talking to there?"

"A friend."

"You don't have friends. You can't have friends if you have no name."

"You're my friend, Hedge."

"Yes," Hedge admitted, and reached out and began stroking the side of Kasteel's face. Beth saw this and smiled for some reason. John cocked his head the other way and watched Hedge touching Kasteel and shook his head a little like he didn't understand or couldn't believe there were those who weren't always trying to batter you up and down your own living room.

Boffo twirled his top hat on the end of his cane, let it drop onto his head, and took another bow. The children cheered. Hedge gave a courteous round of applause. Hedge's dead father, who knew? Kasteel watched John, hoping the kid would bounce back again. He was afraid the Castle would steal him from his mother, and the boy would be another sacrifice standing at the top of the Fool's tower, bone meal for future gardens.

«««—»»»

Three days later, about four am, after Kasteel had checked on Chester Milgrom twice, Kasteel was lying in Operating Theater 3 trying to sleep. The empty stadium seats surrounding the table full of faces from his dreams. He saw cops and pro heisters he'd worked with before, the guys who'd been loyal and those who'd betrayed him, the bulls and the cons, the patients and the doctors. Conrad and Watkins were up there, watching him. The German nurses, Merilee Himes's family members, the hundreds of sick and dying he'd sat with in the ER waiting room. Kathy was there. Eddie wasn't.

Kasteel turned over and pressed his face to the cool pillow, the thin sheets with holes cut out they'd place over a patient. A perfect square so they could make a perfect incision into the chest, the belly, the brain. Kasteel wondered if he lay here long enough if some surgeon's staff would gather around him and hook up the hardware and just start cutting, since that's what they did. If you lay on the table long enough, someone would come along and take away an organ or two, or stick in a pacemaker or a stent, or just start running bypasses.

Kasteel sneezed. His eyes watered. Something was wrong with the air.

He knew what the smell was though he'd never smelled it before. And he knew where it was coming from even though he couldn't have known where it was coming from. The ventilation system was more than powerful enough to keep the air clean. Except it wasn't.

Kasteel didn't think about it. He let the Castle move him to where he needed to be. He followed the perfect walls until they were the crumbling brick of the original hospital. His feet carried him to the elevators and then down, down, down, until he was back in the morgue where he'd made his point to Tracy the candy striper and her deviant friends. He walked among the dead the way he had that night. He passed the vaults and the dead whispered to him, or he whispered to them.

He saw signs around him that were easily recognizable, a splash of blood, an autopsy scale knocked over, a gurney spun aside, a few fibers stuck to a counter top, a clump of scalp and hair. Maybe it had been an accident. Maybe someone had just fought for his life. Kasteel held his nose. The smell was insane. He followed through the twisting chilly rooms of the morgue, past the freezers, to the crematorium.

He heard the attendant humming and laughing to himself. He talked. He cursed. He was hateful, and his actions hadn't bled off any of the venom at all. Kasteel could see how it could happen, alone down here with corpses. A lonely man was an inch away from madness. The poison was all still there, locked up inside him, continually firing up his already overheated mind.

The morgue attendant was still working on the girl. He was sixty, in solid shape, a lot of his hair gone but what was left he thickened with the proper gels, kept it trim, shiny, youthful. Lots of defoliants, his own teeth, athletic movements. A simple gold band wedding ring, much like Kasteel's. The kind of older man that a young girl would go for. Based on his mutterings, Kasteel was able to put the story together. The attendant was a sugar daddy. The girl wanted more cash. She wanted him to get out of the marriage. He was torn. He hated his wife but had the kids and grandkids and neighbors to think about. He was comfortable with his station and status in life. The girl was naive, immature, fucking dumb, really, but she was great in bed. He hated listening to her. He didn't want her except when she was naked, on her knees, under the sheets. Same old story.

He didn't mean to kill her, except he did. The rage built up and tore free of him and while she was putting the touch to him, maybe slyly threatening, maybe just coming right out with it, he was thinking the things he'd thought a thousand lonely nights down here. How easy it would be to dispose of your troubles. This was the place to get rid of the evidence. To hide the flesh, to remove forensics. He should've cleaned up where it had happened first, soaped away the blood, mopped up, put the scale back in the right place. But no one ever came down here to check on things. It was just him and the dead bodies and occasionally his girlfriend. Now she was dead too.

"What did you do?" Kasteel asked.

The attendant turned. He was still grinning a little, happy the deed was done. He didn't jump at the sound of Kasteel's voice, wasn't worried at all. Maybe he'd completely cracked, maybe he was still in shock.

The body was in pieces, along with dozens of others: the amputated arms, the failed surgeries, the tumor-riddled wasted remainders of wasted people. And there, her head, staring back at Kasteel with blue helpless eyes. No older than twenty-one, young enough, perhaps, to be forgiven for putting a man in a bad spot. He should've known better than to allow it to happen.

"You're burning someone alive," Kasteel said.

The attendant shaking his head. "No."

"I can smell it."

"You can't."

"I can. You killed her. Only a few minutes ago. The whole hospital reeks of what you've done."

"That's impossible."

"Not for me. You murdered her. You're planning on disposing her in fire. But that will only make it worse. What you burn will turn to ash and the ash will rise into the sky and fall on you like dark rain for the rest of your life. Don't you know that? She'll be in the dirt, the air, the dust."

"You—"

The attendant turned to the butchered girl, reached out and touched her here and there, her red lips, her arm, her belly, her breast. Kasteel counted fourteen pieces. Once he'd started sawing he just couldn't stop.

Realization was dawning on the attendant. His shoulders slumped. The smile left his lips. His eyes were beginning to spin. He looked at the saws and scalpels and other instruments he had used on the girl, and then looked at Kasteel as if he might try to attack and run. Kasteel just stood there, waiting. It was already over. It was over because the Castle said it was over.

"Go tell a cop," Kasteel ordered.

"What?"

"Go. Now. Tell the police. Turn yourself in. We can't have you in the Castle."

"You can't have…?"

"No. The Castle wants you gone. Oh, before you go, call Admin and have a replacement sent down here."

The attendant got on the phone and called in his replacement. He then called the police and said that he was very sorry. He said he didn't know why he had done what he had done. He gave his name, the name of the girl, her address, and the phone number of her parents. He said he didn't know why he was talking so much except he couldn't stop. He apologized to the police over and over. He said he hoped someone would tell his wife. The attendant sobbed for about thirty seconds and then regained his composure. He explained in great detail exactly what he had done to the girl and her corpse. Kasteel left.

He took the elevator up and moved through the corridors. He took his phone out. It seemed very important that he take the phone out of his pocket. He didn't know why. He stared at it wondering if he was supposed to call Kathy. Except Kathy didn't want to hear from him, not until he was done here, and he wasn't done here.

Kasteel looked at his phone and began to walk faster through the halls. He had no idea where he was going. He glanced at faces left and right. Perhaps one of them would understand. He got to the lobby and watched the police pull up and rush inside and down the corridors. Sweat slithered across his brow. He felt forces gathering around him, colliding, withdrawing, weighing on him, leaving him. He didn't understand what any of it meant. He started to move. He started to run. He sprinted through the halls.

The phone rang in his hand.

1

«««—»»»

The Castle showed mercy and swept him along towards ICU. He picked up speed until he couldn't even see where he was anymore. Faces blurred, the walls were no longer brick and mortar. Kasteel passed into and through them, or so it felt. Many of the faces that had been in the operating theater watching him were around him once again. They populated the hospital, they would never know his name but they were a part of him.

Kasteel shouted, "Chester!"

Chester Milgrom, sixty-two, professor of economics at a local second-rate state university, assorted health problems related to heart disease and diabetes, sitting up in bed with his twenty-eight year old lover, the graduate student who hadn't abandoned him in the midst of the media frenzy, kissing gently. Chester stared at Kasteel and shrugged, gestured, What's the matter?

The grad student said, "Who are you?"

Kasteel looked around the room, asked, "Chester, where's your phone?"

Chester held it up.

"Did you call me?"

Chester shook his head.

"By accident? Did you dial my number?"

Chester checked the phone, shook his head.

Kasteel looked at his cell again. He didn't recognize the number.

IS EVERYTHING ALL RIGHT?

"Sure. Somebody overheard me talking to you and telling you to dial 1-1-1."

Abaddon?

"Probably."

OH CHRIST.

"Don't worry about it. This is all coming to an end. Can't you feel it?"

WHAT'S COMING TO AN END?

"Forget it, Chester." Kasteel looked at the boyfriend and said, "You in for the long haul?"

The boyfriend said, "Yes."

"Good, glad to hear it. What's the prognosis? How much longer will he be in here?"

"They're still not sure. They found other problems when they opened up his chest."

"At least he doesn't have a bad brain."

"Excuse me?"

Kasteel just grinned. He stepped out of the IC unit. The Castle whispered to him. He strolled. He had never strolled in his life before, but now he strolled. He closed his eyes to focus. He steeled his will.

He imagined Abaddon eating charts, choosing his victims well, finding the woman with the bad brain and talking to her all night long. He pictured Abaddon the destroyer in wait before the glass windows of pediatrics, laying claim to the newborns like Tracy had, hoping to bite them. Abaddon and friends shaking pins into pee holes. Abaddon putting up websites. Abaddon on the top floor while Kasteel was at the bottom in the morgue. Abaddon waiting at the bottom while Kasteel stood at the top, wandering around the roof. Abaddon the enemy from out of the ancient biblical lands. Abaddon the brother, another child of the Castle. Abaddon always listening, hidden, like Kasteel, watching, moving through walls, sitting in the stadium seats of Kasteel's dreams.

He walked with his eyes shut, the tides of the hospital drawing him forward, left, right, into the elevator, his fingers knowing which button to push, or more likely the buttons understanding which one should brush against his fingertips.

Finally, he opened his eyes in the dimly lit recesses of the ancient hospital brickwork and saw the wires hanging down from the ceiling tiles. They'd been like that for month after month. They'd been like that forever and would remain like that forever. He moved to the exit and stepped out and headed toward the Fool's Tower.

He looked up and at the other end of the walkway he saw a living shadow. He stared and the shadow stared back at him. The two of them calm and in repose, understanding that this night would be the last night, without knowledge or interest in what would be ending, what would now finally begin. He took a step and the shadow retreated a step into the tower. Kasteel, who only smiled when he was in pain, smiled now, for the anguish he knew was about to come.

He whispered, "Abaddon," and began to chase the angel of death, the destroyer of firstborns.

Abaddon wasn't even in a rush, hardly moved fast at all, certainly didn't run, not the way Kasteel was running, trying to catch up. Abaddon turned and Kasteel had a moment of recognition that faded almost instantly.

"*Look who it is,*" Abaddon whispered. "*I've been waiting for you.*"

The creature Abaddon, with one bad leg, gimping along but traversing the tower the way that few others could, as if the walls gave way. Abaddon sneering bitterly, quietly, slowly laughing, in tune with his pain. Boffo the unfunny clown, carrying a cane with his top hat, without a big pair of shoes. Still with short guy syndrome, Brace Clarke needing to impress himself upon the world, upon this new world he found himself in, this new city of invisibility and power.

"You could've just called me on your own phone, Brace."

"*That would have been too easy.*"

"What did you do to Merilee Himes?"

"*I talked to her. I looked at her. I told her to die and she did. I ate her. The same way I ate the others.*"

"Which others?"

"*The same way I'll eat you.*"

Kasteel tried to suppress a surge of guilt. He had pushed Brace too hard. Brace had been more than an abusive husband and father, he'd been a complete lunatic on the edge of losing his mind. Kasteel should've recognized it, should've noticed the signs. He'd handled the situation all wrong. A man who needed to always prove himself the toughest and sharpest and meanest little prick in the room, and Kasteel had beaten, scarred, and crippled him right in his own living room, in front of the wife and son he resented so much. No wonder he talked of plague and murdering of firstborn sons.

Kasteel followed Brace up the staircase, stone step by stone step.

"It's time for you to be quiet, Brace."

"*You already tried to destroy my voice. You can't. You aren't able. You don't have the capacity. I kill at will. I kill on the wards. I steal homeless children. I eat them.*"

"You should've just started by apologizing to your wife and son."

"*I have no wife and son.*"

"Neither do I, except when I do. One's waiting for me at home. The other is waiting for me beyond the veil."

"*That's where I wait for you too.*"

Step by step, retreating up the stone stairwell, past the windows showing the silver moonlight and stars grappling to fit within human view. Story by story, where the ghosts of the fever victims, the civil war surgeries, the Vietnam vets, all appeared and pushed them up, up, up to where men without names like Kasteel and Boffo suicided off the thin rim.

When they reached the top of the Fool's tower they stared at each, destroyer bearing witness to destroyer, children of the Castle squaring off.

"Do you think you'll ever get better, Brace? Are you trying? Do you think you want to get back to your wife and son? Or should I put you down?"

"*Children laugh at me.*"

"It's a gift."

"*Children die at my touch.*"

"Not quite."

Brace Clarke, Boffo the clown, Abaddon the angel, swung his cane and caught Kasteel across the shoulder. It hurt like hell. Kasteel went down to one knee. He thought he should give that one to Brace. He'd crippled Brace. Boffo had to lash back. Boffo had to get a few licks in. Abaddon was known to men with bad brains. Kasteel saw Brace's arms rise in the night like black blood-soaked wings. Brace lashed out with the cane again. It brushed against Kasteel's skull. Blood spurted. Abaddon sniffed and said, "*Ahhhh.*"

It was all right. Everything was all right. Sometimes you let the other guy think he had you down and a hole opened in his defenses. Like now. Brace doing the little dance around the roof of the Fool's tower. Kasteel could roll to his feet and shove the poor little prick eleven stories down if he wanted. But it wasn't going to end that way. He hadn't come this far just to wind up nudging a man who was already an inch off the ledge.

Maybe there was a chance to save him. Maybe you just had to leave the guy in the waiting room a few more days and something would snap into place. A little therapy, a little indulgence. Kasteel really didn't know. Maybe he was going to have to kill the bastard.

Kasteel turned back to the Castle and asked, "What do I have to do?"

Brace swung the cane again. Kasteel dodged and Brace twirled around twice completely, heading off the edge. Kasteel reached out and grabbed the cane and Brace held on, his ruined leg failing to hold up his weight. Blood ran into Kasteel's face as they remained frozen like that, the breeze rising, Brace with one foot off in space, the other trembling, no big shoes, Kasteel holding him up, keeping him alive.

"*Let me go.*"

"No."

"*I'm nothing but a fool. You've already destroyed the destroyer.*"

"I just gave you more room to move in. In the Castle you could cut loose. They should've locked you up in ward eight."

"*They tried. I slew my opponents. I earned my freedom.*"

Kasteel was going to have to find out what really happened down there on ward eight.

He gave a hard tug on the cane and Brace came flying into Kasteel's arms. Kasteel clipped him on the chin. That's all it took. The angel of death closed his eyes and fell asleep there in the dark wind, in the shimmering mercurial starlight.

Kasteel called Beth Clarke.

He said, "I made a mistake."

"What mistake?"

"I should've found a better way."

"What are you talking about?"

"I should've either killed him or helped him. I shouldn't have crippled him. He was already crippled. I just made him worse. I made him Boffo."

"Boffo? Are you talking about that crappy clown?"

"The crappy clown was Brace."

"No. That's not possible. I would've recognized him."

"He's unrecognizable. I did that."

"You're not to blame. You saved my life and the life of my son. I'm certain of it. But—but how is he walking? He wasn't supposed to be able to get out of bed for three months at least."

"He's insane. Insane people can do amazing things. They can smell a dead young woman burning in the wind."

"What?"

"I don't want to kill him."

"Do what you have to do," Beth Clarke said. "Kill him if you have to."

Kasteel was about to disconnect when another voice came over the phone. It was the boy, John, whose voice Kasteel had never heard before. The boy said, "I hate him. I don't know if I can ever forgive him. But… don't kill my father."

"All right," Kasteel said.

He carried Brace down, step by step, stone by stone, and held him in his arms like a child, like a maimed firstborn son. He hugged the lunatic to him the way he had hugged Eddie to him. Kasteel began to cry for his sins, and a few minutes later Abaddon's body also began to tremble in his arms, also crying. The two children of the Castle sobbed for each other and themselves, and for the others that had come before them and those that would follow. Kasteel said, "Your son wants you to live. Get sane, Brace. For his sake."

"*I don't know if I can.*"

"Try."

«««—»»»

He called Kathy.

"Are you ready to come home?" she asked.

"Yes."

He hung up. He walked out the front door. He could've waited for her to come pick him up, but to hell with it. He found the nearest car with MD tags. He didn't even need to pop the door. It was already open. As if the Castle was inviting him to leave once and for all, like an unwelcome guest, hoping he'd never come back. Kasteel went to break the steering column but the keys were in the ignition.

Hedgwick was in the backseat.

"You don't mind if I come along, do you?"

"Did you see all of that?"

"All of what?"

"No ham sandwiches, Hedge."

Hedgwick reached into the pocket of his robe and pulled out three or four wrapped sandwiches and dumped them out the window.

"No stealing my trash can lids," Kasteel said. "No running around your dad's building. No scaring my wife."

"I promise. Do you remember your name yet?"

"No."

"It'll come back to you."

"Yes," Kasteel said, throwing the car into reverse, pulling out, throwing it into drive, and gunning along. Before he went home he had to stop off somewhere first. "I think it will."

He didn't know where his son was buried, but he knew he would find the way.

About the Author

Tom Piccirilli is an American novelist and short story writer. He has sold over 150 stories in the mystery, thriller, horror, erotica, and science fiction fields. Piccirilli is a two-time winner of the International Thriller Writers Award for "Best Paperback Original" (2008, 2010). He is a four-time winner of the Bram Stoker Award. He was also a finalist for the 2009 Edgar Allan Poe Award given by the Mystery Writers of America, a final nominee for the Fantasy Award, and he won the first Bram Stoker Award given in the category of "Best Poetry Collection".

38861834R00057

Made in the USA
Charleston, SC
19 February 2015